make/manifest

A Life in Art and Craft

by

MIGUEL MENDONÇA

Featuring interviews with:

Kari Barba, Formica Coriandolo, Mike Hall, David Hurn, Corin Johnson, Claudia Kappenberg, Muazzam Ali Khan, Reuben Langdon, Peter Lord, Rama Mani, Miguel Mendonça, Maggie Murphy, Charlotte Mary Pack, Lee Pepper, Lady Pink, Stan Prokopenko, Herman Rarebell, Red Means Recording, Josh Scott, Matthew Shewchuk, Dave Smith, Kazuaki Tanahashi and Eda Elif Tibet

First published 2021 by Miguel Mendonça

Copyright © 2021 Miguel Mendonça

All moral rights reserved

This book or any portion thereof may not be reproduced or used in any manner whatsoever without the express written permission of the authors except for the use of brief quotations in a book review

Cover design by Miguel Mendonça
Front and back cover paintings copyright © Kazuaki Tanahashi

ISBN 13: 9798592695360
ISBN 10: 8592695360

www.miguelmendonca.com

About the Author

Miguel Mendonça is an Anglo-Azorean writer based in Bristol, England. His education has incorporated forestry and horticulture, journalism, a BA in geography and history, and postgrad studies in social science and environmental ethics. He worked as an author and campaigner on sustainability while serving as Research Manager at the World Future Council and Communications Manager at The Converging World. At that time he authored or co-authored three books: *Feed-in Tariffs*, *Powering the Green Economy* and *A Renewable World*.

Following that work, Miguel published a short fiction collection, titled *Quick! Act Normal*. He then studied metaphysical topics, and published a trilogy: *Meet the Hybrids*, *We are The Disclosure* and *Being with the Beings*. In 2020 he published a study of wisdom titled *Wisdom: Now and Always*.

In addition to exploring fresh subject areas in fiction and nonfiction, he enjoys producing music, poetry, fiction, photography and stained glass.

To Dave Bailey

You can't use up creativity. The more you use, the more you have.
—*Maya Angelou*

Every child is an artist. The problem is how to remain an artist once we grow up.
—*Pablo Picasso*

The aim of art is to represent not the outward appearance of things, but their inward significance.
—*Aristotle*

Acknowledgements

As always, my deepest thanks to the contributors. It has been a life-changing experience, and will be an ongoing influence in my creative journey.

And I am equally grateful to Dave Bailey. This book is the result of discussions we had before, during and after I interviewed him for my 2020 book *Wisdom: Now and Always*. Some of the questions are his, and arose from his own curiosity about the lives and approaches of other makers. I encourage all readers to seek out *Wisdom* and read or listen to his chapter. It will edify any maker in important ways. He has a philosophical and spiritual scope to his work, and an ability to articulate it, that is exceptional.

To the actress and activist Chipo Chung for writing the foreword. As a native of Zimbabwe myself, I was delighted to have her share her vision of the role that art plays in building society and the self. Her discussion of artistry in these realms warrants deep reflection.

To Kaz Tanahashi for allowing me to use his magical paintings for the cover.

I wish to thank all those who helped connect me to the contributors. And the guys on the Affinity forum for their help, especially Dex.

I am eternally grateful to my circle, the invaluable folks who keep me grounded, keep me on track, and keep me informed and entertained. Much love to Lou, Matt, DB, David, Darlene and my family.

And Dexter; ever in my thoughts.

Contents

Foreword xi
Introduction 15
Kari Barba 18
Formica Coriandolo 30
Mike Hall 42
David Hurn 59
Corin Johnson 79
Claudia Kappenberg 91
Muazzam Ali Khan 107
Reuben Langdon 115
Peter Lord 130
Rama Mani 146
Miguel Mendonça 163
Maggie Murphy 173
Charlotte Mary Pack 191
Lee Pepper 202
Lady Pink 215
Stan Prokopenko 230
Herman Rarebell 245
Red Means Recording 257
Josh Scott 271
Matthew Shewchuk 286
Dave Smith 299
Kazuaki Tanahashi 317
Eda Elif Tibet 325
Conclusion 341

Foreword

Human beings are distinct from all other creatures, not by their ability to love, but by their ability to create. The artist lives in the world of curiosity, contemplation and imagination, the visionary state of self-reflection, dreams and magic. Scientific minds turn their art to discoveries in astronomy and physics, and feats of architecture and strategy. But even the simplest of workers turns the laying of bricks, the baking of cakes, the polishing of shoes, into an art form. In practice, all humans are artistic creators. Creativity does not exist solely in the realm of fine art, but in the magic of everyday life.

The finest work of a painter comes from stillness: the acute observation of life, the patience to connect the eye to the hand, and vision to action with accuracy. The obstacles to execution exist in impatience, restlessness, and the inability to watch and wait for the hand to move at the direction of the seeing-eye. Through rashness, the colors mix and become muddy; instead of waiting for the paint to dry, more colors are added; finally, in frustration, the artist stabs the canvas and discards the wasted mess.

As in art, so in life.

We live in a hectically-paced world. Each century is accelerating exponentially; within decades, buildings and communities are destroyed and replaced by new ones, technologies become vintage and old visions are cast aside as irrelevant. Transformation becomes a form in and of itself, a rushed process in which 'the new' is all. Can we imagine a world in which the pace of change is matched with internal softness and self-reflection? Would this awareness mean that we could carry more people with us towards the goal of happiness, instead of racing ahead to find ourselves alone?

This collection of artists' experiences is a window into how each human can make a contribution to the collective work of art that is our communities, our society, our marks on the great cave wall of the world, inspiring generations of the future to remain in wonder at our existence, and our survival. Each individual creator marks a path that inspires others to follow. Be they tattoo artists, musicians, calligraphers, or car restorers, they cut paths that I hope will inspire you to consider the art that is your life, and encourage us all to keep stepping forward in creativity.

Each small act adds up to a collective way of being that has either studied vision or a lack of skilfulness. The experience of artistry is the same, whether a head of state or a baker.

Take my home country of Zimbabwe, for example. It was founded by a group of visionaries, and takes its name from a great 14th century kingdom, the artefacts of which still remain. A respect for the past and the vision of a revolutionary future were the lightning rod of the country's founders. In the early years, families worked together with teachers to build schools for their communities. All were looked after by the healthcare system. And the younger generation began to tap against the walls of racial segregation within the social sphere. A visionary society was being created.

Fast-forward 40 years, and there is a hardness to human interaction, born out of frustration, anger and a desperation sometimes bordering on despair. The environment is littered and polluted, the schools have no books. Politics is blocked, living is survival and success is material wealth. The paint has become muddy and we have forgotten that the nation is a collective work of art.

For society to blossom, vision needs to take place at both the level of government and at the level of the artist. Transformation arises out of curiosity, imagination, playfulness and an openness to the world, be that the beauty of the environment, or another person's point of view.

How do we reintroduce artistry into our everyday life? And how do we infuse a nation with it, so that it is shared by all those present? We do this by instilling in each of us the need for art as an integral part of everyday life, both the physical manifestation of art and the processes that allow individuals to turn their lives into art. We need art to heal us, to collectively allow us to meditate on our wounds, as a people. We need acknowledgement of those who have suffered in the past. If we cannot have justice through the harshness of prison sentences, let us have it by having our secret stories heard and respected.

We need art to interrupt us, to make us consider how things could work differently. We need art to gather us together and display our various identities, and celebrate our collective identity – that of humanity.

We need art to communicate to the rest of the world who we are, and be the platform through which we learn about the rest of the world, and dance together.

We need art to make us laugh at the absurdity of life, to celebrate its beauty and the magic of our existence within it.

We need art to fulfil the promise of our power as humans: not to destroy, but to create.

For many years I worked with an organization called S.A.F.E., which uses dramatic performance to encourage social change in Kenya. The organization's most remarkable work has been with the Maasai community of the Loita Hills, where by singing about the need to protect the next generation of girls, poetry and song have opened up a taboo subject and led to the abandonment of the practice of female genital mutilation. A group of community leaders-turned-performing artists have sung the change they wanted to see in their society. Their work is proof that a provocative cultural act can cause an internal drama in the viewer, a change in the way one thinks and acts, just as music changes the way one feels. Their vision, translated through song, has transformed their reality.

I committed to the life of an artist from a young age. It has meant being an itinerant, an outsider, a nomad, and a bridge-builder. I would not be able to survive the choppy waters between acting gigs and personal projects without the community of fellow makers who inspire me, and the cause of social change that grounds me.

In some nations, art is perceived as a luxury. And in communities that live in desperation, the stress of survival and the distraction of hunger make staying creative near impossible. Art is not going to solve world poverty. But treating Life with the same reverence as the artist approaches his canvas is going to make it easier to get there. The less blockage, closed-mindedness and conflict we have between us, the more quickly we will be able to come to solutions that will lift us to a better reality.

It will start in small meetings, art exhibitions, training courses, therapy sessions, rehearsal rooms, in small kindnesses, and in community ownership of a collective vision. Our lives are the art we have been given to create. Our nations, and our world, are the art works we have been given to create together.

Let us observe the beauty before us and breathe, before lifting our hands to paint.

- Chipo Chung, 2021

Introduction

Art and creativity are fundamental to the human experience. Our survival has always depended on channeling raw creativity into problem-solving. From toolmaking and shelter-building to hunting and clothing, we have met essential need with faculties that have found finer expression in art. Some of the oldest surviving images and objects are artistic renderings of human and animal forms. Something stirred in us from the beginning, and we felt a need to represent, to record, to remember. From that moment to this, all cultures have brought decoration and ritual into their world. They may be used in the veneration of nature, of spirit, of the ancestors, of deities. They may bond the group through shared activity, values and gratitude. And these groups may further distinguish themselves through their costumes, flags and cuisine.

Creativity goes beyond function and into a place of enjoyment and expression. It runs through every manifestation of identity. As children we draw, paint, sing, dance and build. In our teens we decorate our rooms and our bodies, and often move through musical subcultures which mandate their own codes of dress, jargon and behavior. In adulthood we define ourselves through a wide range of elements, including clothing, vehicles, home decoration, technology choices, hobbies, politics, spiritual beliefs and opinions in general. In our work we cannot help expressing ourselves. Even the telesales representative with their script will naturally inject some personality into their work. No matter who or where we are, we cannot help but express our uniqueness. Our very presence here changes things, in a million ways. Our ongoing biological functioning necessitates changes in the environment. And much as some cultures attempt to suppress or control it, human nature is going to make each of us make a unique impression in the world. The creative force that runs through all of life is irresistible.

And then there are those who by nature are compelled to draw deep from their well of creativity every day, and pour it into some form that pleases them. Without it they lose themselves. No two paths are alike, but it seems their childhood sense of exploration and play is intact. Some use it to work through pain, some to visualize an idealized existence, some to make a political statement, and others to operate in an uncertain space of complex emotions and abstract forms. A great many makers will simply make. It is what it looks like, and does not represent anything. It is a wooden box, to keep things in. It just happens to be made with supreme technique. Whether the buyer understands the skill and artistic requirements of marquetry or not, they just know that they like this box. And for the maker, that is often enough.

The story of human art and creativity is long and complex. But for each of us that walks this path, we are prey to doubt, to creative blocks, to struggles with time, with balance, with our audience and with making it pay. This study is a journey through the lives of 23 highly accomplished artists and makers, who share an honest portrait of their challenges and triumphs. By walking with them, we are each the beneficiaries of the problem-solving that they have done over the decades. We can gain insight through both the small details and the big picture.

The contributors are active in a wide range of art forms and creative expressions, including tattooing, stained glass, classic car restoration, photography, painting, sculpture, graffiti art, performance art, music and music technology, performance capture, voiceover, acting, animation, filmmaking, poetry, theatre, illustration, and television development and production. They include practitioners of devotional art, political art, public art and collective art. Between them they have won many of the most prestigious awards in their respective fields, and have around 650 years of collective experience in the arts.

Introduction

Their work has influenced more than a billion people. Some are living legends who have helped define their art form and/or industry. Many have taught, gifting thousands of students the benefit of their experience.

They were chosen for their diversity of art forms, their accomplishments, and often because I am a fan of their work and was excited to learn more about their process and perspectives.

These conversations have substantially expanded my sense of the life of the artist and creator, and they have inspired me in ways that will continue to unfold over the years. I anticipate that you, the reader, will find similar fascination, joy and encouragement in spending time with these highly talented people who continue to manifest their creative visions.

Kari Barba

Kari Barba is a world-renowned tattoo artist who has been inking for over 40 years. After selling flash art to other tattoo artists and developing her own style, she opened her first shop in 1983. Kari has since won over 500 awards, including Best Tattoo Artist nationally and internationally, and a Lifetime Achievement Award. She currently owns two branches of Outer Limits Tattoo. The Long Beach location is the oldest continuously running shop in the USA, and the second longest running shop in the world. She works alongside a staff of highly talented artists and piercers, offering a wide range of styles. Kari tattoos five days a week at the Long Beach location. Currently, she most enjoys tattooing realism, portraits, Asian styles and trash polka. She is also a painter working in oils.

outerlimitstattoo.com / Instagram: karibarba

What drew you to your medium?

I'm from Minneapolis originally, and I started tattooing there in 1979, when I was 19. But I didn't see my first tattoo until I was 17 years old. I was hanging out with some friends and one of the guys in the room had a forearm tattoo. It was a couple of ace cards I think. People were talking about it, and my first thought was that it didn't look very good. It looked like it needed something. It was more just an outline. So I thought that tattoos didn't look very nice. But then I started to see more tattoos, and some of them edged on realism, and were more detailed. I wondered if you could do even more detail. I moved to a new place, and had an upstairs neighbor called Neil, who was a tattoo artist. I used to draw a lot then, and as we became friends he saw me drawing. So he said, "I think you should try tattooing." He was pretty fully tattooed, and I didn't know if I would be into it. But he said he thought my style would work really well with it. At that time I was married to a guy who was very into getting tattooed. So I would draw the design on him in pen, and he would go to Neil, who would follow the lines and fill it in. So that was the beginning for me.

I then ordered the setup and gave it a shot. But my initial interest started with him prompting me. I didn't have that interest on my own. When I did my first tattoo it was super fun and very scary at the same time. People saw the first one and I started getting requests. And it grew from there. I started to have real fun with it and wondered if I could make a living from it. I was still very young and didn't otherwise have a specific direction in life. In 1980 we moved to California with the dream of opening a tattoo shop. I started winning awards from about '85, and a lot of punk and rock bands wanted to come in and get tattooed. It was fun.

Do you feel a connection with the history of your medium?

I hated history in high school, dealing with the years, the numbers, all of that. But in tattooing, it just kept getting pushed in my face, in a nice way. I came to appreciate the pioneers, the traditions that helped bring us to this point. And I've come to love history in all aspects. I still don't remember dates very well, and sometimes forget places, but the notion of those who came before us is very important to me.

Does your medium offer something unique?

There are so many people tattooing, and doing so many different styles, but you still see a sense of individuality in every single piece. When I can tattoo freely, doing something I just draw on the skin, I'm making a connection with the person in some way, but it comes from within. So if I can just zone into the tattoo, I can almost in a sense let the spirits take over, and tattoo through me. If I come to a difficult piece, in my head I will invite tattoo artists from the past to help me do a better job. So it's very spiritual. Sometimes in the tattoo process it's better for me to be still and quiet, and just have music. Conversation is okay here and there, but the less I talk, the more I can focus in and become part of the tattoo.

Knowing that the person will wear that piece forever is quite scary and also very exciting at the same time. The biggest honor is that someone trusts me to mark their skin permanently, sometimes without even seeing a design. Often we have a discussion and develop ideas, but I don't show them a whole laid out tattoo like a lot of places. I used to do that in my early years, but my approach has progressed, and it works.

I've been tattooing for over 40 years now, and I can still recognize my work from even the first days. It's got a sense of yourself, and you know it was your piece, even if you don't remember specifically doing it. Sometimes people will come into the shop and ask if I remember doing one of their tattoos in 1980 or whatever. It's interesting to see your progression. It might have the same look, but hopefully it is on a better level now. Yet you can still see yourself in them.

When I look at the Japanese practice of preserving the tattooed skin of people that have died, it's very interesting. They give permission to have the work preserved. But sometimes I think about the skins of animals that are preserved, and so in some cases I think about that as skin, and sometimes as art. Those leaving their skin behind want to share that piece of history with people who will come after them. To me that's a beautiful thing.

Why do you have a need to create?

I don't know why. I think we're all given something that we feel natural with, something that makes us feel calm. And when we do that, whether it's painting, making furniture or working in a machine shop, it becomes less of a job. It makes you feel at peace. I've been driven to draw since I can remember. It was something I did when I had quiet time. I would sit out and draw trees, birds, things like that. When I was about eight or nine I remember sitting on the front step drawing whatever bird would fly my way. So I think we're born with these things, and it's something that helps us feel ourselves, and that's as simple as I can put it. It's just calming for those who have something they like to do.

Why do humans have a need to create?

That's an extremely interesting question. I've never thought about that. There isn't any other species that creates art in the same way. But I suppose it depends how you look at it. A spider creates this beautiful, ornate web. But that's more about survival. The male Japanese pufferfish creates a large, kind of mandala pattern on the sea floor as part of a courtship ritual. But it's not by choice. It's an instinct. In mating season, bowerbirds create spectacular 'bowers' which they decorate with objects they find, often using specific colors. Some species do amazing dances. This is something I'm going to think about. Is it about instinct, or intelligence level? Elephants, apes, dogs birds and dolphins have been taught to draw and paint. So maybe it's a sense of seeing it and learning that you can create things if you choose to. You wonder if the ape, for example, is trying to create an image that it saw in his or her head. They can sit and draw for hours, taking no notice of anything else. And they stick to the paper. It's fascinating.

What sacrifices have you made to pursue your creative path?

There have been quite a few. The biggest and most hurtful one is missing out on time with family. And personal time, in terms of getting out and spending time in nature. In my early years, when my kids were young, I was at work from 10 in the morning until midnight, six days a week. And at the time you don't realize how that's going to impact you or them. But later on you realize that. That's the one that makes me feel the most.

And then just to keep the art going financially, on one or two occasions I had to sell homes to keep the shop running. It's been a battle through the years, at certain times. The in-between times give you the opportunity to reestablish time with your family and loved ones. You realize at some point that you have to find a balance, rather than continually falling into your craft.

How has your work shaped you as a person?

I've learned how to create differently. And it has taught me a lot about other people. I've learned to talk to different types of people, in different ways. People come to me with so many different ideas that it's taught me a little bit about a lot of different things. For example, about different religions, iconography, trees, animals and so on. So it's shaped me in that way.

It's also helped me to stay motivated, to stay regimented. Even in this time, during the pandemic, getting up and creating every day has become really important. So I think that's part of my job, part of who I've become over time. If this had happened in my younger days I would have been in the forest the whole time. So I make sure I continue to develop.

As a tattoo artist you do get a lot of praise for your work, but you have to look at who you are. I strongly believe in humility. There is always somebody better, somebody who is going to top us. I strive constantly to do my best, to keep that going, but it's just not in my personality to be egotistical about my work. I'm kind of a quiet person in general. Some of the artists get into a rock star mentality, and I don't know how that happens. But I think many of them strive for that. We all strive for people to recognize our art, and who we are in some way or another, or we wouldn't be putting it out there and trying to sell it. But to remember where we came from, and who we are in general, is super important. If somebody needs to be the rock star, let them do it. There's quite a bit of that going on now, with all the TV shows about tattooing. But not all of them have that mentality. I know several people who are on the shows and they are fantastic, beautiful human beings and have not had that happen to them. I think it's just who we are inside. Some people have that mentality and some don't. And I do not. It feels very good, yes, when people tell you they love your work. But I don't personally need to tell everybody else about my awards and so on. You have to share that stuff in order to attract more customers, but otherwise I don't think I would put that out there. Showing your accomplishments is basically just to help keep your profession moving forward.

How do you deal with creative blocks?

I do get blocks, but generally when people come to me and tell me to just tattoo whatever I want. I need to at least get a sense of direction in order to start developing a design. The vast majority of the work is about interpreting the vision of the customer. If they come to me with an idea, I find that their spark will spark me. But if someone wants me to just come up with something I can struggle with that.

I do get creative blocks when sitting down to paint. I always felt more like a copy machine. I take an idea or group of ideas and work them into something new. I'm more towards realism in my art. I call it 'illustrative realism' because I like to throw my own flair in there and do it the way it feels natural to me.

How do you stay fresh in your work?

Again, it's the people who come to me. For example, someone might come in and say they want to get a forest, and are thinking of having an animal in there. And in my head the picture is already forming. So staying fresh is about exploring ways to make it unique. That can be about the layout, or some other aspect. I am always looking to find that in myself. Let's say you've done 20 tigers, and you are asked to do another. You want to find some approach to making this one unique, some inspiration to make this a truly individual piece.

And what helps with that goes back to balance. If you get up and take a walk in nature, or go on a bike ride, something rejuvenating, it always brings fresh light into what you're doing.

There are always technical challenges. If you're working off a stencil, you may have to change the drawing, because the surface is stretchy and three-dimensional. For example, if I'm doing a building with straight lines, on a particular body you may have to compensate for its shape by drawing the lines curved so that it comes out straight on the body.

And on those buildings there's a freedom to drawing them. If you zoom way in it looks very detailed, but you may have to simplify it on the skin. So you're not creating every line. It's like an impressionist painting; your eye fixes it, it creates what isn't there. You leave some stuff out, but you still know that's the building. But I love doing them. Right now I'm finishing a painting of a street in Mediterranean Europe. Even on canvas it's interesting to trying to get the texture right. I love those old buildings, the way they don't repaint them.

What is your relationship with satisfaction in your work?

I think that as an artist, if I was ever to be satisfied, I would cease to grow. For me, I'm constantly reevaluating every piece, even after it's finished. And even if you're happy with the outcome, you're not ecstatic, because you look at it and see what you could have done better or different. I'm happy with them, but am I ever satisfied? I don't think so. There's always room to improve. It's super important for us as humans to realize that even if we did a good job, we can still do better.

Although it's my artwork, it's your body. I want you to be able to wear it for the rest of your life and have pleasure and meaning from it. It needs meaning for me, but it's more important that it has meaning for you, and that you're satisfied with it. That's why I always try to get a guideline from the customer. Because maybe on that day I just wanted to do some abstract brushwork that communicates a sense of calm. The person might look at it and say, "What is this? I'm not a calm person. This is just a bunch of lines to me." So I always try to find something that is common ground. I look for what is necessary in your tattoo for you. What feelings do you want to show? Then through my artistic interpretation I try to express that.

What is the relationship between your work and its audience?

It's completely individual, just like any art. A group of people can look at a piece of art, and it will evoke different feelings and meanings for each of them. Some will focus on the colors, or the emotion it brings up. And I feel the same thing with tattooing. But for the person wearing it, when they come in, they're choosing a particular tattoo for some reason that connects to them. Whether it be a nature scene or a portrait, there is a personal feeling and history behind that choice. Other people will look at that piece, say an octopus, and will just see the animal. Others will see it in terms of its intelligence, or another characteristic of the animal. Some people see it as peace, others as chaos. It's all relevant, and it's all individual.

I've had some amazing experiences with octopi, which has influenced my interest in them. I was diving off Florida and the divemaster had caught an octopus which he was showing to the group. All these people were touching it. I stood way back and just felt bad for the octopus. I could feel its stress. I had never seen one in person before and was struck by its beauty. It slithered out of the divemaster's hands, and headed right for me. I was up to my high waist in the water, and it came right up and sat on my chest, and just relaxed. The divemaster was saying, "Don't be scared, it's not going to bite you." And I said, "Are you kidding? This is the best thing that's ever happened to me!" I don't know how long it stayed with me, but after a while it just drifted off. I'm sure it could feel what I was feeling.

I've always loved seeing them, and tattooing images of them. I don't do them completely realistic, but I have my own style. I don't show the whole octopus. I show a portion of the head, some of the tentacles, bubbly water, and make it kind of free flowing so that it fits into the area on the body.

More recently we did a fundraiser for a rescue out in the Palm Desert area called The Living Desert Zoo Gardens. They take in animals that may be injured, or may have been illegally obtained. In return they gave us a tour of the aquarium, and we had a one-on-one with the giant octopus that they had. The tank was very large, but we got to go to the top of the tank, and the octopus, who was called Gilligan, came right up, and we got to touch her head and tentacles. She was massive. Her tentacles look soft, but when you touch them it's this hard muscle underneath. She was very strong, but very gentle. She was doing the same thing as the small octopus I met in Florida, and just relaxing. She was pregnant, and though I didn't know this at the time, once they give birth they will do nothing but protect their babies, which means that the mother will soon starve to death. So a couple of days after we visited her, she gave birth, and a few days after that, she died. So we were pretty much the last people to see her. In the work I've done since, I refer to a lot of the photos I took of her. I think about her all the time. They have another octopus at the Living Desert now, a small male. But her energy was so amazing, just like the little one I met while diving. People always ask me why I do so many octopus pieces, and the reason is that I feel very connected to them.

What is the relationship between yourself and your audience?

I guess it depends on the audience. Some people look at the artist as the interpreter of their vision. I think it's all dependent on the person who is looking. They're trying to recreate something from the past, or maybe it's from a dream or something of that nature. I'm the middle-man for getting the art that they need. Unlike art forms where they buy a piece they like, in tattooing, they have an idea that they would like created. So that's what I am to most people: the translator of their vision.

I haven't tattooed at a convention for around 10 years. But when I did it, the noise around you becomes a kind of white noise. It kind of drops back. The tattoo becomes the entire focus. If people come up to talk for a minute I'll stop working, so that my attention is always on the tattoo. But the noise has never bothered me. We have a very busy shop and I enjoy that. In my mind it's very peaceful, but the space itself can be noisy. We have 12 artists working at the shop, and most are there on any given day. The noise is just a backdrop, and doesn't interrupt what I'm doing.

I do share my work through social media, but my wife does that. I try to add a sense of personality to it, sometimes showing what I'm doing, maybe if I'm out hiking, but generally I try to keep that relationship mostly business, and have some separation between that and my personal life. Some in the profession keep a very strict separation. I like it to be a little more personal. I enjoy people's comments and I love to hear what they say. But I'm not very technical, so my wife does a lot of posting, and a guy at the shop takes care of it there. But it still shows me as me.

What has your audience taught you?

To be myself. To let the art flow. They've also taught me that no matter how hard we can be on ourselves, the work is loved and recognized by someone. Even if I'm not entirely satisfied with the piece, someone else loves it, which is fantastic. It shows you that everyone has a unique artistic eye. They may pull things out of that tattoo that I didn't see when I was doing it. That's very exciting to me. The audience is so diverse, the world is so diverse, and it's shown me how unique art is for every single person.

What has been the greatest challenge in your career?

These days, it's honestly about keeping up with the body. I've been doing the job a long time, but now the biggest challenge is being comfortable while tattooing, in terms of how my body feels. And I use other avenues to relax my mind, like being out in nature. I've started doing yoga, and that helps with my mobility, and helps me continue doing my job.

The biggest challenge is probably how you feel about your art, yourself. I can constantly be criticizing the work, in my own mind. So how do you get past that, and not let that bring you down, and stop? So staying in a place where you can continue moving forward is the internal battle. You have to know that you can, and will, do better.

What has been the high point of your career?

I've been very fortunate in my career and have had many high points along the way. Each time there's a new one I look back to the others and think that it's just different, it's not necessarily better. If I can pick out a couple of things right now, the first would be when I was chosen to tattoo a silicon arm for the Natural History Museum in LA. From 2017 to 2018 they had an exhibition on tattooing there, and it traveled internationally. I tattooed an octopus full length on the arm. The exhibition was in Paris, Chicago, Taiwan, Russia, and it's supposed to go to Brazil. The connection that they allowed, between women and tattooing, was amazing. I started giving talks on the subject.

And secondly, I was asked to be a judge at a convention in France called Le Mondial du Tatouage. As far as I'm aware it's the biggest convention in the world, and the other judges are extremely talented, so I was honored to be part of that. Those are two of the proudest moments of my career.

What is the most important thing your creative practice has taught you?

To just let go. I'm very OCD, and always want things to be squared up and neat and tidy, but in tattooing it's very free flowing. And in my art I can be more loose, and let myself go a bit.

How did it feel to reflect on creativity today?

Every time I have a conversation like this it brings new awareness. It makes me look inside, and it feels good. The feelings that you experience when you talk about art change from moment to moment. Because you're constantly moving around in your thoughts, thinking about what you and other people have done, and what they mean. And it's quite exploratory to look at those feelings. It's been amazing and I appreciate it very much.

Formica Coriandolo

Formica (Angela Toninelli), moved to the community of Damanhur in 1983, at the age of 21. An artist in the fields of sculpture, painting, stained glass and music, she created many of the renowned works of art in the Temples of Humankind and was the composer of many Damanhurian lyrics, inspired by the mythology of the community.

Dreams and art intertwine in her life. From her personal experience as a self-taught artist she founded and successfully managed the seminars 'Discover Your Inner Talent' and 'The Path of Dreams'.

Formica has held many roles in Damanhur. In 1987 she was elected Minister of Culture, and from 1999 to 2007 she held the role of Guide, the highest political and social role in Damanhur. She currently works in the Damanhur Communication team. In recent years she has discovered the art of writing, and her novel *Il Libro di Giulia* was recently published in Italy.

damanhur.org / Instagram: formicacoriandolo

What drew you to your medium?

At the beginning my medium was stained glass. I became an artist after joining the Federation of Damanhur, a spiritual community in Italy. Before then I was living in Florence and working as an electrician. I was probably the only woman who was working as an electrician in Italy at the time! I have never studied art, but in Damanhur we wished to represent our belief system through art. So we Damanhurians spent 15 years excavating an underground cathedral in secret. We dug 100 feet down, and built the Temples of Humankind. We have been self-taught in everything, including the excavation work. None of us was an architect or engineer, but we did our best. We aimed to represent the soul of this construction through art, so art is an indispensable part of the Temples. Our intention is to demonstrate that even a small group of people can do seemingly impossible things together.

The Temples of Humankind are dedicated to reawakening the divine spark which is inside every human being. We want that spark to grow through creativity. When we work for a dream we feel more alive than when we work just for money, do we not? This is not to say that money is evil, but in Damanhur the real purpose is to reawaken the potential in each of us. This means transcending the conditioning of mainstream culture, and creating something which is based on relevant and meaningful values to each of us. We created Damanhur and the Temples to inspire people to consciously choose their way of living, and to do it with others.

What drew me to work with stained glass was the need to create artworks which could survive over time underground. This meant that they had to be able to survive all the elements down there, especially water. At the beginning, when we were painting on the walls, the humidity was really high and we didn't know how to deal with that.

There were around 150 people working in the Temples at the time, and I was one of the people who accepted the challenge to create artworks, even though I had never done so before. I started the stained glass workshop with another girl, and other people started workshops for statuary and mosaics. We created this together, sharing deeply and trying to overcome the lack of experience.

Being born in Florence, I decided to go back there and visit the workshops of stained glass artisans, to learn from them. At that time, I had to lie about the reasons for my visit because the Temples were secret. I couldn't tell them that I was part of a spiritual community who wanted to create art in a underground cathedral. I told them I was a teacher in a school and I wanted to create little stained glass objects with the children. They allowed me to enter their workshops and each of them showed me a few minutes of basic techniques. I'm sure they could never have imagined what I would do with that information!

The first work we created is the Sun door, which is a portal in the Hall of the Earth, which is one of the Temples. Today we reproduce the image of the Sun door in many ways and people like it a lot, even though it was the first work we did!

This is the way I got started. I wanted to find a medium that would still be in place in hundreds of years, because the Temples of Humankind are meant to be there far into the future.

Do you feel a connection with the history of your medium?

A little. I was born in Florence and there is so much art there. In all our churches there are these beautiful stained glass windows. When I learned more about glass making I became aware of the kinds of colors that we no longer have. With some colors, you only get certain shades from glass blowing. This is not generally the way glass is made today. And some colors are formed using precious metals, like gold and silver. Unless you have an artisan that can use that kind of alchemy to create certain colors, you will lose some of those nuances.

I was more connected with stained glass than fusing. We were fascinated by fusing, but it was taking so much time that we focused instead on stained glass.

Does your medium offer something unique?

It's very simple: the light. Stained glass allows you to not only perceive the beauty of what is represented, but something behind and beyond, which is the light. Light means so much for all of us as human beings. When we are exposed to the light, we feel much more alive because it energizes us. Like the plants, we human beings need the light in order to live! Creating art with something that allows light to come through is, to me, unique.

And when the light changes, also the creation changes. If it is a candle, or a ray of sun, it makes a huge difference. The Temples of

Humankind are underground, so we use artificial light. This allows us to use many variations in the light: as a consequence we can modulate the energy in the environment, and this affects us in different ways.

Why do you have a need to create?

I began to create because I was committed to accomplishing our shared dream. I trusted myself as an artist because in Damanhur we trust human potential. I decided to try, to go beyond any prejudice that I could have had towards myself and my abilities. Of course, if you have never done something, you have to develop your skill. We created this collective field of trust that empowered our hidden talents. The man who created the statuary workshop used to work in the train station of Turin. He didn't received any artistic training. The passion and enthusiasm of each of us has largely compensated for our lack of experience. The awareness that we were, and still are, doing something beyond our existence, has helped us to create all the art in the Temples.

Why do humans have a need to create?

It is in our nature. It's like something is pushing us. Our divine essence, the highest energy, the highest purpose, the highest nature that we can manifest as human beings, is pushing us somehow. We can feel a physiological need to create something. Think about giving birth: that is an act of creation. We should not underestimate any kind of creation. In my community, for example, when some of the women cook they are like magicians, or alchemists. They create something alive. It's not just food, it is true nourishment. Every time you use your creativity you offer nourishment on multiple levels.

We can approach what we do, from the most simple thing to the most complex, with the intention to always find something new, to explore something that hasn't been explored yet, that we were not in touch with. Touching this infinite space inside of us gives meaning to everything we do. It's beautiful because every time we create something, we connect with some parts, inside and outside of us, that are, somehow, new to us. I would say that the need to create is the need to communicate what we have inside in order to reach others. It's a deep exchange, and this is at the base of our life as human beings. It's really simple.

What sacrifices have you made to pursue your creative path?

I would never think in terms of sacrifice. I think more about what I have achieved. Every creative process that I have lived, for example when I have composed music by myself or with others, it has always been a very empowering and meaningful process. So I never sacrificed anything. I always get something back. I've always felt I was connected with a powerful source.

Any creative process can be also a huge effort. It can feel like we are giving birth, especially if we are creating something big that we have never done before. When I gave birth to my son, it was like something got broken, something opened in a way that I could have never imagined. During birth a new space is opened. It is such a powerful moment. Sacrifice is not the right word to describe this process of creation. It is like we are in a storm, with a positive purpose. The effort is nothing compared to the result, to what happens a second after we have given birth. We are involved in something greater than us. When we have a baby in our arms we are amazed by what we have been able to do. And as a consequence, when we create something alive, it is no longer ours, it does not really belong to us anymore. This is what has happened to me after I have created artistic works in the Temples. I don't feel they are my works, even if I have done them. They have their own life, their will to create their own story.

And if we think about it, as human beings we are always involved in acts of creation. If we look at what happens in nature, what happens to a seed, how it grows into a big tree, in the same way each of us passes through this process of breaking in order to become something different. It is not a comfortable situation, but it is how it works in order to go beyond. And we live the same process when we make art.

In Damanhur there are some elements that are very important when we make art: we commit ourselves to always add something new in our creations. We look for a constant evolution in what we do. Making art in the Temples of Humankind requires a constant progression; there is always some new technique or challenge that we have to explore. That's a huge effort, but not a sacrifice.

How has your work shaped you as a person?

Totally! In doing, we discover who we are. I am the result of the work that I have done. We say that we dug the Temples, but more than that, we dug inside ourselves. I believe that we, as humans who can access the meanings we have inside us, are the greatest and most important work of art that we can make. Creativity is the energy of life. Life is constant creation. In the moment of creation we are no different to anything else that surrounds us. As human beings, when we create we can feel united with the spirituality of all life. It is like sharing a heartbeat with all of creation.

So, yes, I am what I did, and I am even more than I thought. Because our thoughts are often like storms, in that they have so many elements. But what we have created with our hands, is something that really shapes life. It changes and transforms life. Our hands leave a trace in the world. Probably, because I love sculpture, I could say that I am the best sculpture I have ever made.

I thought about the main difference between being an artist inside Damanhur and being an artist outside of it, because I have met many artists who have come here to exchange and to get in touch with the energy of the Temples. What I understood is that many artists live their art as a way to stand out from others, to feel that they are doing something unique. It is their art, their style, their process. And sometimes this is not an easy process. What is different for us when we make art in the Temples, is that our art is not about distinguishing ourselves from others, but about meeting everyone else – merging our creativity with that of others. We do not focus on our style as individuals, but we look at art as a collective creative container. The indigenous natives have cultivated, through art and symbols, their sense of belonging to their culture and values.

We have a different approach when we don't work in the Temples: we express our individual style and can sell our artworks as individuals.

In the global capitalist enterprise, creativity can commonly be either exploited or disincentivized. If your work does not meet certain market expectations, even if it is beautiful and unique, it may have very limited commercial opportunities.

How do you deal with creative blocks?

I have never had creative blocks. I think that when we have creative blocks it is because our attention is taken more from our thoughts than from our imagination, from our heart, from the inner place where there is pleasure in doing things.

And when our attention is too focused on our thoughts rather than our feelings, it is more difficult to stay in touch with the source of our inspiration. I feel lucky because I grew up as an artist in an environment that helped me to express my creative potential through singing, painting, sculpture and so on.

In Damanhur we do our best to cultivate a culture of non-judgment. We know that being judgmental towards ourselves or others is completely useless. If we don't know how to do something but we do it together with others, the way we look at the result changes completely. In the Temples, on the ground near the walls of each hall, there are sculptures representing all the Damanhurians. Each of us has created a little statue that represents us. When you look at these statues you can't call them beautiful or ugly; together they are really extraordinary, and each one is unique. When you appreciate the fact that we can express our potential, you no longer judge the result, you experience the process. This is true beauty. What is really important is the act of creation itself. If our attention is focused on these feelings there are no creative blocks.

How do you stay fresh in your work?

It's like having an eternal fire inside, naturally very much alive. I speak for myself, of course, but I see all the other people who make art in Damanhur, and I think they feel the same thing. Creating is not a matter of suffering: it is a very living, natural, elated process. Maybe we see it this way because we are all self-taught artists and everything we create is experienced as a gift. I come from an environment where I have not had to deal with competition and where, on the contrary, it is all a matter of cooperation and integration. I think maybe this is the reason why for me creating is always a fresh process. If we live in a safe environment, full of appreciation, trust and solidarity, everything is lighter.

What is your relationship with satisfaction in your work?

When you work the way we do, it is easy to be satisfied. And it satisfies me just to think about projects. Recently I was in Bulgaria to hold a course on lucid dreaming, which is another skill and passion of mine, and while I was there I had a vision of a painting I would like to paint. I saw all the details. I have not done it yet, but I am already satisfied because it is here in my mind.

I wrote a book, the first part of a trilogy. And when I think about the second, and how the story develops and transforms, I already experience the satisfaction of creation. Making art is like walking. One step is creating, and the other is enjoying. You are always in one step or the other. They go together.

What is the relationship between your work and its audience?

It is an interesting question, because my art is no longer 'mine', as

I said before. Even though I have made many works of art in the Temples, I cannot say that this is 'my' art – it is our art. The artworks in the Temples are dedicated to humanity.

My wish is that these works can make deep and meaningful emotions resonate in those who see them. I hope that the Temples can generate energy and inspire those who come into contact with them. Even simply being surprised is a precious feeling. It is not important that these people know who created what pieces. It gives us enormous satisfaction if they can feel a strong connection with what they discover. The Temples are there to inspire people by demonstrating that we can dream big together, and create something that seems impossible. This suggests that nothing is impossible. On the other hand, we are already 'impossible' beings. We are blessed with the amazing complexity that we contain in our bodies, and we can do anything.

What has your audience taught you?

It is so beautiful when I meet the emotions of others. I am a very lucky person, because besides creating art in the Temples, I am also one of the guides for visitors to the Temples, so I can see how much the art of this sacred space is able to move and touch people's hearts.

I always get a lot from this sharing, but one of the most significant understandings is that the real protagonist of a work of art is the one who meets the art. Through the visitors, the work of art becomes much more; it is continuously alive through the perception of others. So what the audience has taught me is to be humble and aware that we are something only when we create something for others. This is probably the most beautiful lesson they taught me.

What has been the greatest challenge in your career?

There have been many, many challenges. Being self-taught, everything was a challenge. I was an electrician, then a week later I accepted the challenge of creating a portal that represented the sun, the male principle, using the Tiffany technique. I needed a mix of strength, madness and wisdom. And at the same time, it was a very positive experience.

I did a project working on the ceiling of the Earth Room, also in the Temples of Humanity. It is a painting about 14 meters in diameter. And we were four young women who took up this challenge. I was about 22 years old and had never done anything like this before. We were not trained, but we used the best of our imagination to figure out how to do it. It is a sort of complex mandala, based on the ideograms of an ancient and sacred language that gives meaning to the ceiling.

Another incredible challenge was when I made the first stained glass portrait. Although the Tiffany technique was very difficult, I wanted to create something really alive. I love this portrait; it is so beautiful to me.

It was also very challenging to make the first portrait with the grisaille technique. It is a technique where you use oxide, so it is a kind of sculpture while painting. You put the oxide on the glass, then you pull out the shadows, the face, with a brush, and then the image you want appears. It's a demanding technique, but very beautiful.

We also made a dome in the Hall of Mirrors, which has a diameter of 10 meters, all with the Tiffany technique. The walls of the room feature a glass mosaic, another thing we had never done before. So it was all very challenging, but very exciting.

What has been the high point of your career?

Perhaps it was when I collaboratively composed polyphonic compositions with a group of five women. We did some concerts in the Temples. I love this kind of creation. Its intensity is contained in a few moments of time. The music doesn't stay in front of you like a painting. The moment you listen to it, its vibrations transform your emotions, and when the music ends there is almost a nostalgia for the music itself. This is something that really moves me.

Writing has also been an extraordinary experience for me. The book I wrote is inspired by my life in Damanhur. Writing this complex story was another high expression of my creative career. It is another creation that becomes more alive when people read it.

What is the most important thing your creative practice has taught you?

This creative journey to Damanhur has taught me that we are extraordinary beings, and I think I am an extraordinary being! Not because I am special, but because I am human. Probably if I had never come to Damanhur I could have been a very happy electrician, because I really enjoyed doing that job. As a child my dream was to become a plumber, but nobody ever hired me as a plumber because I am a woman. So I became an electrician. But getting to live in Damanhur has been an incredible adventure. It has given me the chance to discover how incredible we are as human beings, when we live collaboratively.

And my creative practice has given me more awareness and appreciation of the creativity in others. Life is hard in this world and we are the lucky ones. In poor countries there is a lot of dignity in the way people do their art. I have been to Senegal, Morocco, India and other countries, and I have seen these women create their art and crafts with pride. They are aware of the beauty of what they create with their hands.

In Morocco I discovered that women, who did not have the chance to go to school, have their own way of writing, especially through their carpets. They weave their stories in the weft of the threads. According to the ancient tradition, women used to make a carpet for the man they were going to marry, and the carpet told their story. Some of these are simply incredible. In some of them I left my heart. Women who have never seen Kandinsky or artists like these, were able to weave abstract, wonderful carpets. They are artists. So, even in poverty, our souls can fly.

How did it feel to reflect on creativity today?

I feel great. I am totally grateful to have the opportunity to express my creativity, to enjoy the creativity of others, to live with the senses that can perceive this. Yes, being grateful is how I feel.

Mike Hall

Mike Hall is the self-made owner of a construction company based in 'rust valley' in BC, Canada. For over 40 years he has been collecting old cars, particularly from the muscle car era, with the dream of restoring them. In 2012 he built a workshop and committed himself to bringing as many back to life as possible. In 2016 he was approached by Matt Shewchuk and Tyson Hepburn to make a TV show about his restoration mission. Now in its third season, *Rust Valley Restorers* is seen around the world on The History Channel and Netflix. Mike and his team continue to make the dreams of car owners come true, and inspire others to get to work on their own car projects.
rustbrosrestos.com / Instagram: rustbrosrestos

What drew you to your medium?

I was born in 1957, so when I was around 11 or 12 years old, that was the peak of the American muscle car phenomenon. Mustangs, Chargers, Barracudas, Cameros, Firebirds, Challengers. Canada is a big country so you have to drive everywhere, and on the car lots or driving down the street, I would see those cars brand new. When I was 16 it was '73, and that era was just starting to fade, but those cars were still out there. And when I hit 20 I started buying old cars. I had to move three times because I was getting hassles with the city. So finally I bought a 26-acre farm and moved 200 cars out there. Then I bought an auto wrecker and now I've got over 400 cars. I kept seeing them getting crushed and destroyed, and I decided to save them.

I tell people I suffer from what I call 'metallic hallucinations'. I look at a rusty car and I see it painted, restored, driving down the road. It's a disease. Some of the cars we want to restore, people just shake their heads. They say, "Mike, don't do it." But there's nothing cooler than dragging one out that's been parked for 40 years, that looks like there's nothing there, and in two or three months it's driving down the road looking brand new.

I'm not a techie. When you open the hood of a 60s car, there are eight spark plug wires, there's the wiring harness to the headlights, there's the coil wire and the alternator wire. That's it. But if you open the hood of a new car, unless you've got $200,000 worth of computer analysis gear you can't do anything except change the oil. I think the whole restoration phenomenon is that people want to get back to a simpler time and place, and the cars are a way to do it. You can actually work on your car. If something goes wrong, as long as you've got compression, fuel and spark, it's going to run. You don't have 200 sensors, that if one goes your car doesn't run. I'm almost a luddite, but not quite.

If you're restoring cars from the 30s, 40s and 50s, and bring them up to modern-day suspension, handling and power, that's called a resto – a restoration mod. But the muscle era started with the Mustangs and the Barracudas in the mid-to-late 60s. It ended around 1972. Now they're doing it again. You can go out on the lot and buy cars with 800 or 900 horsepower. But the technology involved has come so far that you can buy it, but unless you're trained on these systems, or a genius, you can't work on it.

What ended the muscle car era was the pollution and the gas wars. In the old days you could buy a HEMI for two or three thousand bucks, and now they're a quarter million for the same car. Because 50 years later people realize the rarity and scarcity of those models. It's supply and demand. One of the highest-priced cars right now is a '68-'70 Dodge Charger R/T, like the one in the TV show *The Dukes of Hazzard*. They made 270,000 of them in those three years, but now a rusty piece of shit is selling for up to $10,000. And you've got to spend around $70,000 to bring it back because right now everyone wants a *Dukes of Hazzard* car. Or they want a Challenger or a Camero, or the

Mustang Fastback that Steve McQueen drove in the movie *Bullitt*. And the people that are my age—late 50s to early 60s—they're the boomers, the ones that grew up with all this stuff, and can afford to relive their foolish childhood.

Do you feel a connection with the history of your medium?

Basically these things are a piece of art. We've worked on stuff back to the 30s and 40s. The generation before us built stuff to last. I cook out of cast iron and stainless steel pans. I don't have one of those teflon-coated pans. It's the same thing with the cars. They built things to last and it was their gift to us. I'm sure there are a lot of old cars driving around Great Britain, where you are. People cherish the simplicity and the fact that they were made to last generations. They didn't make throwaway garbage like today. That trend is why the planet's in such bad shape. We've become accustomed to disposable products. You use it once then throw it away. People aren't buying silver flatware, they're buying plastic spoons and forks. Some people don't even want to do dishes. They eat off paper plates. We're clearcutting our forests for chopsticks and paper plates.

Does your medium offer something unique?

I bought a car off a buddy of mine, who is a Dodge freak. He loves Mopars. And he explained it to me in a way that almost brought me to tears. He said, "Mike, we don't own these vehicles. We're caretakers. And if we do our job properly, the next generation gets to enjoy them and take care of them." That's why you see cars that are a hundred years old. Generations of people have taken care of that vehicle. So I think of myself as a caretaker, not an owner. I've saved them from being destroyed and lost forever. I can bring them back and preserve them. Before I didn't even sell any. But I'm 65 years old now. I'm not going to live long enough to restore 500 cars. But now I'm getting to the point where I've saved them, and it's time to let them go to somebody else who is going to restore them. Or at least sell them the dream. Because I'm pretty sure that half the cars I own would not be here if I hadn't dragged them out of farmer's fields, bought them from scrap yards, hauled them home and parked them for 40 years.

The beauty of the old cars is that you can restore them if there's enough bones left. You go buy a truck today that's 10 or 12 years old, and the fenders are already rotted off half of them. The steel they use is not very good. They're made to be worth nothing in five or six years. The whole culture right now is about planned obsolescence. In 50 years people will still be driving '67 Cameros, if we're still driving at all, but we won't be driving 2015 cars. Number one, the complexity of those cars is just overwhelming. And the cost. When those muscle cars were brand new they were around two to three thousand bucks. If you buy a new truck today here it's $110,000, and in five years it's worth next to nothing.

Why do you have a need to create?

I don't consider myself an artist. As I said, I grew up surrounded by these cars, so I know what they should look like when they are restored. You wouldn't buy a Picasso then say you don't like some part of it so you're going to change it. Those cars were designed beautifully. But I don't mind upgrading the musculature, shall we say. For example, taking something from the 50s and making it handle like something modern. Or making it go faster or stop easier. But to me they aren't cars, they're automotive art. And that's gone today. Unless you see the name of the car, you don't know what it is. It could be a Toyota, a Honda or a Ford. But back then you could identify the make and model half a mile away. So to me the cars are the art. I'm just a restorer, not an artist. Like old paintings will have people who restore them. They don't change it, they bring it back to its original glory. That's what I'm trying to do. I don't think I can improve on them. People like Chip Foose are artists. They have their own vision of what the car could be. But I more or less want to bring them back to their original design, with some upgrades. So I'm more a conservation specialist than an artist.

My wife is an artist. She can see things in her mind. I can only see the vision of what I want the car to be because I saw them growing up. She says I have 'aphantasia', which is an inability to visualize mental imagery. I'm good at numbers and remembering things. Even though I know what I want the car to look like at the end, I don't really see it. I can't draw. People like me are meant to subsidize artists. I'm good at making money. Except when it comes to cars. That's my downfall. But I run a successful construction company. I can stabilize a cliff. I'm great at blowing things up. I'm more destructive than reconstructive. I also have ADD like a sonofabitch. I'm really bad. So I'm great at taking cars apart, cataloging the parts, but then I hire my team to fulfill my vision. Just to stay focused long enough to finish things is tough. That's why I have 500 cars. It's easier to collect them than restore them. But now that I've assembled a team and we have the show, I'm finally able to get serious about restoring them. When the show came along it gave me the kick in the ass I needed. I have $2 million tied up in rust, and it's finally time to do something with it. Or what was the point of my life? Basically, as the show says, these cars are my legacy. And if in the end I don't restore them and they end up getting crushed anyway, then what was my legacy?

Originally, the show was supposed to be about my work on rock slope stabilization. Then I got an eight-year contract with the Canadian National Railway, doing all their slope stabilization work. And they would not let film crews on the railroads, for liability reasons. But the guys came to my place and saw my field of cars, and said, "Why don't we do a restoration show?" I said, "Are you guys nuts? I have a car addiction. I'm not a restoration shop."

I do know some things about restoring cars, and I know the history of them, but I said 30 years ago that I would never restore other people's cars. I did it once for my brother, and spent more on materials than what I charged him. So I said, "If I'm going to do it, I'm going to play with my own cars." But once they had the funding for the show, they wanted to see the payoff, the moment when the client receives the car. I had a 20 by 30 foot shop at the time, but they wanted to do 10 cars a year, enough for a season. So I had to build this bigger shop, with enough room to work on more than one at a time. Then we hired some people, and as I like to say, the rest is history – because we're on The History Channel.

My whole life, apart from collecting cars, has been hanging off ropes stabilizing cliffs. So it's kind of funny how it turned into a car show. That wasn't the original idea. It was going to be about me and my son Connor blowing up cliffs, stabilizing mountains, but then the long-term contract with the railroad meant that I now work for the railroad almost exclusively. So that's how the show came about.

What sacrifices have you made to pursue your creative path?

The fact that I own 400 cars does in no way qualify me to run a restoration shop. So my learning curve has been incredibly steep. You know what they say about experience: you can't buy it, but goddamn is it expensive to obtain. Well I've obtained a lot of experience in three years doing the show. I used to imagine that we could turn out a car in three or four weeks, and now I know that to do a proper job it's 800 hours, or a thousand hours, or more, depending on what you start with. But my problem was that I wasn't out preserving pristine cars that are easy to restore, I was out collecting the ones that people were going to throw away. These could be $500 cars, or $1,000 cars. That's where my metallic hallucinations come in. I look at a rusty piece of shit in the guy's field and I see myself driving down the road having restored it. It's a bad problem to have.

This year we were going to sell a lot of stuff and have an auction. Honest to God I was seriously considering having an unreserved open auction. And then Covid hit. So that's screwed all the plans. I used to smoke and drink. I have ADD and a very addictive personality. It's why I have four or five hundred cars. But 10 years ago I woke up one day and said okay, enough of the alcohol and cigarettes, it's time to grow up. But I've never been able to get over the car addiction. I've lost so much money to my son, betting that I will never buy another car. Two days later I'm buying three. It's the last hurdle I have to get over in my life in terms of addictions. But it's also because I am so numbers oriented. People see hundreds of rusty cars in a field, but I also see a couple of million dollars in potential. So it's not just the preserving, there is money there. But that's not the prime reason. I often sell cars for less than I paid for them when I know they're going to a good home. It's a complex thing. There's the history, the beauty, the artistry, the emotional side and the monetary value.

If it wasn't for Covid, and the fact that the planet is so screwed up, I probably would have sold a lot more, because right now the boomers are the driving force in the economy. They own probably 80% of the world's wealth. And they're the ones that love this stuff. I never thought of that 40 years ago when I started collecting, but I was born right in the middle of the boom. So I'm part of that generation. If we do the show one more time there is going to be an auction, because I finally realized that I have to let them go. My wife and kids don't want 400 cars. I have to do something with them in the next couple of years.

And the world is changing. We are going to electric cars. The days of driving 700 cubic inch HEMIs is coming to an end. It's not sustainable. I never thought about it until the last three or four years. But you grow old and look at the way the planet's going, and you look at what you want your kids to have, and their kids to have. I can see the day coming where people will be putting electric motors in these cars. This is probably the next wave of restoration. GM is already making electric motors that look like V8s. Right now they cost $50,000 for the power plant. But they're making a power plant that plugs in, so you can hook it up to your standard automatic transmission, and it's an electric motor.

But there are no guarantees in life. I'm 65 years old, so I'm already five years older than my dad was when he passed. I don't want to die and have my legacy crushed. You see it every day. There was a guy we knew in a little town about two hours away from us. He had over 700 cars, and when he died, the kids would not even let people come and make offers. They just called in the squishier and squished them. They were piled four high. Cars going back to the 1930s. The kids didn't want to deal with it, so they just crushed millions of dollars' worth of cars. This is really common. My son Connor loves this stuff, but he's not going to give up his job running my construction company to come and build old cars. That's not his passion. The younger generation want a better work-life balance. That's what he always tells me. I spent 40 years on the road working. I'm retired, but now work seven days a week. That's why I have a hard time making this a business, because to me, restoring cars will never be a business. This is my hobby, my passion, my love. So it's really hard to just break it down into a dollars and cents enterprise. That's not the point.

Once we start a car on the show, we have to finish it. So it doesn't really matter what the cost is, we have to finish the car or there is no show. Some days I wake up screaming, and others I'm happy to come to the shop. What do you do?

People have a very special relationship with cars. You see old people go down into my field of dreams and they'll stand in front of a car, and you don't know where they are, but they're some other time, some other place. That car has taken them into a memory. That's why you can drive around the prairies and see the occasional field of old cars. Why? Why don't they just crush them? Why do they save old cars? Or old pictures? It's an embodiment of a time and place, or a person or a memory. And there are very few things in life that do that. Maybe it was just that generation. But maybe in the old days they would have saved old buggies for the same reason. The car is a vehicle from our generation and our parents' generation. But my grandparents went from horse and buggy to a man on the moon. The car is something that carries memories for everyone. It could be a memory of a camping trip with their family. In fact we just bought a van off some people. They got married in this van in Ontario, drove it out to BC, then back to Ontario, then back to BC, and it's been sitting in their backyard since 1989. They sold it to me because I said, "This thing is rotting into the ground. If you sell it to me, I won't sell it, I'll bring it back to life, and park it in front of my yard and sell tee shirts out of it. So the whole world will see your van." I've already been offered twice what I paid for it. But I'm not selling it. What's the point? Sometimes you make a deal, but a lot of times it's not about the money. They wouldn't have sold it, but they know how I love cars, and that I would restore it and look after it. We were supposed to do it this year, but couldn't because of Covid, so next year, when the van is all polished up and running and sitting in front of my gate selling tee shirts, I'm going to have them come down and see it. They'll sit in that van and think about the day they got married, and their memories of driving it back and forth across Canada, and I know they'll be crying like babies. Vehicles are an emotional thing.

Right now we're working on one for a friend of mine. It's a '47 Merc, mounted on a '76 three-quarter ton Chevy 4x4 chassis. He bought it 40 years ago. Connor played in that car when he was a little kid. The guy got crippled at work, so he's been on long-term disability, and he couldn't work on it. He rebuilt the motor 14 years ago, and there it sat. So this spring I said, "Bill, let me have it, because I've been looking at it for 40 years and it's time. I'm going to make sure you drive this thing before you die." I realized that he can't finish it, so we're going to do it for him. We just painted it, we're putting the chrome back on it, and next week we're going to invite a bunch of his friends and do the reveal. He knows nothing about it. I'll be outside the shop and the truck is going to drive out, and four of his best friends are going to get out. It's going to bring him to his knees. It's going to be a great episode and there won't be a dry eye in the house. It'll be cool.

How has your work shaped you as a person?

Basically what shaped me most was 18 years of going to church and good old Roman Catholic guilt. So I know what's right and wrong. My mom talked directly to God. She just died last Christmas, God rest her soul. She was a union organizer. You can bet that right now she's upstairs trying to get the angels on five-day weeks. She's pushing hard for it. So I always try to be upfront and honest. Because I've got ADD, I learned a long time ago that I don't like to lie, cheat or steal. And I don't have to. It's also really hard to remember lies. It comes down to wanting to do unto others as you'd wish them to do unto you. So when most people come to ask me to restore their cars I'm honest with them, and I tell them not to do it, because of the cost. It's like you buy a house, and just want to swap out the sink, but before you know it half the house is torn apart. You could have spent the same money on a new house. And that's the way most of these builds go, because you're dealing with stuff that's so old. Nobody's got X-ray vision, and as you start to work on the car you find more problems that need fixing. Doing the show I try to stay true to who I am. I try to be honest and upfront with people. And a lot of times I'll take the financial hit if I know the people can't afford it. I'm a firm believer that those that can afford to give, should. My grandparents were very involved in the Salvation Army. It feels good to give, if you can help people out. It's about paying it forward. Most restoration shops that you go to, there are 10 projects out back that never got finished. People started them, then got in over their heads. I said that no matter what it takes, we're not doing that here. I'm lucky enough that I have a secondary income, so I know that if we start a build we're going to finish it, even if we do take a hit. Once we make a commitment, we see it through.

How do you deal with creative blocks?

Due to my background in construction, when you're stabilizing a mountain, things can go sideways in two seconds. So my philosophy on getting any job done is 'cork in the water'. You hit an obstacle, you bounce off it and keep going downriver. You have to get the project finished. There might be arguments over the direction of a build, but we keep going forward. With my background as a contractor, we don't get paid for problems, we only get paid for solutions. So there are no problems, only solutions looking for a place to happen. There can't be a block. The biggest block is waiting for parts, or looking for them if we can't order them. But if you can't work on one aspect there's something else that can be done. So if we can't work on the engine, we'll work on the chassis, or do bodywork, or upholstery.

Normally the client is right, but not always. So you might have to persuade them to see it your way. Based on experience, you do your best to get them to understand the likely outcome of doing it their way. It doesn't feel good to say I told you so, especially if it just cost them thousands of dollars.

How do you stay fresh in your work?

Every once in a while I tell the crew to fuck off and I go and hang on a rope for a week or two. When I get really stressed I go blow something up. The problem with working in a shop is that you're not really living in the now. If you're grinding or painting, maybe, but when you're hanging on a cliff on a rope, it's like you're downhill skiing – you don't have time to think about anything else. And I like living in the now, being focused on what I'm doing. When you start getting eight members of staff, and client builds, and conflicts, you're not living in the now, you're living in 300 different places at once, and that's what stresses you out. When we go fishing in Bella Coola and a grizzly bear is swimming across the river towards us, we're living in the moment. You feel like a piece of meat, and that's a cool feeling. Everybody should feel like a piece of meat once in their life. You're absolutely living in the now. It's the same when you're rock scaling. If you're not totally focused, that's when that rock's going to come down and pick you off. You don't have the luxury of daydreaming. So when it gets too much, I tell them I'm bugging out. Or I hop in one of my cars and go ratbag the shit out of it.

When I get back from one of those trips, all that pressure has been blown off. All that conflict and inner turmoil has been blown out the door. You can ask my crew: when I come back from a couple of weeks' work I'm a way nicer guy.

What is your relationship with satisfaction in your work?

The most satisfying thing is when you see it going out the door. I have a saying when we do rock work: we're only as good as our last job. It doesn't matter what builds we've done, what cars we've turned out in the past, the only one that counts is the one we're doing now. And in rock work we say, "It's over when it's 100% done." Because it's the 1% that can kill you. The 1% you forget. That 1% can kill someone who drives under that rock job you've just done. The last 10% is 90% of any job. That's when you've really got to bear down and stay focused. That's when shit goes sideways.

And with cars, you don't want it coming back. There are probably a couple of thousand pieces on any car. Once we've torn them apart and sandblasted them, we've basically disassembled every part. You can strip a car in a day or two, but it takes around 200-250 hours to put it back together. And everything has to be torqued, everything has to be adjusted and set up right. Our windows guys can spend a day or two trying to adjust the glass on one door. They took it apart in 20 minutes, but putting it back together and getting it to work the same is a lot more complicated. And when it rolls out the door, you want everything to work. When you're dealing with stuff you can't get parts for, you're trying to refurbish parts that could be 50 or 60 years old. There's a lot of pressure.

We do two cars per episode. And on the average restoration that's a thousand hours. Sixty thousand minutes. And we get 17 minutes for each car on the show. You do the math. We get very little time to show all the work that has really gone into bringing that car back to life.

What is the relationship between your work and its audience?

It's a character-driven show, with the cars as the hook. We get fans from ages three to 80. We'll have grandmothers tell us how they love the show. And Connor recently sent me a photo of a pair of toddlers wearing our tee shirts. Our demographic range is pretty wild.

What is the relationship between yourself and your audience?

The most pressure that the show has put on me is that people recognize me wherever I go. We could be pulling into a gas station and someone comes up and starts telling me about their car. I'm a pretty personable person, so I'll talk with them. But I can't imagine being super famous, and having paparazzi and hordes of people swarming you. It's bad enough just being on a car show. This is British Columbia, and we'll be at some gas station in the middle of nowhere, and there are people getting out of their cars saying, "Mike, we love the show! You guys are amazing!" And you have to be nice to everyone, and talk to them, and listen to their story. But I can see how it would drive people nuts beyond a certain level. I like talking to people so it's not a big deal, but now with Covid, it's pretty hard to say to a fan, "Stay the fuck away from me." So I don't. And then I get shit because people are posting pictures with their arm around me. But what do you do?

The biggest compliment I get is when people come to the shop and meet me, and the first words out of their mouth are, "You're the exact same as you are on TV." And I say, "There's a reason for that. I'm not an actor." The reason the show is so popular is that people can relate to me being me. It's the same for all of us. So when people meet me it's like I'm their next door neighbor. It's not like they're coming up to Meryl Streep or somebody and asking for an autograph. They'll tell me they love the show, and I walk them through the shop and give them the tour of the cars. I don't know how other car show guys do it. There was a show called *Orange County Choppers*. It was one of the first automotive reality shows in the States. He was on for 16 years. Paul Teutel Sr., the boss of OCC, phoned me up one day and said he'd watched the show, and loved it. He said we're the most real guys on TV, and we shouldn't change a thing.

I want to remain true to who I am. I think I'm the same person that I was five years ago. To me that's important. I'm a self-made man. I don't owe anybody anything. If the show ended tomorrow, my life would go on as usual. I'm not going to be blowing my brains out because my fame as gone. It's been a cool thing, I'm riding the wave, and when it casts me onto a sandy shore, well, it was a good ride. The most that you can ask for in life is a good ride.

My other philosophy in life comes from my college basketball coach. He said, "Mike, life is a game. And the best thing about the game of life is that you get to make as many moves as you want. If at the end of the game you've made no moves, whose fault is it?"

What has your audience taught you?

My audience has taught me that there are way more car-crazy people out there than I thought. They are everywhere. There are people that love and cherish these cars. We get letters that have my daughter in tears, from guys saying that watching the show has made them dig their grandpa's car out of the garage, and start working on it with their kids. Just watching me drag a piece of junk out of the field and restore it has inspired them to try it. The thing is, when you come to my shop, we don't have a bunch of fancy tools. The work we do here relies mostly on relatively basic skills. We have some specialists, like my metal guy, but most people can do what we do in their own shop. We don't have high-end equipment, or do million-dollar builds. So that seems to have motivated a lot of people to start working on their cars. They think, 'If that bunch of clowns can do it, I can do it.' Because the show spends a lot of time showing off our mistakes, as well as our successes. That's one of the main differences with our show. We do screw up, but we fix our mistakes. People can totally relate to screwing up, because that's what happens in real life. We aren't perfect. Most shows won't show the guy screwing up a $20,000 paint job, but we will. And then we do it again and get it right. Or Avery dropping and smashing the brand new transmission on my Roadrunner. Or us flipping the engine hoist over.

Avery and I are good friends, but we're both alpha-type personalities. We both like to be in charge. So when it comes to stress, I often tell him to go pound sand. If you've got a best mate you can tell him to fuck off, and next day it's all good because you've said what's on your mind and blown off steam. That helps make it work.

What has been the greatest challenge in your career?

The greatest challenge is having employees that I can't yell and scream at. Because I'm used to running construction jobs. I'm spending $50,000 per day on wages and equipment, so if something goes sideways I lose it. I'll scream at them until I lose my voice. But they have the right to turn around and tell me to go fuck off and sit in the truck, because we're all equal up there. But I can't do that here. So my biggest thing is having to work on my interpersonal skills. I'm pretty good at dealing with people, but I'm used to dealing with governments and railroads. You do the work, send them a bill and that's it. So I have to be careful what I say. I guess it's a matter of acquiring a seven-second tape delay. It's a different industry to what I'm used to.

When we did the '66 Pontiac Parisienne, that was the first time we did the LS, and the six-speed transmission. It was the first time, as my son would say, we got dragged kicking and screaming into the 21st century. That was a very complex build. Right now we're doing one for Connor that's going to be 700+ horsepower, supercharged. A level higher than the Parisienne. But anytime you do something for the first time you're a little bit leery. It was a very expensive build, and a lot of money was on the line. And we really wanted it to turn out well. The client was heavily invested, and the shop had a lot of time into it. When I let off my first blast I said a hail Mary when I pushed the button, just in case. It's the same thing with cars. But once you've done one it gets easier, and you're no longer an automotive virgin, so to speak. And you go onto the next one.

The body and paint is basically the same as it's ever been, it's just the technology has changed. You start to go with four-wheel disc brake sets, with computer-controlled transmissions. I am PC, which means pre-computer. I remember when the first electronic calculator came out. It had four functions and cost $100. I remember it was a big deal when we learned to use a slide rule. I've come a long way. Now I have a cellphone, and send texts and do emails. I still don't have a computer, or a television. So I don't watch the show. I think I've seen two episodes. But it's like I don't take a lot of pictures. I've seen it and done it, and don't need to relive it. There's enough going on in my life that I don't have to relive the past. Maybe that's just part of my ADD. I don't have photo albums. It's a memory, I've got it, and I move on. I don't worry about what I've said or done on the show. I don't have time for that. I'm living it, and I don't need to relive it.

What has been the high point of your career?

The high points are really the moments of emotional satisfaction. It means a lot when you do a build with a story, and the story comes to an end. Especially the builds we do that involve a tragedy, a family loss. And then you feel that these people are finally getting their closure, because they were going to restore that car with their kid or their parent. It means a lot to help them close that chapter. All the time the car is sitting in their garage unfinished, it's like that book is still hanging open. And they have to relive it every time they see the car. Closure is a good thing. It's like a wound that can finally heal.

What is the most important thing your creative practice has taught you?

It's just been another chapter in my life, and a continuation of my belief that if you do good unto others, good things will happen to you. I've learned a lot about restoring cars, and the time and cost involved, but that's just technical stuff. It's not really a life-changing thing. I thank God every day that I'm still here, and able to live my life. And my passion, all the time I've spent collecting cars, has finally come to fruition. Forty years of collecting junk, and now they're coming back to life, one at a time.

How did it feel to reflect on creativity today?

I reflect when I see the builds done, and I can go back and look at the journey. Because every vehicle is a journey. It begins when someone drops off their dream. Or we go down to my field and pull out some rusty piece of shit. And when you see the job finished it's a sense of relief, and happiness that we've done that job well. It's the same thing when we do a rock job. You start with a cliff that's just a nightmare, and when we leave all the loose rock is done, the shotcrete is sprayed, the bolts are in, the mesh is hung, and we know that people can drive under that cliff safely. I like knowing that the job has been well done. It's a total sense of satisfaction.

David Hurn

David Hurn established his international reputation with his intensely personal coverage of the late 50s and 60s. He became a full member of Magnum Photos in 1967. In the 70s he returned to his home country of Wales to explore what the word 'culture' meant to him. David works from his cottage in Tintern shooting a few selected stories, working on his archives and being in contact with the world's major museums and collectors. In 2020 he was awarded the prestigious Lucie award for Documentary.
magnumphotos.com/photographer/david-hurn
Instagram: davidhurnphoto

What drew you to your medium?

It was a kind of bizarre luck. I'm extremely dyslexic and when I was at school, there was no such word, so you were just called 'thick'. But I was extremely good at sports. And so I sailed through school on the back of being in the school team and that sort of thing. My career preference was to be either an archeologist or a vet. But with dyslexia it's very difficult to write well, and in the 50s, exams were nearly all written essays. So, I have no qualifications whatsoever. I therefore decided to go into the army. At that time you had to do 18 months of national service. And because I was good at sports, I found myself not having to do a lot of normal things in the army. I ended up at the Royal Military Academy Sandhurst, which is like a university for the military. I was there almost as a professional sportsman, but I enjoyed it immensely because the standard of lecturers and people there was very high. So for me, it was like going to university, but you were studying things like military history. And so there I was, destined to be an officer and a gentleman for the rest of my life and I was enjoying it. I think I would probably have been a pretty good army officer. I had the ability to break things down into their component parts, and be very clear-thinking and focused.

One day I was in the officer's mess, and as I was looking at a magazine I burst out crying. And crying is not something you normally do in the officer's mess at Sandhurst. I was looking at *Picture Post*, which was a wonderful visual magazine. And in that issue there were pictures from Moscow. At that time we were fed the propaganda that all Russians ate their children. They were the enemy. And the picture that made me cry was a Russian army officer buying his wife a hat, in a department store in Moscow. When the Second World War ended, I hadn't seen my father through the whole of the war. And the first thing he did when he came back to Cardiff was to take my mum, with me in tow, to Howell's department store, and he bought her a hat. And so my first real memory of the love between my father and my mother being demonstrated, was the buying of a hat in Howell's. And when I saw this picture, I thought it extraordinary that it could produce in me such emotion. But not only that, the picture was more powerful than the propaganda I was getting from experts in that field. I believed that this was a decent human being in the department store buying his wife a hat. I found that ability to counteract propaganda, and to create some kind of emotion, whether it be sadness, happiness, laughter or anger, to be an extraordinarily powerful combination. And even though I'd never shot a picture before, I suddenly thought that this is what I want to do. I would like to spend the rest of my life basically photographing army officers buying their wives hats.

And that's what I've done ever since, or the equivalent of that. It's to do with trying to find moments that I think are significant in life, that create emotional impact, that show the world as being either decent or unpleasant. It's a matter of trying to be as factually accurate as a human being can be. We all have foibles, we have prejudices and so on, but it seems to me that if you're reasonably intelligent and you're open-minded and you research well, and you try to read well, you can come to some kind of decision in your life, which you can justify. And I wanted to do that in pictures. And so I left to be a photographer.

I come from a valley background, where the honorable thing is that you get a job so you can pay your way in life. So I went up to London, and got a job selling shirts in Harrods. This allowed me to buy a camera, a little folding Kodak. I still have it. In the evenings I used to go to the coffee houses. I don't drink, so I didn't go to pubs. I soon discovered that there were two groupings in London at that time. There was the pub crowd, which tended to be painters and sculptors and people like that. And then there were the coffee bar types. Coffee bars were just beginning to explode at that time. They were much more to do with the writers and the composers, and to a lesser degree, the photographers. There weren't that many photographers around at that time. And I fitted into that crowd. I learned to take pictures by going into the coffee bars every night and just taking pictures. This was the late 50s and early 60s, and you met people. I learned what networking was about. I think the main thing that I learned, very early on, is that by and large, in the sort of activities that I'm interested in, there are two types of people. There are the doers and the talkers. And the doers attract doers, and the talkers attract talkers.

As I shot pictures, I would make little prints and show them to people. I suddenly got this little grouping of friends around me. I met Ken Russell very early on, who at that time wasn't a filmmaker. Bizarrely he was actually a ballet dancer, originally. But he went into still pictures and then into movies, with a windup Bolex. His 1959 short film *Amelia and the Angel* got him his BBC contract. And Colin Wilson was there, sleeping out on Hampstead Heath. Michael Foot was there too; I think he had just become the editor of *Tribune*.

And I discovered that these people tended to gravitate together, if you were a genuine doer. And therefore the conversation was not about what you pretended you were going to do, but what you had actually done. And as you were showing what you'd done, it attracted a group of people that I liked very much, and I found incredibly constructive. And I discovered at that time that the best way to improve is to be with people that are better than you are. It doesn't matter what they do. If they do what they do better than you do, you learn. If you are with a whole lot of people that do nothing but talk about things all the time and philosophize about it, it's like being in a mud pool. They might enjoy themselves, but it's not very constructive.

Do you feel a connection with the history of your medium?

I do, because I started to be interested in it. I didn't know anything about it at all. I literally hadn't shot a picture when I went up to London. I didn't know any photographers, and I didn't know anything about photography. At that time there weren't many photographic books. When a new book came out you grabbed it, but because there were so few photographic books, the ones that came out were really high quality. So you don't have this thing now where everybody goes and does their own little publication. It's charming that they do it, and I suppose it gives them a bit of confidence, but it's usually crap. And the book is never going to be seen again after two weeks. But when the publications were coming out then, because they came out so rarely, they came out through some major publisher, like Thames & Hudson. And people at that place had done a lot of research to find the best people. So I began to look at the books that came out, for example by Henri Cartier-Bresson, Richard Avedon, Ansel Adams and Bill Brandt.

I suppose I almost instinctively understood that if you're going to make your living out of it, you've got to produce something that somebody wants to buy. They've got to be interested in it. So very early on, I would pretend I was the perfect editor. And when I started to do something, I would say to myself, would I buy this? Would I be interested in it? And that helps you to develop.

The other thing I discovered is that the people that seem to be the most successful, had something which you could loosely call 'authorship'. In other words, if you looked at work by Bill Brandt, and if you knew a little bit about photography, you recognized that Bill Brandt had shot those pictures. Likewise, if you saw something by Cartier-Bresson, you would know it was by him, and not by Brandt. In a way that's irrational, because they've all got a box with a hole in the front. That's all a camera can possibly be. It lets light through, which makes a trace on the back and that's it. Now, how on earth can you have that same instrument produce such different results? For example, if Ansel Adams, Koudelka and Robert Frank came and stayed with me, and we went to take pictures of the village fête, they would all take a different set of pictures. That's why there's no such thing as competition among the very good people. The only competition is among the crappy people who all shoot the same picture. I hope that's not what I do. I rely on somebody somewhere saying we want pictures taken by David Hurn.

Does your medium offer something unique?

The thing about photography is that it uniquely has a technical tool that does the craft work for you. You don't have to learn to paint or draw, you have a tool. Now that's not coincidence. That came about because in 1839 photography was invented. We're talking about the time of Darwin and these sorts of people, and the scientists at that time collected and analyzed a great deal of information. And what they desperately needed was a very quick, very accurate method of record. And basically, like most scientific inventions, if you need it badly enough, somebody invents it. The Egyptians had observed that if you had curtains, you had to open and close them because if you didn't do that, the sun would, for some reason, bleach lines down the curtain. That's photography. That's light affecting a material. And then there were other people that invented the pinhole camera, and the camera obscura. So if you begin to link all that together, people like William Henry Fox Talbot then introduced a chemical process, and fixed images using silver salts. And as more people worked on various aspects of this, you end up with something called photography, which is basically a box with a hole on the front, that lets light through, and a method of fixing the trace of light at the back of that box.

So what it does terribly well, is it records what the camera lets in through the lens. It does that better than anything else does, and that's its unique quality. I would argue that because that's its unique quality, so don't abuse it, don't try to pretend it's painting. If you want to pretend it's painting, go and paint, because painting does it better. Painting is much more flexible. Or if you want to get into metaphor, go and write poetry. If you get want to get even more abstract, write music. So I would argue that you should pick the right medium for what you want to do. Use its strengths. And the strength of photography is the recording of what is in front of it, accurately and honestly. And it happened that what I want to record is relationships between people, which was based on an emotional response to a photograph in *Picture Post*.

Why do you have a need to create?

When people talk about creativity, it sounds like some God-like thing that only you have. I don't buy that. It's a job. But it's a job that I love doing, that I think is important. It's a bit like deciding to go into medicine, and making up your mind whether you want to be a nurse or a surgeon. And if you want to be a surgeon, boy oh boy, do you have to put in a lot of hours. I don't want to be operated on by a surgeon who does one operation a month. I want to be operated on by a surgeon who does five operations a day, and therefore works at it. And to me it's a bit like photography. You might just want to be a wedding photographer. Why not? It gives an enormous amount of pleasure for somebody. It's just not what I want to do.

The most important genre of photography certainly isn't what people now call fine art photography, or journalism or anything. I had a really bad cancer back in 2000. And my life was saved because somebody stuck a sigmoidoscope up my bum and took a photograph inside me, which was accurate. A surgeon could then look at that photograph and say, "This is where we cut," and save my life. So the most important type of photography is very technical. It's to do with medicine. Or it's to do with Rosalind Franklin's work on X-ray diffraction which in a way allowed Crick and Watson to discover DNA. It's a very technical sort of thing.

What I do is a small offshoot of photography. I'm now going to sound very pompous, but in a way, what I'm trying to do is to record accurate memories, that in a hundred years' time, people can say, "Because David Hurn took that, and because I know that he did not manipulate his pictures, that's what it looked like when he took that picture." And hopefully that particular person will know a little bit about me, and can say, "And he did it as honestly as he possibly could." It's very difficult to be totally honest in photography, because you don't always know the facts correctly. But as long as you've done your research and you try to get the facts right, and are willing to admit afterwards when you don't get your facts right, then it seems to me that you could be reasonably objective.

But some people have this ability to be what I call 'subjectively objective'. And that's what I call authorship. Bresson has the ability to take pictures that look like Bresson. And that is obviously reflecting his personality, whatever that means. I just happen to believe that personality is the sort of combination of your life happenings. It's as simple as that.

I'm uneasy, particularly when young people start talking about creative stuff, because it's so often linked with what they think is going to make them some money from a gallery or selling a print. They want to call themselves artists. I have no idea what they mean by that. I have a plumber in the village here who calls himself an 'artist plumber'. I can understand why he does it: he gets paid more money for it. Everybody thinks he must be very sincere about what he does.

People call themselves an artist, but to me it should be a bit like being knighted: it's something you say about somebody else who has achieved something supremely good. Like, "By gosh, he's an artist."

But when people describe themselves as creative it just seems to me a little bit silly and pompous and unnecessary. It's designed for academics to talk to each other.

Why do humans have a need to create?

I have no idea. Is it something to do with the desire to try and do something as well as you possibly can? Certainly that's the case for me. The fun that I get out of photography is that it's so staggeringly difficult to get really good pictures. And therefore, all the time you're up against something which is difficult to do. And trying to do things which are difficult to do is fun. Doing things which are easy to do, I would think, is extremely boring. Being locked down at the moment, I am frustrated because I can't get out and stretch myself, and try to improve, whatever that means. So I know that when and if I wake up tomorrow, it's a new world. And therefore in theory, there's something to look at that's different from today. And that's wonderful. But in a little village like this one, today is very much like yesterday, and the day before that. And then suddenly there comes a time when that's all just a little bit flat. I was out today trying to shoot some pictures, but in the village there's so little happening, and I just find it difficult.

During the lockdown I gave myself an exercise. I said to myself, let's pretend you're an estate agent photographer, and I'm photographing my cottage as though I wanted to sell it. So I gave myself a whole new type of photographic challenge. I thought, okay, I'll learn how to do that. I'll look at some books that show architectural photography, and then see if I can do that. And I was okay. I'm sure I could have made a living as an estate agent photographer, but I didn't enjoy it that much. I enjoyed the realization that I could do it. And I enjoyed the fact that I felt I could learn to do it better, but I didn't have that sort of satisfaction of the end picture, and thinking that in 50 years' time, somebody will still want to look at this picture.

David Hurn

What sacrifices have you made to pursue your creative path?

I was married to somebody that I loved very much. We lasted for seven years. I could speculate that perhaps one of the reasons we broke up was that I was continually charging off. I think it's reasonable to say that if you try to do something at a supreme level, you can only do that if you have the freedom to be able to do it. Whether that inevitably puts a strain on relationships, I don't know. There undoubtedly have been people that are married and it worked. But it seems to me that in those circumstances, somehow the idea of what you do being in any way competition, has to not be there at all. And I find that very difficult. For me, it was always the case that if I needed to go and shoot something, I needed to go and do it. And my guess is that that probably put a strain on our marriage in all sorts of ways.

And there were other, more trivial things. I had to give up playing rugby. When I came out of the army I was playing for a team called the Wasps, which was a very good team at that time. But on Friday, I'd suddenly need to go to Afghanistan or something. So the night before the game, I'd have to tell them I couldn't play. But you can only do that twice. So then they suggested I play for the second team, but I didn't want to do that. That's the nature of wanting to do something well. At one time I started to learn to play the guitar, but I only did two lessons because I was too busy with photography.

How has your work shaped you as a person?

I hope it helps you to be a decent human being. One of the things about photography which to me is wonderful, is that you have to be there to do it. You can't do it over a phone. You can't sit at home and speculate. And if you're doing the sort of thing I'm doing, which is usually involving yourself with other people, you need to be able to get on with people. People very soon pick up if you are being rude or anything like that. I hope I've never been rude. But maybe it smoothes you out a little bit. It teaches you a terrific amount, and you have to participate with what you are photographing. That makes you think more about what other people do, etc.

So you tend to be a participator. You tend to be interested. You tend to research a lot. If you don't do your research, you don't get the pictures. I've done a little of what is usually called war photography. When people think about war they seem to think they're going on all the time, but it's not the case. You can be somewhere like Beirut and be drinking coffee in one street while they're shooting the hell out of each other in the next street. And if you don't have the experience to know that, you'll miss the moment. So these are things that you learn. If you are genuinely interested in other people, and genuinely trying to record moments which you think are going to be relevant in 50 years' time, I hope that makes you a better human being.

How do you deal with creative blocks?

I don't have time for creative blocks. To me, the world is a wonderful place. I often think, "I wonder if cows wonder?' Because the mere fact of wondering is one of the most lovely things that human beings do. And I am very aware that if I wake up tomorrow, and I hope to, it's a new day. Everything's changed. And so you can't have a block. I don't know what that implies. I certainly have days when I don't find any pictures, but that's not because I've got something in my head which is blocked. It's because the type of picture I take seems not to be happening. So that's annoying. But the idea that there's some mystical thing which isn't happening today because the vibes are not right, I've never understood all that stuff.

How do you stay fresh in your work?

As I say, the world is wonderful and all you've got to do is go out there and look at it. And by definition it changes every day. People say, "We must do something new." But I always do something new: I get up each morning.

What is your relationship with satisfaction in your work?

I like to get a picture which I feel combines two things. Firstly it has a sense of design, because I happen to think that people look longer at something which is well designed, or has good geometry or good composition. I think that draws the person to look at something for five seconds rather than one second. And I don't think it's any coincidence that painters have a sense of composition and design in what they do. I think that's because they want to grab the audience. And that good design has got to be projecting interesting subject matter. Getting those two things working together is difficult because everything is fluid and moving.

And then on top of that, what you want to get is something that is almost instinct. And again, instinct I don't think is a mystical thing. My guess is that instinct just has to do with having done an incredible amount of research.

And what you get is something which I find absolutely wonderful. If I look at you now, my guess is that 99.9% of people that would be looking at you would say, "That's a man, wearing glasses and a plaid shirt, and he's got a forest backdrop." Most people will pick up that kind of information, but what everybody would do differently is to put that information into the reading of the picture. They would make some kind of assumption about you based on these things. I find that interesting. It's why I love working with poets. They are very precise, and very tight with their language. John Fuller is a great friend of mine, and we do a lot of things together. I would take a picture which I like, and then he will write a poem about that picture. And I can see exactly how he feels about the picture, because he's such a good poet, and so precise with his language. And I find that wonderful, that he obviously reads my picture in a subtly different way. He gets all the technical information the same as everybody else, but he comes to a unique conclusion. I love that. I think that's a very exciting thing to do.

What is the relationship between your work and its audience?

My hope is that it creates two things. I want it to create some kind of emotional impact. I don't care if that be hate, laughter, anger or whatever. And I want it to give accurate information. I don't want it ever to be economical with the truth. I don't want it to be pretending that there's only two people dead in this field when in fact there's 300 people dead, simply because I've cropped it in a way to make it look as if there's two. That is what I hate most in what is loosely called 'documentary'. It's a very bad word. 'Reportage' would be better. But when it pretends to be that, but obviously isn't, it's propaganda. It's trying to distort what is there for some particular end. I detest that.

In my work I'm trying to say to somebody else, "This is what I saw, and hopefully you understand what I feel about it. And this is my honest opinion." Now that picture could have been set up, but I'm presuming that it wasn't. So you make presumptions which might be incorrect, and they might come back to bite you. And certainly nowadays with silly things like Twitter, you basically can't make a mistake because there's always some bugger who's going to find it. You may have shot a million pictures but they get hold of one picture and accuse you of staging it or whatever. You can only be as honest as you can. And if you discover that something doesn't fit that kind of way that you would like to be working, you say so. I'm a human being, and obviously I'm going to make mistakes in life.

What is the relationship between yourself and your audience?

As little as possible, to be honest. I want a big audience, and I need the pictures to be out there. That's why I like them to be published, or be on a gallery wall. Although a gallery wall is probably my lowest priority. My preference is to have it in a book or magazine. A friend of mine who works with the BBC is a whizz with the web, and we've done a few things. One of which is almost like doing a whole issue of *LIFE* magazine. It features 30 pages of pictures. And it goes out to four million people. That's a lot of people. I much prefer that than some book that I do and self publish, which goes out to 60 people, and they're going to forget it in two weeks' time. I wouldn't compromise for an audience, but I want the maximum possible audience I can get. Now whether I'm going to communicate directly with that audience is another thing. Luckily people are lazy. So I don't get that number of people sending me emails. But I'm very lucky. Most emails I get are pleasant and polite. And so I tend to reply. I use Instagram, but I don't socialize on that. I just post the picture and write some little pertinent text by the side. If somebody does ask a question which I find interesting, I reply back by email.

Students doing their thesis will often write to me. I'm not exaggerating: I get at least 40 people write to me, saying, 'Could you kindly answer the following questions in detail for me?' So I now have a template which has 20 books on it. And I write, 'If you read these 20 books, you will find the answers to all your questions in there. If having read them, you still have a question to answer, please get back to me.' I've never had a single one follow up.

What has your audience taught you?

Nothing. I'm not being disparaging to the audience, it's just that I don't really have that contact with them. My Instagram profile, which is really quite tight, has over 43,000 following it. When I did that, I thought I was going to be able to analyze the data and work out what sort of pictures people liked. But I have no clue. I have absolutely no idea why one picture gets some phenomenal amount of hits, and another picture doesn't. It's very strange. And the history of photography is very much like that. It's very interesting to see which pictures really stand the test of time. There is the little Vietnamese girl running down the street being burned by napalm. The little Syrian boy washed up on the beach. George Floyd stuck on the ground with the police officer's knee on his neck. These are pictures that have had really major effects. And very often nowadays they're by people we've never heard of. So in that way, photography is very democratic. If you're there when something incredibly important is happening and you can record it, it's a very powerful medium.

But there's another kind of photography, which as I said, relies on the fact that it's taken by Koudelka, and somehow you know that when you see it. And that's a different thing. But that's in all forms of communication. You don't have to know very much about music to know that Beethoven is not Mozart, for example. But why? They're all working with 12 notes. That's a miracle. And thank God it's there, because it gives us an enormous amount of pleasure. But they all have something in common. At one time, I was very friendly with Daniel Barenboim, who is considered one of the truly great pianists. I knew him quite early on when we were both reasonably young. I remember going with him to a concert at Wigmore Hall that he was giving. Afterwards we had dinner, and I was staring at him. And he said, "David, you're staring. What are you thinking about?" And I said, "Well, two things, Daniel. One is, I do not understand how human beings can play the piano like that. It seems to me it's beyond the ability of human beings. And I love that realization that somebody can do something so well that you can't conceive that it's possible to do it that well." And that's what I would call an artist, when they achieve that. They do something that you just can't conceive of. And then I said to him, "Daniel, what is the essence of being a concert pianist?" And he said, "David, you play the piano a lot." And that was the best bit of early advice I've ever had. A surgeon becomes a great surgeon because they do lots of operations. Painters become great painters for the same reason. I knew Lucian Freud quite well. You could go there early in the morning or late at night, and he was painting. You look at David Hockney. He must be producing 10 bloody drawings a day or something. They don't stop. The people that are mediocre talk all the time. They discuss all the time what they're doing. What's the theory behind this? The theory behind this is that you get off your arse and do it.

David Hurn

What has been the greatest challenge in your career?

At the moment, the greatest challenge for me is that I am getting older. And it's very frustrating because my head is very clear. If I lie down in bed and don't move, I feel like a 30-year-old. In fact I feel better than that because I have more thoughts and more experience and I feel great. But the second I sit down in a chair I can't get up. And it's a struggle. When you're young you don't think about physical things. But at my age, 86, every movement is difficult. And it distracts from what you're doing. You have to learn little tricks to compensate. And you have to slow down a lot. In fact, one of the things which is really depressing about this whole lockdown thing, is that it will have taken a year out of my life, at a time when a year in my life has a major effect on me physically.

And I'm coming to the conclusion that it would be silly to try to travel much. It's okay in Wales because if I fall over, somebody will pick me up and I'll go to the hospital and I can speak the language. But if I fall over in Dubrovnik, for example, somebody might pick me up, but I would have no idea where they're taking me. I can't speak to anybody. I would be anxious. So photography in the future is going to be a certain amount in Wales, particularly if I get people to come with me and drive me. And certainly I could photograph in the village. But boy oh boy, it's a change of lifestyle.

I was friendly with André Kertész, the Hungarian photographer. I remember going to New York and he had bought an apartment overlooking Washington Square so that he could photograph it with a telephoto lens from his window. And he was 92. And so I said to him, "Well, if you can do it, André, I can do it." It's as simple as that. So I'm pretty certain that I will find a way of photographing when I'm 92, but it won't be the same as when I was 22. It will be different, and you just have to adapt. But the core is the same. The core is trying to record something which you feel has a value permanently. I'm in a profession where I can leave something behind. I have no religious beliefs. I'm an atheist. I don't decry anybody having their own beliefs, but I don't. My feeling is very simple: I have no idea what happened to me before I was born, and I feel that after I die is probably exactly the same as before I was born. And if I don't remember what happened before I was born, I can't get that interested about what happens after I die. So that sort of thing doesn't worry me. I'm pleased for people that believe there is an afterlife, and if that makes them happy and less anxious, good for them. But what I do have is a sense of legacy. The work of Shakespeare, for example, is still around and it continually gives enormous pleasure. And people continually participate in it. There are a few professions like that. Beethoven is going to be around forever. As is Mozart. And some lesser composers. And I strive desperately, so that when I die I will leave something behind. I know that in half a dozen museums around the world, it's part of their job to look after my work. The government tells them they have to do that. If it's a museum it's got to be archived and looked after. And I like that. It's a bit vain to sit back and think that way, but I really have worked pretty hard and I have been very tight in my beliefs. And if it's important for me that I leave something behind, I'm okay with that.

What has been the high point of your career?

I had a simple little high point just recently. If asked by small galleries to do shows, I tend to say yes, particularly if they are in Wales and if there's a reason for doing them. And then I push them hard to work with the local school, to make it a community project. The Worker's Gallery is in the valleys, and we did a show there. I've shot so many pictures in Wales over the last 50 years that I could have a show anywhere in the country and show 20 pictures from within a 25-mile radius of that spot. So that makes a little exhibition like that a community exhibition, because it's dealing with the past, the grandfathers of the kids that are in the school. I love doing that and we had this show and it was very successful. We did all sorts of things. Like I spent a day shooting portraits of anybody. It was well organized, and we shot 25 portraits, and we charged not very much money. But that produced a lot of money for the gallery. It was good. We also did a couple of things with the schools. And then we took the pictures around the various old folk's homes in the valleys and things like that. I'd love to do more of that. So that's one level. I find that incredibly enjoyable.

I was in a cafe in Bangor recently and two young people very politely came up and asked if I'm David Hurn. I said yes and invited them to join me. They were nice and genuinely enthusiastic and they weren't bullshitting. And I found that incredibly enjoyable.

And then I've just got this Lucie Award, which is pretty much the biggest award you can get in photography. It's a bit like the Oscars in film. It's at Carnegie Hall and so on. It has been given for achievement in documentary photography. That was wonderful. And there is something about being accepted in America. I'm not complaining, but I've never been asked to give a talk in the village here. I find that fascinating. I can't think of another country where if they had in their village somebody who had some kind of reputation in what's loosely called the arts, that that person wouldn't be inundated by requests to do things. And then suddenly my peers in America say that they'd like to give me this supreme award, which Cartier-Bresson was given before, and Bruce Davidson, Koudelka and others. It's kind of good for British photography as a whole. I was debating whether I should go, but then Covid arrived and I'm off the hook.

In the 60s I had a flat in London and Peter O'Toole stayed with me for some time. I knew him as a struggling actor who was just out of RADA. And the same happened with Richard Harris, Julie Christie and Claire Bloom. They were just friends. And I took happy snaps of them. The pictures are fine, and they have a relaxed nature to them, which I think works quite well. But if I have a regret, it's that I didn't photograph friends and people more than I did. Sometimes I do get carried away. I did quite a lot of stuff with the Beatles. And one of the things we'd do is to play Monopoly together. I have no pictures of this, because I was so competitive that I wouldn't get up to take a picture. And looking back, that's crazy. The lack of pictures I have of people that I was really quite close to is a shame.

One of the things about photography is that you get very close to people for limited amounts of time. It's the nature of it. But because you're moving so much you lose contact. It's a bit easier now because we have email and things like that. Often I would be close to somebody and write a letter to them. And I remember one particular person that I loved dearly. You'd write a letter and it would take seven days to get to Rome, and then to write back it would take another week. That soon drifts away. But at that time, that was the nature of being a photographer dealing with portraiture. It is a kind of regret.

But as you get older, sometimes you invent memory. And so I often think I must have photographed a particular person, but when I look back through the contact sheets I realize I never did. Or if I did, it was an out of focus picture, which was taken by mistake.

Against that, it's a real jog to memory. I love looking at the contact sheets because everything comes back. I had an instance of that recently with Don McCullin. When we were much younger, Don and I often would go off shooting together. And I was looking at a picture of his and commented that I liked it. And he said, "Yeah, we were together in Rhyl in North Wales when I shot that." I didn't recall it, but because I had the picture with the number and dates and everything on the back, when I came home, I could look at my contact sheets on that date. And instantly, looking at my own contact sheets, the memory came back of the event. There's an extraordinary link between the taking of the photograph and the memory if you see that photograph 50 years later. It brings things back.

What is the most important thing your creative practice has taught you?

What the people I most admire have in common is that they work their butts off. They are obsessional workers. When young photographers ask me for a tip I say, "Go shoot lots of pictures. And be very self-critical." If you are self-critical, you will begin to not take the sort of pictures that you don't like. And if you start doing that for a couple of years, you will discover you're shooting more and more pictures of a certain type that you like. And by definition, you're getting better. But you can't do that if you're not shooting pictures every day for two years.

The only other advice I give—that I think is very good advice—is to wear good shoes. I learned very early on that really great photographers might walk for 12 hours a day. If you do that you get very bad feet unless you've got good shoes. So the first thing you buy is really good shoes.

How did it feel to reflect on creativity today?

To be honest I don't enjoy talking about it very much, because so often you're talking to academics who don't do much, they just talk a lot. And in my opinion, they discuss everything which to me is totally unimportant. And they don't discuss enough the need to go and walk and take pictures for 12 hours a day. I find that young students are being taught all sorts of things which I think are totally irrelevant to shooting pictures. They might be useful if they want to be writers about photography, but they don't help them shoot pictures.

It's nice to converse with people, and occasionally something happens and you find it interesting to reflect on. The people that sparked me in that way are usually people like scientists. I remember I did a thing on the vice-principal at Magdalen College, Oxford. And so I was having dinners every night with the fellows. So you'd be sitting next to a Nobel Prize winner or somebody, and I found it fascinating talking to them. But they weren't talking about the photography. They weren't talking about some mystical approach to creativity. And it's that I shut off against, this idea that there's some sort of mystical aura floating around somewhere; I just don't believe that. I have enough problems trying to work out why, when I flip a switch on the wall, the light comes on. But I do know that I could find somebody that could very precisely tell me. And it could be peer reviewed, and I could learn why the light comes on. I don't like anything which can't be peer reviewed.

Having said all that, sometimes I feel as though I've been injected with a gramophone needle, and it just pours out, because I've been interested in what I do for 60 years. And if you've been absorbing information for that long, and thinking about it, and refining and clarifying it in your mind, you're going to be a bit thick if you don't have something to say at the end of that time.

But you don't get into that conversation with photographers. If I go to see photographer friends, we will only be discussing what we've done. Or maybe about being able to carry less equipment as we get older. We'll talk about the practicalities of the job, not fairies in the Glen.

Corin Johnson

Corin Johnson is a sculptor in stone and wood. His work incorporates larger public sculpture commissions, restoration projects, personal artwork for exhibitions, drawings, letter design and modelling, as well as stone, marble and woodcarving.

Corin was born in Warwick and lives and works in London. He has exhibited at the Tate Britain, the Mall Galleries, the Snow Gallery, Arts Centre Melbourne, Kings Place Pangolin Gallery and many others.

Major commissions include two Christian martyrs on Westminster Abbey, the Bentley Fox, the Lady Diana memorial at Althorpe, St. Andrew for Exeter College Oxford, Pair of Ounces for The National Trust, two large marble sculptures designed by the artist Paul Noble and a relief carving for the Clarkson Memorial monument at Wisbech.

corinjohnson.co.uk / Instagram: corinjohnsonart

What drew you to your medium?

This first thing I recall was going to Greece when I was around the age of six, and finding a piece of marble in the sea. And I treasured it. It was my favorite thing, as much as an Action Man, but it was just a square of marble. So I think I had some intuitive attraction to stone. I grew up in Warwick, which is a very historic place. And I remember an old guy pointing out to me a face in a wall, and I used to love it. It must have been a medieval carving.

I think I was always drawn to clay, stone and wood. I wanted to do something that I liked, that was both artistic and environmentally sensitive, something that was nondestructive to the Earth. And use materials that had been used for centuries, instead of adding to the plastic detritus of the world. And I like really old sculptures, and architecture. I generally prefer it to modern works. But I didn't get the sense that I would be working in sculpture until I was in my late teens.

Do you feel a connection with the history of your medium?

I do. In the days before print, it was a way of recording things. We had stone tablets that we carved information into, and statues of Egyptians and so on. My auntie was a bit of a hippy, and she lived in London. When I was a kid we used to visit her and she would take us around the British Museum and places like that. I remember seeing the mummies and that kind of thing, and I absolutely loved it. Maybe I never grew out of that early fascination. It has so much mystery and wonder, and records things that we would otherwise have no idea about. And that goes into the architecture as well as the statuary.

And there are so many things that are portrayed, from Louis XIV to the alabaster knights lying down in the church with a dog at their feet. It's an old form of record, of depiction. Gravestones to a certain extent offer the same thing.

Does your medium offer something unique?

This is not unique, but it has been used in spiritual settings, in churches and monasteries, and in ancient rock carvings. It communicates spiritual wisdom. I've read that churches were used to depict to the poor and illiterate the stories of the bible. Statues and carvings would give them an image of Jesus, or Jacob going up the ladder to heaven, which you can see on the front of Bath Abbey. And it could give a sense of the higher realms. The large cathedrals and temples would put people in awe. The church has been accused of attempting to control and sublimate citizens, and I'm sure that went on, but they also created a sense of wonder. I've been to some amazing temples in China, which are completely made of wood, and they have huge clay Buddha statues which are astounding.

So they've been used to express a continuance of the soul as well. I was very attracted to that when I was young. I got into meditation and wisdom teachings, and the supernatural and that kind of thing. And a lot of that has been carved in wood and stone, and modeled in clay. It's also been used for the veneration of monarchs, which is not so interesting.

The physical presence of a statue occupies a space in a unique way. And if you add a load of beautiful color to it, it becomes something else. And then you have the baroque theatrics, with the marble detailing. And they would stage the central figure by surrounding them with other figures. You might see this with Christ, or the Madonna in ecstasy. It was powerful – an almost otherworldly experience. I remember going to a temple in Ladakh, in Northern India. It was originally part of Tibet, but it's not now. And you would walk into these rooms and there would be 10 Buddhist monks or deities portrayed, in these painted wooden temples. It does make you feel like there is another realm that is above the mundane. Having those divine focal points in a space can put people in the zone, in the headspace that aids meditation and reflection.

Sculpture often lasts longer than paintings and other forms of representation. The Native Americans had totem poles. The Polynesians created the moai. There is something about having a big, physical, three-dimensional thing that focuses you into that spiritual belief system that you are a part of. It's a powerful medium.

I work a lot with churches. I'm not a Christian, but I'm very open-minded about spirituality. I love sculpture, and feel very lucky to do it. It's hard work though.

Why do you have a need to create?

Perhaps the urge to create is either part of you or it isn't. But I'm not sure. I don't intellectualize it. Though I do sometimes wonder why I do it and other people don't.

I've been told by mediums that I have artist spirit guides that work with me, but I've never felt any evidence of that. Who knows?

A lot of the people my age who started in this kind of work no longer do it. So I don't know why I'm different. I just love the work. And I enjoy looking at other people's work. I suppose I've had enough affirmation of it, that it's wanted and enjoyed by other people, to confirm that it's worth doing. People ask me to sculpt things for their buildings, so they and other people can enjoy it. I always have commissions to work on, and I collaborate with others, which is inspiring.

And I'm asked to do a variety of things. I did an anti-slavery relief carving in 2010. It was created in honor of Thomas Clarkson (1760-1846) who was a central figure in the British campaign to end the slave trade. So sometimes I get asked to do things that I have a strong interest or belief in.

Why do humans have a need to create?

I think it speaks to human benevolence, though some people do create very negative things. I also think it's a way for humans to process things. It transmutes energy. And it comes through us. Often you don't have that much say in it. You just do it. But I think it's a bit like wanting to have kids – it's just innate in some people.

It also demonstrates our alliance to certain things.

And if you're good at it, it's a way of earning a living. People like adornment. Some people might like making clothes that other people love, so it's a way of making people happy. And it makes you happy to do it. So I think it's a human thing about society, and trying to make things better for everyone in a way, by making nice buildings, paintings or sculptures. And bettering yourself. The better that you do, the better you feel. And you can share it with other people as well. You can be proud of something you've done.

I think it's very difficult to be totally original. We borrow a lot from other ideas, and process them a little bit, and put our life experiences into them.

I also think it depends on what you're into. If you're into environmental things you want to put that across, to use your existence for something that's positive. I think there's a spiritual element to it. It's something that comes through us.

What sacrifices have you made to pursue your creative path?

There's quite a lot. Certainly time. Most of the stuff I do is carved out of stone or wood, and it takes a very long time. So you could be doing other stuff, like going away for the weekend. And for quite a long time I didn't earn much money doing it. It takes a long time to get good. And it took me a while to find people who could help me improve. It hasn't really felt like much of a sacrifice. But I certainly didn't live very luxuriously. I lived in squats until I was about 27.

How has your work shaped you as a person?

I think it's probably done so in quite an unconscious way. The work is a product of who you are. It's a two-way thing. You grow together. And then other people commission you to do stuff based on what you've done before. It's quite an organic process.

I've definitely grown in confidence as my work has got better. And you get more respected. When I started out, the sculptors that I worked with used to treat me like shit. And the same goes for the clients. I certainly wouldn't let them now.

But someone else could probably tell me better how the work has shaped me. I'm too close to it.

How do you deal with creative blocks?

I have experienced creative blocks, where I just don't have a project idea for several months. And it's pretty awful. But that's one good thing about how long it takes me to make things, because I've normally got a commission, and by the time that's done I have an idea for something else. So I just work through it. I'll just keep going with my commissioned work until my own ideas start to flow again. And that works, because if you did have an idea you were really excited about, you might not want to finish the thing you're working on.

Big artists, like Damien Hirst, get other people to make their work. So you can have lots of ideas and have people create them. But I'm not in that position. I make my own work. If I am really stuck, I like to do some meditation. That's normally quite good for letting stuff in. And working with other people is good. You can talk, and get inspired by their work. And socializing helps. For example, I can get an idea while talking to people at the pub. So I think it's quite good to do a variety of things. Like reading or even watching films. You never know where the next idea is going to come from. Sometimes just walking around the house an idea will strike you. So you just have to be patient and trust that maybe it's not the right time yet.

How do you stay fresh in your work?

I hope I do stay fresh. In terms of technique, working with different people helps bring in new ideas. It's good to work with new people, and not stay in the same studio with the same group. Sometimes just talking to a lorry driver, as much as someone who is artistically celebrated, will give you inspiration.

Again, a bit of meditation works well for me, as do walking and eating well. Just keeping yourself in a good place can be productive. Happiness allows things to flow. If you get down for a long time, you can stagnate and get into a negative groove. So taking yourself off for a few days and having a change of scenery helps. I was recently working in the countryside for a couple of weeks, which was nice. Getting away from it all, and being around some different people helps keep you fresh. Just going up to Norfolk for a day can make you feel completely different, like you've been on holiday for a fortnight. So you have to have a break, and have a bit of a balance in life.

Here's an interesting little story. I used to know this old American mystic, and I would help him out with things, and we would meditate together. And one day we were doing some meditation, and then he said, "Spirit wants you to do a statue of a saint. And it will manifest it for you." I'd never done that kind of work before. But the next day I get a phone call asking me to go to an old church at Exeter College, Oxford. It was a statue that was so eroded you could not tell what it was by looking, but they knew that it was originally a statue of St. Andrew. So things do have an interesting way of working out at the right time.

What is your relationship with satisfaction in your work?

It's nice to be pleased with your work. And if you can be satisfied with it, all the better. But it varies. I don't call a piece finished if I'm not satisfied with it. However, sometimes you can look at something and feel satisfied, and other times you can see something you'd like to change. But if it's already installed you have to make your peace with it. Yesterday I saw a couple of statues that I did about seven or eight years ago. I won an award for them. And one of them I was happy with, but the other, I thought, 'That leg's a bit dodgy.' But I can live with that. The Muslims have this philosophy where when they create something, they always make a mistake, because only Allah is perfect.

I had a weird experience at a Buddhist retreat I went to, again around eight years ago. I had taken some alabaster, and in some downtime I made a little sculpture of a flute player. And that piece was in a little show a couple of years ago, and a flute player came along, and he told me that one of the hands was the wrong way round. I don't care too much about that kind of detail on a piece I made to please myself, but he put it on Facebook, and I heard that some people didn't talk to him for a while afterwards. If you always go for perfection you'll always be a bit frustrated. You can't win them all. I can always do another. But in sculpture you never know what's around the corner. You can always get a bad bit of stone. Or clients can be difficult. You have to learn to be patient and philosophical.

What is the relationship between your work and its audience?

I don't really know, because I don't have much to do with it once it's out in the public domain. So I don't get much feedback personally. When I finish a job they generally say they like it, and often that's the end of it.

There is one that comes to mind. When I go past Westminster Abbey I always see people taking pictures of some of my work. I did a couple of statues for the front of the building. It's nice to think that people enjoy them enough to take pictures of them.

I did a piece for the musician Nick Cave, and he's now interested in working on something together. So it's nice if people like your work, and they treasure it.

What is the relationship between yourself and your audience?

I used to put a bit on social media, but I don't do that much anymore. The work generally got positive responses. But when I see other people doing it all the time, I sometimes wonder why they're doing it. Is it a bit of insecurity? An indulgence? It's nice to get positive feedback, but to do things just to get lots of likes seems a bit childish, in a way.

On the other hand, it could be that you create something priceless, yet it gets measured by this weird metric of likes. I've seen people who will do a piece of art in a couple of hours, then mess about with it on their phone and it will get over a thousand likes. And the work is not that great. So it's a bit of an illusion I think. It seems like a bit of an ego trip. It doesn't feel very genuine to me.

What has your audience taught you?

Feedback can help you to improve. As long as you don't let it become a self-destructive thing. Constructive criticism is useful. And it may be that you want to make something that pushes people's buttons.

But as I mentioned, I don't have a lot of interaction with my audience. I keep getting commissioned, so I keep working. In a positive sense, this teaches you to keep going.

What has been the greatest challenge in your career?

There are different levels. The greatest challenge is when you're feeling like shit and you've got a mountain of work in front of you, and you have to keep going because you've got a deadline.

I've had a few challenges over my career. I worked with a very well-known sculptor and we took on a few commissions together, but he gave up working and I was left to finish them. Then those pieces were being covered in the press and he refused to pay me. And I was buying a flat at the time. So I had six months to a year of borrowing money, only to end up not even having my name on the work, and our friendship broke down as a result.

I had a commission to do work on two ounces. They call them 'ounces' but they're big pieces of stone, the size of a car, in really hard stone. And I had the statue of the saint to do at the same time. And I only had a three-month window to deliver them all. I've had a few of those situations, where there's not enough hours in the day.

I did one a couple of years ago. It was a tree made out of a tree, an abstract, like a Matisse-style tree. The guy I'd agreed to do it with basically didn't do anything, and I had to put a team together to finish it on time. I worked through the last night available as it was getting picked up at five in the morning. I got help from a young African guy who didn't have much experience, but he was like an angel. He just turned up to help me, and if it wasn't for him I would not have had it ready for collection. I've had a few tight finishes like that, where the shippers are coming first thing in the morning to take it to the exhibition.

One commission was for a famous artist, and he wanted these huge marble sculptures made. I went to Italy to make them, and we bought

30 tons of marble and put a team together. I took them all out to Italy to help, but they just kept going on holiday instead of working. Only one or two of them actually bothered working. And that again was down to the wire. That piece actually got nominated for the Turner Prize.

But in a funny kind of way I quite enjoy those challenges. Even the one I'm working on now is a bit like that. I'm doing some gargoyles. It's just the nature of the beast.

When you asked about sacrifices, probably my relationships take a knock. Because it comes down to a question of: do you go away for the weekend with your partner, or do you finish your commission? I would probably have had a family if I didn't enjoy my work so much.

What has been the high point of your career?

There have been a lot. Working with great people is a highlight. Doing that piece in Italy with Paul Noble was special. The Westminster Abbey statues too, and the statue of St. Andrew at Oxford.

But the present moment is important: I'm doing what I like so I'm happy with what I do. Recently I've been cutting these square blocks of alabaster for an artist. And funnily enough, they're probably the most valuable things I've worked on. I've been doing something with him recently, these sculptured benches. They're huge. Some of the world's wealthiest art collectors buy them. I also enjoyed doing the moquette for Nick Cave. It's a guy riding a horse, which is the basis for a monument to be erected in his home town. That was in the press a lot. Funnily enough it was in the quiz in the *Financial Times*.

I've recently been asked to do work for Buckingham Palace. And I taught sculpture and carving at an art school for eight years. That was good. The anti-slavery sculpture is also something I'm proud of.

When the saint got put up at Oxford University my mum came to visit. She said she wanted to visit the chapel, which is a copy of a chapel in Paris. And as you walk through the door, there is a sculpture of J. R. R. Tolkien, by his daughter, Faith Tolkien. When I was about 20 I met Faith, and she told me that she would do anything to help me in my career. We worked together for a while, but then we lost touch. And it was a nice coincidence to see that we both had sculptures in the same church.

I worked with an old stone carver for years, a guy called Michael Black. He died last year. He was into literature, and had fields full of vegetables. We used to go and meet up with his environmentalist friends in Cornwall, and plough fields with horses. And I stayed with him while I did the statue of St. Andrew. And he would kick my arse, making sure I always kept my standards high. But when he saw the finished piece he gave it his approval. That was a nice thing. So I've had many great experiences in my career, and met lots of nice people.

What is the most important thing your creative practice has taught you?

Trust, probably. Trust that if you do your best and you're true to yourself—and that you're doing it for the right reason—that something good will come along next. Trust in the universe, and the great spirit. The right thing will come along.

And try to be a bit generous in spirit, if you get a bit frustrated with people, or think someone may be taking advantage. These days we're taught not to take shit. A lot of people I know who go to psychotherapy are taught to be assertive, and realize that they're replaying childhood dynamics with their parents, and so on. But sometimes I think you should give people the benefit of the doubt. Maybe they are wanting more than I want to give, but I will sometimes just decide to give them that extra bit of time.

Funnily enough, a friend talked me into getting an old washing machine from someone's house. And this French guy was sent to help me, and he turned out to be an amazing writer. He does loads of books on musicians. And through him I've met loads of wonderful people. So sometimes it's better to think that even though you don't really want to do something, there might be a reason why it's presenting itself. If they're being persistent in needing something, maybe just be a bit humble and generous. You're not always the all-knowing being. It's a bit like the Buddhists, where they get the monks to sweep the garden out as part of their practice.

How did it feel to reflect on creativity today?

It's good to stop and think about it for a change. It's nice to talk to someone who is very interested in art and creativity. But I'm better at making things than talking about it. In the end, if you love it, you'll do it. Love is the real driving force. Love is the answer.

Claudia Kappenberg

Dr. Claudia Kappenberg is a performance and media artist, and Principal Lecturer at the University of Brighton, UK. She has published widely on performance and screen-based work, including *Art in Motion* (2015), *Oxford Handbook of Screendance Studies* (2016), *Syncope in Visual and Performing Arts* (2016), and *Performing Process: Sharing Dance and Choreographic Practice* (2018). She curated an online film season titled grounded in 2020. Her performance work borrows from the everyday; it appropriates, recycles and remakes, to challenge the familiar credo of productivity and purpose through a deliberate squandering of effort and time. Her projects have been shown across Europe, North America and the Middle East.

ckappenberg.info / Instagram: kappenbergclaudia

What drew you to your medium?

It would be impossible to define what performance art is. One of its characteristics is its polymorphous nature. It appears in all kinds of places and states, and does all kinds of weird stuff. That's part of its essence.

I came to it through a long journey, starting off as a dancer. As a child I wanted to dance and I was always interested in movement. That was a key fascination for me. Movement in all its forms; real movement, implied movement, the idea of movement. After some years as a professional dancer, something about dance felt too limiting. It is highly codified, driven by aesthetics, and it didn't satisfy me creatively. So I stepped away from dance and studied fine art. And through that I was able to come back to movement, but from a different perspective. That's how I got into performance art. It's another kind of dancing, but it's more conceptually-driven, more interrogating of its forms, its place in the world, its ideas, what it wants to do. Now I work with performance, film and photography, but at the base is a performative engagement with the world at large. In other words, the medium itself is not so important to me.

I came to England in 1991, did a foundation course, and went to Wimbledon School of Art to do a BA, studying in the painting department. They also taught performance and one of my tutors was the wonderful performance artist Richard Layzell. He organized an exchange for me in Canada, with the Nova Scotia College of Art and Design in Halifax. That's where I got in touch with a local gallery and proposed my first piece. That was in 1995. The work was a meditation on transience. I collected all kinds of things, including cabbages, swivel clamps, and made dodecahedrons out of mylar. I then hung those from the space and projected light through them, setting up a kind of landscape installation in the gallery space. The clamps are normally used by scaffolders to connect poles, but they look like little people, creating a sense of population in some ways. The dodecahedrons were bubbles of nothing, but suggestive of something elemental. I stuck the cabbage leaves into my clothes, but as I was moving through the space the leaves gradually fell off, creating a slow, minimal soundtrack when they hit the floor. I was performing entropy.

It is hard to describe the intention behind this work, in that as an artist you don't necessarily know what you're doing when you're doing it. You have to follow a hunch, some kind of vague sense. Twenty years later, I can in hindsight reconstruct my strategy, and I can say that there are certain things that have become part of my approach. For example I'm very interested in the idea of recycling. By this I mean taking something which is there anyway, and displacing it, bringing it into a different context and working with it in an unusual way. I play with it, to see what else it can do. Swivel clamps normally live on scaffolding, but if you take them out of that context and put them in a white space, they can become something else.

And a sense of something ritualistic is important for me, in that I'm less interested in producing something which can be bought or sold. I'm interested in the essence of art, to ask questions like: What can it be for us? What can it do for us? The ritual as a form has become a way of structuring my work. And here I can bring in my dance background, selecting a gesture or a set of movements which I can repeat and play with, to build a composition in space and time.

Time is also very interesting for me. Maybe I'm so interested in movement because it makes time visible. We tend to relate to place, but time is hard for us to understand. Giving ourselves to time, finding a way into time, or into presence, is something I'm very interested in as a practice. And as a life experience. We are so concerned with the past and the future, that we forget to be in the present. Kids tend to be in the present when they play; some might experience this when they play music or read a book, or when they meditate. I'm pursuing this through making performance. All together this is not a direct explanation of what I did in that first performance in Halifax, but this is probably what I was looking for as a young artist.

Do you feel a connection with the history of your medium?

Yes, hugely. There are a number of older performance artists who paved the way and developed this art form, which in itself has many different cultural roots. For example, Alastair MacLennan has been a significant inspiration. He is an Irish performance artist who is in his 70s now and based in Belfast. I've seen him working in old buildings or the streets, setting up a table with objects, perhaps domestic objects, some oddities, and what we might call memento mori like a pig's head, always wearing black. He might have a stocking over his head to obscure his face so that he is more of a figure than an individual, and spend a long time working with the objects. Everything is familiar, ordinary, and yet everything is made to be strange. Another time he found a piece of plastic sheeting, probably from a building site, and he just worked with this, holding it and allowing it to respond to the wind, exploring its lightness and movement. Imagine an old man dressed in black, quietly standing on a street corner next to a building site, entranced with a piece of plastic sheeting. It was very beautiful to watch, and touching. This kind of work, and this kind of sensibility, to go to ordinary places and to respond to it in a surprising way, is something that a lot of people have taken up since. The strategy behind this work is to provoke attention and curiosity, and is part of a quest for greater criticality.

Does your medium offer something unique?

As a mover, as a performance artist, I focus on site-specific work, which is located in and devised for a specific place. In general this means that it is not work in a theatre or in a white 'box' or gallery. And it's quite close to audiences. I am interested in going to places where the audience is anyway, going about their daily business. So I might be on a street, a park or a bridge and do something to explore the qualities of this particular place, and work with the passers-by as my preferred audience. With this kind of project there is generally no obvious label or sign that this is art, and no description of how one is supposed to look at it. It is something that is encountered in the middle of the everyday. This choice of public spaces is partly to do with the sense that art is often there for the converted. People who go to galleries already know what to expect. It's again a codified experience – everybody knows how to behave. I'm more interested in the element of surprise that happens when you walk down the street and see something you haven't seen before. It's not a car going down the road or someone walking their dog, so what is it?

Disruption, in a positive sense, is at the heart of the work I'm interested in. And it is to do with a sense that we as people, as citizens, are very much dominated by values that often are not our own. That we are instrumentalized within a system, within mechanisms that serve other people's purposes, be that making money, or upholding an institution or a nation. And I think we've become blind to our own possibilities, to who we are, who we could be. Hence my interest in art, at this point in time, is that it can perhaps create a little space or pause, a brief interlude, and open something up around this straightjacket of constraints and inherited values. The work, or the encounter with the work, has to challenge the status quo in some ways. It has to be somewhat disruptive. But I'm not interested in violent action. That's another way of doing performance art, doing something really shocking and painful.

I like to make work which is poetic, and slight, maybe absurd, and playful. It might look like what we understand as 'work', but isn't. For example, one piece I did some time ago was called 'Flush, or the Possibility of Moving Towards an Impossible Goal'. I did this in Geneva in 2002 for the Centre D'Art en L'Ile. The gallery is situated on a narrow island in the middle of the Rhône in the centre of Geneva. A low footbridge runs down the middle of the river connecting the island with other bridges that cross the river. I used this little footbridge, which is called the Passage of the Washerwomen, and was perhaps used by women to wash clothes. I invited another performer to work with me and devised a ritual. Geneva is a very wealthy city with banks and headquarters on both sides of the river. And in this spot we had a bucket each on a long rope, and stood facing opposite sides of the bridge. We would drop our buckets down into the water, wait for them to fill, pull them up, then walk past one another to the other side of the footbridge and pour the water out. We repeated this, over and over again, always working in opposition. At times we would freeze and halt the movement, then would start again. The work is a kind of clockwork, implying the possibility of producing something, but the whole thing is completely absurd. All we do is take water from one side of the bridge and pour it out on the other. We did this for four days, always at lunchtime, when people were using the bridge to go to and from work. So people had to walk past us and between us as they crossed the bridge, and most likely wonder what on earth we were doing. Our movements mimicked the work and the systems in which they operate, but the activity doesn't make sense. And that moment of puzzlement is something that interests me. Curiously, there was a passer-by at the time who said this spectacle reminded her of Israel and Palestine.

We are not only born into these systems and become used to them, we are also complicit in them. We have desires and hopes and needs that feed into the machinery, providing us perhaps with some kind of satisfaction, but making us compliant above all. It's not for no reason that this functions so well; it is insidious.

Hence I am exploring the idea of disruption, and there is an interesting model for this kind of artist figure, which is the notion of the trickster. Lewis Hyde has written a fascinating book exploring this role called *Trickster Makes This World*. The late writer and art critic Jean Fisher also wrote extensively about the artist as trickster. If we look at the Native American trickster for example, he is a joker, he is mischievous, and an opportunist. When he sees an opportunity, he does something naughty, kicks up dust and then disappears. And that's a very interesting model for the artist: disruption is not intended to be destructive. The idea is to unsettle relations, so that things can perhaps settle in a more holistic, beneficial way. And that's the jolt or disruption on a street corner that I'm interested in. Maybe somebody slows down their step and hesitates or stops for a moment.

When I work on the street, I often find that children are very curious. They don't behave 'properly' like the adults do, who go past and shake their heads. Children start looking and get interested, and they will come up and ask what I'm doing. As a performer I don't want to be a closed, unapproachable entity, which you often see in the more traditional art venues. I have tried to find ways to allow for some interaction, and I could give a couple of examples. I also did 'Flush', the bucket piece, for an event in Walthamstow in East London, which was arranged through the William Morris Gallery. Artists could use the park around the gallery which also has a small bridge. During the performance, a group of kids came and watched the piece for a while, walking with me from one side of the bridge to the other, observing us taking water from one side of the bridge and pouring it out on the other. Eventually one boy asked me what I was doing, and I said, "It's a puzzle." This is something that kids understand. When they put together a puzzle, they know how to look for pieces to eventually create a whole picture. And I think this answer was all the kids needed. They continued to look for a while and then headed off.

There is another example, from a performance that a group of us did in Bow, again in East London, part of Sight/Sight, a project led by the performer André Verissimo. This is a very mixed community of different ethnicities and religions. We chose a large public square and inhabited it with what could perhaps be described as a physical and sculptural approach, relating to the architecture of the site. We were exploring the surfaces and materials, responding through movement and through stillness, also seeking to just be present within that place. I had again a bucket with me, an object I have worked with in many different situations. And I noticed that there were a couple of kids who were completely fascinated. Most people stayed at a distance, but these two kids, one with a turban and the other with a hoodie, came over. I was sitting on the pavement and balancing the bucket on one of my shoulders and contemplating the weight of it. One of the boys asked me, quite surprisingly, "Are you talking to the devil?" I tried to respond based on what I was doing at the time. So I said, "No, I'm talking to the air." The response seemed to make sense for them, and he replied, "What is the air saying?" I welcomed having an exchange but I didn't really want to get into a long conversation. I preferred them to just watch and experience this. So my response was, "The air isn't saying anything, it only listens." They seemed to appreciate my comment, looked for while, and then moved on to listen to one of the other performers who was singing a song. They mimicked his song for a bit and then walked off.

These interactions are rather special. They create a connection but don't impose any kind of meaning. That's maybe where performance art can be difficult, or elusive, because it's often not clear what the message is. And it often doesn't have a message. Instead it's interested in opening doors, inviting questions, challenging patterns and habits.

Why do you have a need to create?

I've always done that. My way of being in the world is to be an artist in some way. Being a maker of sorts.

Why do humans have a need to create?

What really fascinates me is the mindfulness of who we are as bodies. Bodies are fantastically intelligent entities and the desire to explore, play, investigate and understand is part of our nature. We are somewhat philosophical animals, and therefore we create.

What sacrifices have you made to pursue your creative path?

I have sacrificed at least half my life for this, because it is so important to me, and because it gives me so much pleasure. I've sacrificed the time that it occupies in my life, the time I give to my work instead of earning money, or hanging out with friends. My happiest moments are when I am working creatively.

How has your work shaped you as a person?

I have learned a lot through the work. Through the wonderful aspects, but also the difficulties, the challenges, the complexities. Working with other people is an important part of my work, but collaboration is also very complex. What I've learned over time, and what has become a real value for me, is the importance of graciousness. Graciousness, as a way of being in the world, is a positive energy. It facilitates connections, it can resolve things in a way that is gentle. I've learned that frequently there is no point in fighting, or being angry, or hanging on to things. So I practice being gracious, and the older I get, the more I am able to have a lightness of touch.

If we are talking about reflection on the work itself, this happens sometimes in the moment of making it. When I plan a live intervention, I'm never quite sure how it's going to work out. It's an idea that develops as I am doing it, particularly for durational pieces when I am doing something repeatedly or over several days. A live event is an encounter, not something that is just delivered. So the reflection is part of the work and an intense process of constant adjustment, learning and development.

I'm personally very interested in reflection, and in understanding why I'm doing what I'm doing. I did a PhD and spent quite a few years thinking about my work. I studied the work of the French writer Catherine Clément in particular, George Bataille, and many others, considering the impact of market-driven, capitalist societies, and trying to articulate the purpose of the performances. For me it was important to think about the role of art at this point in time, and in particular, the role of performance art, as something which can disrupt our everyday. In order to think through the absurdity in the work, I focused on the notion of uselessness, devising useless interventions as a way to disrupt the constant pressure to be useful and productive which we have to bear all our life. So my question for the PhD was: what is the use of uselessness? In that sense I am now Dr. Useless.

My conclusion was that uselessness is a useful tool for performance practices, or for art making in the wider sense in this point in time in our society. And that it is a means to challenge given values and what we think is a sovereign structure in which we live. In its uselessness, art can create a space of play, an interlude of possibilities.

How do you deal with creative blocks?

One aspect of being an artist is hard work, because of the constant navigating of the unknown. Also there is something as basic as perseverance. Having to stick with it, even when you don't know where to go next. That is very often the challenge. What is my next step? What is this about?

Perseverance sometimes means looking around. Therefore, lateral explorations can be very useful. I remember an exhibition at the National Gallery called Monochrome: Painting in Black and White, on grisaille paintings through the ages. The paintings made me look at images in a new way and profoundly affected a video I was editing at the time.

On rare occasions there are eureka moments, which are of course lovely when they happen. Occasionally they happen under high anxiety, when one is under stress. Adrenalin can help to pull in extra resources and create a moment of insight.

How do you stay fresh in your work?

In the work I do, the polymorphous exploration of space, time and people, it's the work that keeps me fresh. Because there's very little repetition. However, there can be a tendency to fall back on old patterns and ideas, particularly when I'm stuck. Which of course raises my own suspicion.

But another way of staying fresh is collaboration. I love collaborating with other people. That could be with other dancers, designers, writers or non-creatives. The conversation with other people always brings up something else. And what emerges out of a collaboration is always fresh in some ways.

What is your relationship with satisfaction in your work?

Satisfaction is very elusive but it's a fuel, and compared with the struggle and the sense of hard work and perseverance, satisfaction is one's wings. It creates lightness, and it moves you on.

What is the relationship between your work and its audience?

It varies a lot. For a while I was a member of a large association of performance artists called Infr'Action, who would descend on a city and improvise performances in public places. In 2011 about 60 of us self-funded and went to Venice during the Previews of the Venice Biennale. I was there with an artist friend, Dorothea Seror, and we found a canal that seemed quiet and ideal as a place to perform. We decided to work with the wind that was traveling through the space and over the canal, as a constant given and freely available material. The point being, it was a response to the elitist and expensive Biennale, and all our performances took place in the streets and gardens round about the Biennale. Dorothea and I devised a kind of counterbalance with both of us standing on either side of the canal, stretching two long ropes between us onto which we tied a feather pillow that was ripped in the middle. Leaning back into the ropes we were able to suspend the pillow in the middle of the canal, just above the water where the wind was strongest. The wind then picked up the feathers and deposited them on the water where they drifted slowly down the canal. It was a quiet, poetic piece, playing with the environment, and the audience enjoyed it.

We had noticed that there were police boats on some of the canals, but thought that this one was a dead end, so assumed it was fine to do this piece. However, the canal turned out to be the VIP access to the Biennale. When the first police boat came along, we were able to lift the pillow up and the policemen on the boat ducked under and went past no problem. It was hilarious and the audience was laughing and clapping, and the feathers were blowing in the wind. Some time later a boat came with someone on a loudspeaker shouting at us aggressively in Italian, most likely telling us to get out of there. But we couldn't move away, because we were tied into the counterbalance holding up the pillow. When setting up we had used a little bridge in a complicated process of unfolding this whole contraption. Now we couldn't just walk away.

So this boat was coming closer and we didn't know what to do or where to go. The boat moved toward Dorothea and after much shouting an armed guy jumped from the boat onto her side, and began grabbing her and pulling her away, which was crazy because all he was doing was pulling me towards the water. I tried desperately not to fall into the canal as he was wrestling her, in order to not escalate the situation. He then took a knife from his belt and slashed the ropes. The pillow fell into the water, to the loud protest of the audience, after which he got back on the boat and they drove past the soaking pillow and ropes and vanished. It was intense. When the pillow fell into the water there was a groan of disappointment from the audience. That was the main sense, that this performance was disrupted in a way that was both brutal and ridiculous, and downright scary. It turned out that the Argentine Prime Minister had been on the boat, visiting the Biennale, and the armed men must have been her security guards. Clearly they didn't know how to cope with us. In that sense things can get out of hand very quickly. And it was a very inoffensive piece, quiet and poetic, Zen-like, but it disrupted their schedule, which would not have had a feather pillow on the list of things to see. Dorothea had a few bruises on her arms, and one passer-by took a couple of photos of the wrestling scene, which we still have.

What is the relationship between yourself and your audience?

There is a fellow performance artist from the Czech Republic named Tomas Ruller, who calls his work 'the school of attention'. Which I think is lovely, because it's a very down-to-earth, common-sense description of what this work is. I would be quite happy to be seen as part of a school of attention in terms of what I do with my audience. The work is designed to help us attend, to notice, to observe, to witness, to reflect. So I like to facilitate this in the audience.

Also over time my work has become more participatory. I do less performing now, and instead hold a space and create a set of tasks and invite the audience to participate. This can also happen on the street, or in a gallery, or even as part of an online project. In other words, these days I'm more a facilitator than a performer.

I'm also getting older, and my desire to perform has diminished in some ways. I've become much more interested in other people, in observing them.

Claudia Kappenberg

What has your audience taught you?

Certainly one can never predict how something will be seen or received, as people come with their own stories.

I made a series of works called Slow Races, in which I play with the familiar notion of the race and our obsession with speed, but devise tasks which slow the audience down. For one of the Slow Races I borrowed an exercise I had done in a workshop with Alastair McLennan, where we give people a beaker that is filled to the brim with water and asking them to traverse a space without spilling a drop. In a performance festival in Wellington, New Zealand (titled Performance Arcade 2017), I inhabited a shipping container which is very much a symbol of a modern global world of productivity and commerce. I declared the container to be a A Space Without A Use, drawing on the writing of Georges Perec who thought that it may not be possible to even conceive of such a space. And I invited participants to travel through the container, balancing a beaker filled to the brim with water without spilling a drop. This Space Without A Use gave rise to many different reactions from the participants, and one man, who had spent a long time in the container being quiet and silent, told me the following story when he re-emerged:

Once upon a time in India there was a King. A group of Iranians wanted to immigrate but the King was concerned that the country was already full. He had a glass filled to the brim with milk and sent it to the Iranians. When the Iranians received the glass, they added a sugar cube and sent it back to the King. The King was surprised that the glass came back to him and took a little sip, and realized that the milk was sweet. He then welcomed the Iranians into the country.

I am paraphrasing as I can't remember all the details of the story, but I was very moved by it.

In terms of how my work affects people, legacy is a big word. I imagine some interactions will have been memorable for the viewers or participants and I can recall many moments over the years, and how people have responded. One woman who participated in Slow Races in Wellington told me she had never concentrated as much! I also made a version of Slow Races in Hastings in the UK, declaring an alleyway as a Space Without A Use, and a homeless guy with PTSD who took part told me afterwards that this experience had been better than any therapy he had tried.

Maybe legacy is something one doesn't have time to think about. Particularly now, when everything is so urgent and uncertain due to Covid. I teach at the University of Brighton and we are about to start a new semester, but how are we going to teach the students? To find space to think about my work is difficult. And the more elusive the practice is, the more difficult this becomes. Sometimes I wish I could have a retrospective, or gather it all in a book. But this was a problem with my PhD: how do I represent this work? In the end I selected four still images of the key performances and interspersed them throughout the pages, as a sort of glimpse of something. Because in the end that's what the work is about, this instant of something. In some ways the industry wants me to have evidence of this body of work. The institutions of arts, the funders, the Research Councils, they all want evidence. But this work isn't about evidence, it's the opposite. As an artist I feel like I'm kind of resisting that system, but at the same time I'm in it and I have to submit to it.

What has been the greatest challenge in your career?

There are probably many answers to that, but to give one would be to stick to the work over time. Because in the end it is very hard to justify this kind of work. It's hard to believe in it sometimes. And to take it through the decades. I've lived in different countries, and the world is changing all the time. To say that this is what I believe in, that this is the work I want to do, is the greatest challenge.

What has been the high point of your career?

I wouldn't say that there is one in particular. There are many little high points along the way. Brief encounters, connections, a particular response or moment of engagement are kind of ecstatic instances, beyond words. They are beautiful and fulfilling and meaningful. Sometimes it's about taking a risk and trying something new.

Since the pandemic the whole area of performance and live work has become incredibly difficult, so I devised a very different project recently, in which I co-curated an online season of films in response to the closure of all the local galleries and arts venues. I collaborated with Fiontán Moran, curator at Tate Modern in London, and with a local arts organization here in Hastings called Coastal Currents. We devised a program of films which explored questions relating to our embodied selves, how we are conditioned and confined by the social and political environment, and the losses we experience right now. Shifting my work into a curatorial role, and working very quickly with new partners who I never met in person, was a bit of a gamble. But the collaboration was a real pleasure and enriching in many ways, in terms of the discussions we had and the many films we shared with one another, and in terms of the journey we devised for the online audience. Being able to continue to explore ideas and to engage in a new collaboration was an important experience at a time when the arts are under huge strain.

What is the most important thing your creative practice has taught you?

That there is a lot of pleasure in little things. The possibilities of pleasure are endless.

How did it feel to reflect on creativity today?

As a university lecturer I am generally in an instrumentalized state of responding to demands. There is little time for this kind of conversation, which seems rather sad. Because that's what we're there for, particularly in a school of art and media. That's what we want to teach the students. But for now we are mainly figuring out how to deliver education during a pandemic. So I very much appreciate your time and the invitation.

Muazzam Ali Khan

Muazzam Ali Khan and his brother Rizwan are singers of Qawwāli, the Sufi devotional music of Pakistan and India. It is a vibrant musical tradition with a history of over 700 years. Often listeners, and the artists themselves, are transported to a state of wajad, a trance-like state where they feel at one with God, generally considered to be the height of spiritual ecstasy in Sufism, and the ultimate goal of the practice. Muazzam and Rizwan are nephews of the late Nusrat Fateh Ali Khan, the world-renowned Qawwāli singer. Their family is part of a lineage of Qawwāli musicians stretching back over seven centuries. Their group, Rizwan-Muazzam Qawwali, have toured worldwide, and produced four albums with Real World Records, founded by Peter Gabriel.

This interview was interpreted by Rashid Ahmed Din.
rizwanmuazzam.com / Instagram: rizwanmuazzamalikhanofficial

What drew you to your medium?

It is in the family. As children we listened to our father Mujahid Mubarak Ali Khan, and to our uncle Nusrat Fateh Ali Khan. We wanted to follow them, and they both taught us as we pursued this path.

Do you feel a connection with the history of your medium?

Our family has been involved with the history of Qawwāli for the last 700 years. That is our connection, and it is a spiritual connection. We don't know about the very beginning of Qawwāli, but we have that long-term connection with the music.

The word Qawwāli comes from 'qual', or what is being said by the prophet. So in Qawwāli, we convey the message of Islam, the message of peace and love from the Sufis, and the words of our prophet. To unite people from all walks of life in peace and love is the meaning of Qawwāli.

Does your medium offer something unique?

What it offers that is rare, if not unique, is the improvisational nature of the music. We plan a composition, and there is a choir of 10 people singing that composition. We have the tabla drum, the harmonium, the hand clap and the choir singing. Everything is then improvised. We don't know what we will play and sing based on that composition. The mood can change along with the audience, and we start to improvise among ourselves.

The improvisation was added later on. Originally they used to almost read the lyrics. But our family introduced different approaches, like improvisation of lyrics, not just classical ragas.

We may have a verse that relates to someone in the audience, and then we have to add on other verses conveying the same meaning. This was introduced by our forefathers. This makes the music more entertaining. Qawwāli was limited to performances at shrines in the beginning. Our grandfather Mubarak Ali Khan and our uncle Nusrat Fateh Ali Khan introduced Qawwāli into social events. This is how it has become so popular. It now has a much wider audience. And they improved the style lyrically and musically.

Our family has two different classical trainings. One is called Durpad, and the other is called Khyal. Mixing them together and presenting them to people is only done by our family. Which makes it different and more entertaining.

Our father always taught us, as do all fathers teaching their children who come into the profession, that when you sing, don't sing for yourself – sing for God. When you sing for Him, and get involved, and you are improving in your life, that shows that God's presence is there. It's like your prayer has been answered.

It's difficult to say how you feel the presence of God. Because He will not come in front of you and say that He is God. You sense it in your feelings, and your involvement during the performance. Sometimes you see the presence in the air wherever you are, and your feelings change. Even the singer himself has gone into a trance. If he sings for God he feels His presence. And it is the same if he sings for the Prophet, or for his mentor. Sometimes when we sing we start crying. This also signifies the presence of the person you are singing for.

Why do you have a need to create?

To create the music, number one it is our passion. Secondly, it is never enough; you can never be satisfied. It is bigger than the sea; it is never-ending. There is always a need to do more and more.

Why do humans have a need to create?

Number one, it is good entertainment that gives you peace; it helps to release tension. There was a time in the olden days where people used to be treated therapeutically with music. And now you can see that some people have been healed through the medium of music.

What sacrifices have you made to pursue your creative path?

I have had to sacrifice basically my entire life to achieve this. From my childhood, I never played. I have always been working. I didn't sleep much in the early days. I was kept awake to learn, to practice. So then you have to sacrifice everything else, and be committed to achieve this. You have to be separated from the outside world. You can't have both. You can't run a business and learn this at the same time. You have to totally commit to it. And I had many sleepless nights. I was always training, learning and remembering what was taught. But I have a family now. They fit in with the music.

How has your work shaped you as a person?

The music makes you very humble and dedicated, and it teaches you to love all human beings, all living things. To be kind and loving.

How do you deal with creative blocks?

Sometime we will try to create something and it just happens within moments. Sometimes we do get stuck. And the only way we deal with it is to not give up, just keep working on it, and it will get done.

How do you stay fresh in your work?

Along with our own music, we listen to other artists, and foreign music, like jazz and folk. And we pick up what attracts us and try to adapt it to our style. Our music has some similarity to jazz, in terms of the improvisational qualities.

When we perform we have to keep in mind the first song we have sung, so that the second does not sound like the first. And this continues through the performace. It also depends on the lyrics, and the mood of the lyrics. The composition will be made accordingly, so that it will differ from the other songs. Sometimes we have the same raga, used for perhaps three different compositions, but when we sing, it will not sound the same. That comes from the knowledge of the family. This comes from the training we receive. So this gives us a lot of variation in the sound of each composition.

Usually you will hear Qawwāli groups making a similar effort to make the music sound different. But as I said earlier, we have two different classical trainings, and that is what makes us unique. We apply those skills into our Qawwāli, which is not easy. Even people who know our music will sometimes get confused and not know if we're singing the same raga. And this is not taught to every member of the family. We have to see who has the talent to absorb it. Then they will be taught those secrets in their training. It's like students in a class; they all have different levels of capability.

What is your relationship with satisfaction in your work?

I don't think I will ever be satisfied. It feels like I've just started this profession, even though I've done it all my life. There is always room to do more and better.

What is the relationship between your work and its audience?

There is a big link between our work, and ourselves and our audience. If there is a good audience, and they have a good response, it encourages us to sing more, and even better. So if there is no response, then obviously our performance won't be that great. So we always want more people to come, and enjoy it more, and inspire us to a better performance.

In gatherings, there has always been a tradition where members of the audience will get up and shower the stage with money. In the olden days, there were no entrance fees. Musicians were invited, and they would be given some token, and full hospitality and have all expenses covered. But there was no fee. So it was down to the artist to perform well enough that the audience will give them more money. They may be listening, and come to a point where they feel they want to get up and give the artist something. The family has been well known for getting people's pockets empty.

There is a difference between the religious and the social performances of the music. At a Sufi shrine it is obviously all spiritual music that is played. And a person could be touched at any time, not just at the end, during the last song. The music can take people into trance, and they will dance, and cry. They are all different moments of trance. At social events, at the end people want to enjoy and dance, so that last song becomes the dancing moment. All the way through they will just be listening, but now they want to dance. Especially when we perform in Europe, the audience doesn't understand the language, but we try to convey the message of peace and love. And they will very respectfully sit down and listen. But we want to entertain them as well. I know they want to dance, so we have to get them to that moment.

We do sing spiritual lyrics, but along with that we also sing non-spiritual lyrics. It depends on where we are performing. If we are going to the shrine, it is basically going to be a spiritual performance. But if we do social events, they want to hear love songs. Some poetry can be taken either way – spiritual love or materialistic love. Even the spiritual songs, which are written by the Sufis, they are spiritual love songs. And they can be interpreted according to where the individual's love is. And again, our family introduced the non-spiritual lyrics into the social events, to make it more popular for a wider audience.

We sing poetry by Rumi, Jami and Amir Khusro. They are the main pillars of Qawwāli poetry. They have always been part of this music. It is very meaningful and all Qawwāls sing it. It would not be complete without their work.

What has your audience taught you?

Sometimes when there is not enough response, we have to try to work out what the audience may respond to. So we try different things to see what they like, and work out what kind of audience it is. Then we will sing and perform accordingly.

What has been the greatest challenge in your career?

The greatest challenge is always that someone is keeping the name and reputation of our family alive. Nusrat did not have a son, but fortunately someone else did. Someone in the family will have to do it. Music is in our blood, it's in our genes, so that talent is not hidden, it always comes out. We will see which child has an interest, and has the talent. We will then give him the training, and it carries on like this. In our case, we had the interest ourselves. We were not taught until our father saw that interest in us. First we were practicing ourselves because we were interested, so then our father started to teach us.

We learned from our uncle Nusrat, after the death of our father. We became disciples of his, and had the ceremony of studentship on the third day of our father's death. We had a limited time with him, because he was very busy, but we had a few months with him and we put it in our practice. And if he was still alive today we would still be learning from him.

The moments we spent with him were the best moments of our lives. I cannot even describe how it felt. Those moments cannot be put into words. With the way he taught, the information would go straight into your mind. His teaching style was so good that you would learn very quickly.

We feel the presence of our father and of Nusrat when we perform. Sometimes what happens is we will try to recall what we were taught, if we forget it. And they come and correct us in our dreams. So we maintain that spiritual link with them. It never goes away.

What has been the high point of your career?

The high point was when we did our debut tour with Peter Gabriel's company Womad. Then we did some recording work with Peter.

Our goal is always to continue the work of our family, which has been unbroken for generations. That is my ambition.

What is the most important thing your creative practice has taught you?

What we learn in our career, as we said before, is firstly humility. And secondly, you have to be away from other parts of the world to create. You have to give time to this, and practice. But love and humility are the most important things this music teaches us.

How did it feel to reflect on creativity today?

    I am pleased to have this detailed interview, which has discussed in detail Qawwāli music, our family, our audience and our work. As long as I live I will always be performing, and I want to get better at it over that time.

Reuben Langdon

Reuben Langdon is an international stuntman, martial artist, actor, motion capture artist, filmmaker and video game star. He has worked on many highly successful films, TV shows and video games, and has worked with some of the biggest names in film, from actors Jackie Chan and Andy Serkis, to directors James Cameron, Peter Jackson and Steven Spielberg. In the video games industry he is internationally recognized as Ken from *Street Fighter*, and Dante from the *Devil May Cry* series.

While working on James Cameron's *Avatar*, Reuben had his first UFO sighting, inspiring him to research the subject. In 2013 he co-produced the historic five-day event at the National Press Club in Washington, DC, called the Citizen Hearing on Disclosure. He is now the host of the popular TV show *Interviews With E.D.* (Extra-Dimensionals) on the Gaia Network.

reubenlangdon.com / Instagram: reubenlangdon

What drew you to your medium?

The term the industry is pushing towards is 'performance capture', and away from 'motion capture'. Because ultimately that's what it is: a performance. In the early days it was just about capturing your body movements, but now the technology also captures your facial movement and your voice – so all aspects of the character's performance. And that will then get put onto a computer-generated model. That may be a one-for-one body and facial scan, or it could be a giant monster, or some kind of augmented character with five legs or something like that. But it takes the full range of your physical and vocal performance. So the terms used are 'body cap', with no face or voice, or 'full p-cap', which is the total physical and vocal performance.

Before I got involved in the games industry I was a gamer. I grew up playing games on Nintendo, Sega Genesis and Super Nintendo. I spent a huge amount of my childhood and early teens on roleplaying games like *Final Fantasy* and *Phantasy Star*, and fighting games like *Street Fighter*.

When I followed my passion for martial arts to go and study aikido in Tokyo, action cinema became a new passion. As a kid I had loved martial arts movies, especially with Bruce Lee and Jackie Chan, but I never imagined I could be a part of that. I was a video game nerd. I was not physical at all. So it was kind of surreal and weird when I got to Japan, and found myself doing modeling and acting as a means of paying bills. The concept of me having to stand in front of people and perform was like walking the plank and diving into shark-infested waters. For me, and who I was as a child, I would much rather just play video games by myself. I was a pretty antisocial kind of kid.

Living in Tokyo, I had to find a way to earn some money, and a lot of caucasian people in the city had opportunities in modeling. Someone told me that without having any real talent, I could register with some agencies and book gigs doing commercials and television. They made it sound so easy that I decided to give it a try. I went to my first audition, and was the only guy without a professional portfolio, but my agent said I had forgotten mine. Standing in front of these guys, posing, it was the last thing I wanted to do. On the train ride home, I was thinking it was the worst thing ever, and I never wanted to go through it again. But the next day, the agency called to tell me I got the job. My heart sank. Now I had to go stand in front of more strangers and be judged, for a full day? Doing it for five minutes was bad enough. But they said I would earn $300 for a few hours work, so I gave in and went. I think it was for a Suzuki car catalog. Two other professional models were there, and they had flown to Japan especially for this job. So I watched them and copied what they did. I told them it was my first job and they gave me some pointers. They said, "It's easy. When you hear the camera click you change you pose. That's it." They were super cool and didn't make fun of me as a noobie. So I thought this isn't so bad. I then got called in to be an extra in a commercial. It was for Brooke Bond tea. I was dressed up as an English soldier, in the background of a palace. It was ridiculous, but easy, and paid well. So I was very reluctant to get involved initially, but I was getting paid and I decided to see where it went.

I then met a woman on a job who was taking acting lessons in Japanese. This seemed like a great way to learn the language. I really wanted to learn Japanese, and acting was just a way to do that. I had to learn lines, and understand the emotion that went with it, which would help me remember the words and help me advance quicker. It was stage acting mainly, and we had to do lots of warm-up exercises in projecting your voice and so on. I loved every second of it. And I was learning the language so much faster, and getting more immersed in the culture. This also helped me prepare for my first audition for a Japanese-speaking part, which was on a show called *B-Fighter Kabuto*. It's kind of a Japanese version of *Power Rangers*. My role was an American exchange student from New York. There are a couple of terms that are associated with these shows. 'Sentai' is the word for *Power Rangers*, and 'tokusatsu' is the word for the *Kamen Rider* TV show, and similar shows in that genre. So this was a tokusatsu show based on the lineage from the *Kamen Rider* show. I was a huge *Kamen Rider* fan, and because I was so familiar with the show and the poses, I could throw those poses in the audition. That impressed them, and I got a callback, and then got the job. The role was written for me, and I did a season of that, with six months of filming on and off.

That was an amazing experience, and got me immersed in the Japanese film industry. It improved my language skills a lot, and also got me into the physical aspects of acting. I was already a fan of Hong Kong action cinema, and Japanese 'chanbara' action cinema. And now I was doing it, not just watching it, or playing video games. I had wonderful Japanese stunt teams, and they invited me into their stunt schools. So I was learning to perform my own stunts. I was so excited about all that, that I decided to study it in school. You would essentially learn how to do Jackie Chan-style fights, or *Power Rangers*-style fights. That was quite unique at the time, but eventually a lot of that spilled over into Hollywood. So it was a real gift to study that in those days.

I kept working, and in 1997 one of the action schools invited me to do the motion capture for a video game called *Resident Evil: Code Veronica*. That was one of the first games to incorporate motion capture in the game and the cutscenes. The Sega Dreamcast was just coming out, and it had the power to handle this kind of data. It was a collaboration between Capcom and Sega and we did all the motion capture at the Sega studios in Tokyo. Again, I had kind of a secret key to this world before any other caucasian. At this point, I may well have been doing motion capture for longer than anyone else on the planet, in terms of being still active in it today.

At that time it was body only, like the Power Rangers, who all wear helmets. It wasn't until later that they animated the mouth and eyes. We had to accentuate our physical movements in a cartoonish way in our performance, but that was already familiar to me.

Do you feel a connection with the history of your medium?

I do. If you look at the history of motion capture, there is Reuben Langdon along the whole thing, from the early days to today. After that work and study in Japan I moved back to the States. I was living in the back yard of the martial arts movie star Sammo Hung. I was working with him in the martial arts arena, and driving him to work on the *Martial Law* series. One day he told me that the creator of the *Mortal Kombat* games reached out to him to work on a new game, but Sammo didn't want to do it because he knew nothing about games – it wasn't his world. So he suggested I do it. I said, "What? They want Sammo Hung, and you want to give them Reuben Langdon?" But he persuaded me, and connected me to those guys. The game was *Tao*

Feng, and it came out in 2003 on the first Xbox. The amount of motion capture for the game was extraordinary. We did months of capture. And I was in charge of choreography and hiring the talent for the project.

When I started motion capture in Japan we used a magnetic system, and your joints were tethered by wires. So your movement was somewhat impeded, because you had people holding these wires and following you around as you did the movements, and you had to try not to get tangled up. Doing stunts was therefore pretty challenging. But by the time I did *Tao Feng*, the studio was using the system you see now, with infrared lights hitting reflective balls on your joints. That's still pretty much the industry standard. But at the beginning they were made of wood, because they had to be perfect spheres, and smooth. The technical people were thinking about the technology, not the performers. As you can imagine, when a performer falls, even on mats, those wooden balls hurt. I would come home with bruises and welts all over my body. Luckily the industry moved on from those wooden balls. Us performers just refused to use them, so they changed them.

I then started a business called Just Cause Productions. In Japan we were pitching to video games companies that we could get motion capture talent from the States and do the casting and take care of all the logistics. We did this because we noticed that many of the Japanese games, like *Final Fantasy* and *Metal Gear*, and even the early *Devil May Cry* and *Resident Evil* games, were using Japanese performers for caucasian characters. They only spoke Japanese, so the studio would then dub the English. I called it the 'bad kung fu movie effect'. You would get a movement, and the dubbed English didn't quite line up with the movement. Dialogue and movement always go together closely, and if they don't sync up, it's very noticeable. They did a good job with emulating the essence, but the timing was off. Many of the companies were excited, and said they had been looking for this service. They had tried to hire local talent, but were not finding people who were performers. So we filled that niche. Our first project was *Resident Evil Outbreak*. I also had an advantage, in that I had already done the motion capture for the character Chris Redfield, which became an iconic role. So I had those connections. And then we started getting hired to bring through talent and coordinate that. It's important to know the specific, technical kind of performance that is required to work in motion capture. So we would educate the talent on those things, so that when they get on set they're not like a deer in headlights. And we just kept getting more jobs. I then got cast as Dante in the *Devil May Cry* series, and ended up doing a whole series of them.

Over time I became known as the go-to guy on motion capture. I was back and forth to Japan for work, and running the company, and doing stunts in Hollywood. I worked on *Pirates of the Caribbean* and different TV shows like *Dexter* and *The Office*. Then, around 2003 or 2004, through the grapevine I heard that James Cameron was doing *Battle Angel*. That was my dream show. I was a big fan of the comics in high school. When I heard Cameron had bought the rights I was super excited. I was then called to do some technical and performance tests, as I was by then a trusted figure in that industry. A few months later, I heard that one of my friends was working with James Cameron. I asked him if it was *Battle Angel*, but he said no, it's *Avatar*. I'd never heard of *Avatar*. So my buddy kept recommending me to the stunt coordinator, as someone who really knows the technology, however the coordinator didn't know who I was, so was reluctant. But one day my friend couldn't get to set, so I got called in as a replacement. This was before the movie was greenlit. Cameron was doing technical tests, especially on new technology that he was developing for the film. I lived in that virtual world, so was very comfortable. But Cameron had been firing performers because they weren't as familiar with it. I was already a 10-year veteran of the motion capture world at that point, and was naturally doing a lot of little things that the technical people usually have to spend time training performers on. So I was making their jobs easier, and they kept asking to have me brought back. Sure enough I got called back day after day, and eventually they cast me as the stunt double for Jake Sully, the male lead. I ended up doing that on and off for a couple of years.

At the same time I was still running my company, and we had got the bid for *Resident Evil 5*. I was reprising my role as Chris Redfield, and also working behind the scenes. We had to build out a motion capture studio for that project. And I was hanging out with the *Avatar* crew, and getting tips from them on the latest and greatest technology. Having been in the right places at the right times over the years, I built up my resumé. I've stepped out of that motion capture medium a bit, but even during Covid I was one of the rare actors working on projects.

Does your medium offer something unique?

It's very expansive because you're working in a virtual world. It's like stage work 2.0, because once you're in the suit, you can do one shot in which you're the hero, and in the next you're the zombie attacking the hero. Then with the push of a button I can be a warlock or a space marine. So the variety of performances that you can slip in and out of makes it unique. In regular acting you have to sit in make-up sometimes for hours, then do your thing on set for a couple of hours. But on motion cap there is no make-up, and the only costume is the suit. You can work on 10 projects in the same day. It's fast-paced and very creative. Where else can you be so many different characters in a day? Many times I've been a woman, because they had no women in the suit and it was just a background thing. So they taught me how to walk like a woman, and how the anatomy of that works. Not many jobs could allow you that much range and creativity, so it's a really fun medium to work in.

In one day I did five characters, on three different games. But when you've done it enough, it becomes like the flick of a switch, and you just switch characters naturally. This saves a lot of time on set, because the animator doesn't have to explain the details of the kind of character it is and the performance they're looking for. Experience counts for a lot when it comes to time.

Why do you have a need to create?

We're all creators, we just express through different mediums. This Earth experience is ultimately a creative one. We're not really told or taught this, but if you think about it, we're in a constant state of creation. In spiritual terms, we hear this idea that we create our own reality. At first that can sound odd, as we are given this idea that we're just trying to navigate the world as it is, that we don't change it. But in a sense, in order for you to navigate this world, to do anything in this reality, you have to create the story. Just like in the motion capture space, you have to behave according to your character. You get some instructions on your objective, but you're going to do it your way. Great performers are given a set of rules, and they go to the limits of those rules, or even break them. So as performers we create the life of that character. And in our day-to-day lives we are doing the same thing. How we act and react is down to us. In that sense we are creating our realities. We do not have to be victims of circumstance. Even in a prison we still have some agency in how we choose to behave each day, and that means you're a creator.

What sacrifices have you made to pursue your creative path?

Ultimately, I wouldn't say I've had to make sacrifices. But in the moments when you're in it, you might think you're making sacrifices. For example, my relationships were really put on the back burner. The amount of time it took to be on set, to study the craft, to learn the technology, to run a company – that's a huge commitment. And I would tell myself this story that I had no time for a relationship. But again, that was me making the conscious choice to pursue this work, at the level I did. Running a studio and working on the biggest film ever made, and some of the biggest video games ever made, that's a lot of moving parts. At some points in time I was just exhausted, and I would tell myself that I was sacrificing any chance at sustaining an intimate relationship, in order to live in that world.

Looking back at it now, those were choices, not sacrifices. I was passionate about my work, and entirely committed to it. And that's kind of how I see my entire life. It's been a series of conscious and unconscious choices that took me towards a specific goal. So from one perspective, yes I made tons of sacrifices to pursue the craft and run a studio. The entire time I worked for my company and worked on *Avatar*, all of the money I made went back into the company. I paid myself a very modest salary, about $3,000 a month, to cover rent and food. I did that for a decade. I didn't care. I was having fun. People might be confused by that, and think I got nothing out of it, but they don't understand. I got *so* much out of it. Financially it was a disaster, but it was rewarding in ways that money can't offer. I spent millions of dollars on building the studio, and it's one of the top motion capture studios in Hollywood. If I walk in there, my picture is on the wall, and it's like Granddaddy Reuben Langdon is in the house, and people actually applaud. It's crazy. Sure, I could have taken other steps and lined my pockets better, but at this point, looking back, I had a great time. What an amazing experience that was.

How has your work shaped you as a person?

Man oh man, the lessons! For one thing, the craft of acting is for me a spiritual path. We have this kind of default programming of who we are, our background, a basic canvas of who we are. But going back to this idea that we're creating our own reality, when you are performing another character, another archetype, you get to try on many other kinds of personalities and characters that you wouldn't normally have contact with in regular life. So you get to in a sense empathize with and understand all these different characters. The first question as an actor is: what's my motivation? So you get to discover the mechanics of how these archetypes work. What creates this type of person, or monster? As a performer, you get first-hand experience of those mechanics. I always want to know how things work. What makes things the way they are, or people the way they are? So I got to learn, at a young age, whether I was aware of it or not, the functionality of these different archetypes. And I had the opportunity to play these different roles, from good guy to bad guy, to just a background zombie. There is a specific template that they're all working with, and you get to try all those on. To me, it expands your empathy, your awareness of what is. And if you can take that back and integrate that into your regular life, I think it can make you a better person.

I have to say I did fall victim to the forces of ego, which can suck us in sometimes. But I've always had a good discipline from my martial arts background, that has helped me navigate that, and have an awareness of when it comes up. Having good friends around me, solid people, they could see when things got out of control, and I would get a little schooled. These are key people to have around you, in any endeavor, but especially in the acting world. There is a lot of ego in that world, especially when you start getting a fandom. You can get fans who are willing to give you anything, or do anything for you. And there are a lot of fans in the industry. For example, I was a huge fan of Jackie Chan and Sammo Hung, and I would do anything for those guys. So it's very easy for people in those positions to take advantage of that power. And that's when the ego begins to do manipulative things to other people. It sees an opportunity to take advantage of people, and begins to project things it wants. And if people are willing to do those things, the ego naturally asks how far it can take this. And that's when you see these monsters that get created in the Hollywood film industry. You can get it anywhere, but Hollywood is notorious for it.

What helped with all that was not paying myself. That kind of protected me from becoming too much of a diva. I had a good business partner, and we were both super dedicated to building a company. That required money and devotion. And we were always looking for opportunities to expand. If you're constantly taking, it's hard for something to expand, but if you're constantly giving, it's easy. And it got really big, really fast. We were quickly working on multimillion dollar projects. A lot of hard work and dedication went into that. That also helps keep the ego in check. But then the company became a monster. We got carried away with it. It began to form its own ego, and need constant feeding. It came to a point where we had to make some big adjustments, and that's when I left the company. So it's not just people that have egos, it can happen to companies too. And it takes a strong group of individuals to say no to the company. Probably having the martial arts background, and good people around me, has helped keep the ego under control.

How do you deal with creative blocks?

Another reason I had to leave the company was that it was draining my creativity. What you find is that when you get up into the higher realms of Hollywood, financially, there are two groups. There are the guys that have proved themselves, and can get finances fairly easily, and they can use their creative genius and do something important with that. That's your Spielbergs and Camerons. And because of their creative genius you want to support them, and everything flows quite easily. But then there's a whole other group made up of financial people, that don't have creative genius. But because of their financial power they want things their way, and it's really just a power game. And there is a lot of that in Hollywood. So then the actual creative people get squashed. They may have been hired for their creativity, but what a lot of people find out once they get involved in the industry, is that it doesn't matter how creative you are. What matters is how much power you have. So you're getting hired for just a small amount of your creativity. If you try to put any more of your creativity into the project, you'll find it gets obliterated by those with the real power. And then you get in this creative rut, and you're stuck. You need to pay your bills, so you go along with it. There's a lot of that, and I've been in those situations many times. It's so draining that a lot of creative people quit Hollywood, and go do something completely different with their lives, just to leave that stress and frustration behind.

How do you stay fresh in your work?

Attitude and gratitude. Whenever I would get a call or go onto a new set, I would stay in the state of gratitude, for the opportunity to be there. I would think about all the other places in the world I could be, the other jobs that are out there. I would be there on a virtual volume, helping to create these characters, and drive a video game project that I loved as a kid, knowing that there are millions of other kids out there that love this game as much as I did when I was a kid. What an amazing opportunity. Every day I was just amazed that this is what I do for a living. Staying in that state, through constantly reminding myself every day, is really important. I'm living the dream, and there are so many other people who would want this position, yet here I am. That always kept me humble, and kept everything feeling fresh.

What is your relationship with satisfaction in your work?

The acting world is probably one of the most satisfying jobs you could have, in my opinion. A stunt coordinator I used to work for would say, "Reuben, you're a stuntman, and you've got one chance to do this. Make it good. Go all out. Because what you do in that moment is going to be there for the whole world to see, forever. And if you get hurt, well, chicks dig scars." So that was the motivation he would give me, to go all out in every take. His name is Garret Warren. He was the stunt coordinator on *Avatar*. He's been shot six times, and is missing an eye. He's a crazy man. He's awesome. I loved that saying of his. There's no other industry that documents and distributes what we're doing around the world in the same way. The satisfaction from that is huge. Obviously there are many elements that go into each shot, each frame, but your movement is right there, often in the heart of the action. And that film went on to become the highest-grossing film in the history of cinema, for nearly a decade. So my movements are being seen millions of times around the world. We all believed in the film and the story and gave it everything we had. The lasting success of that film gives a constant sense of satisfaction.

What is the relationship between your work and its audience?

That's a tough one, because you kind of have to ask the audience. I go to these anime, comic book and science fiction conventions, and I get hired to give talks and sign autographs. Sometimes there are lines out the door, people waiting hours to get my autograph. That still blows my mind. Like, why would anybody want that? Often that is in relation to *Devil May Cry*. A lot of them say, "You have no idea. This game saved my life. I was going through some really dark stuff at that age, and this game helped me get through those times." That fascinates me, so I'll ask them to tell me more. They have a lot of issues in their families, and the game is an escape from all that. It gives them a release for a while. Distraction can be healthy in that situation. It can be like a drug, but without the harm to your body. It may be that there are harmful sides to this hobby, but I've heard so many positive things over the years.

In the movie *Avatar*, you can see the positive effects it's had. Just being part of that triggered a major spiritual transformation in me, because I was connecting with the messages in the movie, and connecting with our planet. By exploring the idea that our world is alive, and that trees communicate, that film is another way to talk about the connectivity we have on our planet, and which indigenous people retain. And I was oblivious to that when I started. I just wanted to be an action star and an actor. So it had a profound effect on me, and the box office numbers tell us that a huge amount of people have been affected that way around the world. This medium has an incredible reach. It's a big part of how we've created this reality. These stories can have a big impact on our reality. So this has had a big impact on the kinds of stories that I want to put out there and tell.

Although the games I have made have their place, in understanding the role of the storyteller, and this medium, I have decided to become a more conscious storyteller, and put out stories and ideas that can uplift humanity in a positive way.

What has your audience taught you?

They've taught me that we as storytellers have way more impact than we could imagine. Ten or 15 years later, I'm still getting these messages from people saying, "You have no idea how much that affected me." And I didn't, until they told me. The effect of these stories on the individual and the collective is huge, and we therefore have a real responsibility to become conscious storytellers.

What has been the greatest challenge in your career?

I think it goes back to that creative suppression. Those are the times when you want to detonate. The frustration is unreal. As creative people, we want to create. When you're getting told no, that's totally fine when there are better ideas on the table. But when you are getting told no just for the sake of someone else's power trip, it just drains you. And eventually you start to question what you're doing in that industry. It's the ultimate buzzkill for a performer.

What has been the high point of your career?

I would say that it's the fact that to this day, people are still getting positivity from these performances. Again, I'm just a cog in the greater machine of the project, but being recognized for your contribution always feels good. And anytime someone can take something positive from your work and apply it in their lives, that's double the reward. It's hugely gratifying.

On *Avatar*, Jim would screen clips during production, but most of us didn't see the full film until the premier at Grauman's Chinese Theater. I remember sitting there and being blown away. I had no idea it was going to be that good. Right there, we knew it was going to be a blockbuster. It was a big celebration. Then we went across the street to the Roosevelt and had a party. We were just shaking our heads, because it was so surreal that it was finally finished. It was an amazing experience, to work on that for four years, then see it come together like that.

What is the most important thing your creative practice has taught you?

That we're creating reality. We are creators. Most of us are unconscious creators. And the acting medium is a great tool to remind us that we're all creating, at every moment.

How did it feel to reflect on creativity today?

Like a trip down memory lane. I love it. It feels really good. For me I'm always focused on the next thing, and taking time out to reflect on the past only really happens in interviews. But because we've had these very spiritual conversations in the past, going down memory lane with Miguel is a whole different trip, because I get to see it through this lens of spiritual growth. And the way the questions are worded, it has a much bigger impact than the standard questions I get asked about my career. So thank you for that, and helping me connect the dots to the work I'm doing now.

Peter Lord

Peter Lord co-founded Aardman Animations with David Sproxton while at school. They began making animated short films using modeling clay, and created *The Amazing Adventures of Morph* in the late 1970s. They then produced many successful short films and TV commercials. They were joined in 1985 by Nick Park, who brought great success to the company with his creation *Wallace and Gromit*. Aardman has produced a succession of award-winning and hugely popular films, TV series and shorts. They have also expanded into new media with computer games, VR and AR projects.

As well as the *Morph* series, Peter directed music videos including *My Baby Just Cares For Me* and films in the *Lip Sync* and *Conversation Pieces* series. He co-directed the hit *Chicken Run* with Nick Park and directed *The Pirates!* In addition to the four Oscars won by Nick Park for Aardman, Peter has also been nominated for three Academy Awards. He was awarded the CBE in 2006.

aardman.com / Instgram: petelordaardman

What drew you to your medium?

My medium is animating with modeling clay. I remember quite clearly playing with Plasticine as a three or four-year-old alongside my mother in the basement kitchen. In my day, you naturally encountered Plasticine at primary school, but I really came back to it with enthusiasm at secondary school. I love three-dimensional expression. And then when I was a teenager, I was watching TV one day and I saw an example by somebody else, an American called Eli Noyes. He had made a film using clay animation. He called it clay but I think it was

Plasticine. Young people may not understand this, but back in those days, when you saw something on TV, you could only see it once. There were no repeats, there was no recording. So it was just pure chance that I ever saw this film. And at a glance, you could see that this was made by animated modeling clay. It struck me as a great idea. So I've had a long-standing relationship with the material—because in my day, kids used to play with Plasticine a lot—and I was inspired as a teenager to see that it could be animated.

Do you feel a connection with the history of your medium?

I do. By about 1980, my partner Dave Sproxton and I had been animating using Plasticine for a few years. Although I've mentioned Eli Noyes, I didn't know his name at the time and didn't see his film again for about 30 years. In the early 80s, Dave and I were doing this thing, using this material, and we felt like we were the only people in the world doing it. And possibly we were. And so it was special. Business-wise, it was very smart, because we had a unique selling proposition, as they say.

Interestingly, Plasticine was created and made in Bath, not too far from where I lived. And so in the early 80s I went to visit the Harbutts factory. That gave me the sense that the material was special. It's intimate, and as a tool it's infinitely flexible in the same way that a pencil is. That technology goes back into the mists of antiquity, but with Plasticine you could point to the man who invented it: William Harbutt. He developed it in 1897 in Bath. And in that mill factory, by the canal, they had a museum. There was a gallery of all their packaging over the years, from around 1900 through to 1980 when I saw it. So there was 80 years of commercial graphic art in terms of the packaging. That was very interesting. And they also had some models in the factory. I vividly remember a large goat, which in my mind was two feet high, in a giant glass case. It had all the detail of its hair, its coat, beautifully sculpted and rendered. And it was made in this modeling clay, which I know is soft. In fact I have a packet of

Plasticine on my desktop here. It's soft and malleable. But this goat was cut right through, hard, sharp, as if it was cracked. The Plasticine has oil in it, and when all the oil leaks out or evaporates it becomes as brittle as plaster of Paris.

We started animating in around 1972. And that was the first time that I ever bought Plasticine in this larger quantity – a one-pound packet. Previously you would get a set of small strips in different colors. But when we decided that this is going to be our medium, we started to buy large quantities. And they came in large cardboard boxes. It was printed in two colors. On one side of the box, there were two idealized children who were making a clown in the modeling clay. On the other side of the box there was an artist with a goatee beard and a smock. He was making a bust, a sculpture. And this was to celebrate the fact that this magic material was useful for both artists and play.

Does your medium offer something unique?

It actually does. I've said before that it's kind of like a pencil, because a pencil is this wonderfully simple device, with which you can do anything. It's really cheap, but you can draw like Raphael, if you're able. Or your three-year-old can do some scrawls on paper. So it has an incredible flexibility, from doodling to comic books to high art – anything is possible. And I always think Plasticine is a little bit like that. Although if I'm honest, it's rather harder to work with than a pencil. You buy this lump of material that has these very special properties. It doesn't set hard. Although as I mentioned with the goat, over the years it will do. But over days and months it doesn't set hard. It's got a rather lovely surface to it. You can more or less polish it if you care to with the ball of your thumb. This modeling clay I have on my desk here, which is made by a company called Newplast, is softer than what we used in the past. They must have gradually changed the formula. On a cold day you'd break your hand trying to warm it up and make it workable.

So it's not easy actually, as a medium. But it is very flexible. And as a performer—I'll use that word rather than artist—as a performer animating modeling clay, the special pleasure I think, is that when you've got it in your hands, this three-dimensional object, it suggests things to you. It seems to almost lead you. It has weight, it's subject to gravity. It's got mass. And when you put a character in a pose, the model itself, and its physicality, seem to suggest where you go next. I find that anyway. I like it very much.

Why do you have a need to create?

That's a huge question. I don't know. I just always have. My next-door neighbor has a five-year-old boy, and she told him to go outside and draw. And I heard him saying to his mother, "What should I draw?" I remember asking exactly that question of my mother. And I still think it today, actually. My drawings are never finished things. They are just en route to an idea, or a story or a design.

If I didn't draw personally, it wouldn't affect the work of our company. Nobody depends on my drawings. But I like it. So I have to do it. Along with my Plasticine I have my book of drawings. And so probably I am thinking, 'What should I draw, what story shall I tell?'

So why is it important? Because it's always been a part of my life. And at a certain stage in life, it's helpful to define yourself. It may be lazy, or a sign of cowardice or something, but practically it's true. Like, "I'm Pete, I'm the guy that draws well." Or, "I'm the guy that makes cartoons." I think we tend to do that, don't we?

I must've done that quite early on. I must've decided that I was a creative person. So it's very important to me. Even though today, I don't do very much. I doodle in various books. I make Morph. There's always a few versions of Morph around my desk. I was about to say that I don't do anything for its own sake, but that's not true actually. Especially working with Morph, working on stories, it's kind of for pleasure. But I'm not driven to produce tons of stuff every day. I wish I was. I'd quite like to find more time in my life to do that.

Why do humans have a need to create?

I find the question very interesting. We were on holiday in the Orkneys a couple of years ago, and the prehistory, the archeology, is fascinating, and spectacular. There's a place called Skara Brae, which is most extraordinary. It's a village that was buried under the sand. It's around 5,000 years old. In 1850 a huge storm tore away a lot of the earth and exposed this place that had been hidden for thousands of years. And what is so extraordinary about it is that you could see how the people lived. In England we don't get that at all. You might get an archeologist pointing out holes where posts once stood, or maybe a hearth. But at Skara Brae their beds are still there, made of upright stones. And there is a strange watertight sink in the floor. And most incredibly of all, opposite the door in each hut is a dresser with three long shelves and uprights. And you think, 'What on earth did they put on that dresser?' This is rather a long way around to answer the question, and say that I don't really understand why humans have this creative urge.

At Skara Brae there are flints, bones and things like that on display. And then there were two or three rather beautiful objects that are highly carved. And what was that about? My instinct is that it must be ritual. Somewhere there may have been a thought process that connects ritual to permanency through carved, ritual objects, which takes a huge number of hours. And so somehow creativity, in my understanding of prehistory, must be tied up to ritual.

But then you'll look at those cave paintings in France, like those at Lascaux. Extraordinary, beautiful, faithful recreations of animals. I find that fascinating. Most people assume that it related to ritual. How did they get from that to an illustration in the margin of a manuscript, that's got a monkey dressed as a Friar, farting? Creativity has so many functions.

I can tell you that there are many things that I don't understand. And one of them is, I'm fascinated by the artists with a capital A. I saw something on Instagram the other day. A friend of ours paints studies of birch woods. And on his Instagram he's got about a hundred of them. They're all kind of similar and they're very nice. And I think wow, that compunction to do it again and again, and again and again. I don't really understand that. I wish I had it, actually. If you're a potter, you've made a lovely pot, and now every day you keep on making pots. And if you're trying to sell them, that's fair enough, but still every day, you go back to the clay and make more and more pots.

And then there's abstract art where someone paints, and they're just feeling for something, reaching for something, experimenting with something. Something pure, but presumably irresistible. You just have to keep going back and scratching that itch. I look at that with great admiration, thinking, 'That's not me. I'm too lazy.'

What sacrifices have you made to pursue your creative path?

Not very many, honestly. I suppose the classic one for people is that, when the kids were small, it coincided with being extremely busy, but also not having that under control. Since then we have the business under control, but in those early days, in the 80s, we would work ridiculous hours. I was away a lot when the kids were small, and I think that's a sad thing. I don't think I was too bad because again, not being the absolutely driven artist, I knew the importance of getting home as well.

But apart from that, I can't really point to any sacrifices. And I'm probably really annoying other people who are artists. They'll say, "You jammy sod." I do think I was very lucky. Lucky in the choice of what I do, and the way it's turned out. And if there's anything missing in my life, I don't think it's because of the career or the art at all. It's really been a pleasure, most of the time.

One thing comes to mind, that would probably draw a snort of contempt from somebody else. At a certain stage in my career, I stopped being a prime creator, and became what you'd say in filmmaking is a producer figure. Then your job is not to make, but to help somebody else to make. And I know the pure artist stays making the ideas. I have done quite a lot of that, I suppose. In not doing it yourself you don't get the satisfaction of working on a single project wholeheartedly. And you don't get the credit either. But that's not much of a sacrifice. Was it a choice? It just kind of happened over time.

How has your work shaped you as a person?

That's an interesting question. I think I must have learned to become more empathic. And learned to be, if I may say, good with people. But the 20-year-old Peter Lord was very shy, and not at all outgoing. And not particularly confident, except in my art. When I graduated I was about 23. And since then I have become a bloke that will happily stand up and speak to 200 people that we employ, and move them sometimes, and inspire them. Or I will stand up and talk in a public arena in front of a thousand people. Those are the things that I certainly wouldn't have been able to do when I was younger.

I mentioned previously about the way you define yourself: "Oh, I'm the guy that's an animator." I know how lucky I am with that. Because most people don't have that in their career. A lot of people do jobs which probably don't say much about who they really are. Jobs that aren't very sexy. And probably those people then define themselves in what they do in their spare time. Like, "I'm a delivery driver, but I'm a footballer, and that's what I really love." So the funny thing is that if you do somewhat define yourself by what you do, which I do, then you wonder what happens when that stops. And maybe you'll choose not to think about that, to blank that out. You hear it talked about in different contexts. Like people who are driven, and obsessed with their work, and define themselves that way. And it's often spoken of as a bad thing, as a weakness of some kind, that you can't just be happy to be you, you have to be the animator or whatever it is. But no, I'm pretty happy with it. It's just natural. It feels right. It feels satisfying to me.

How do you deal with creative blocks?

Drawing is my way into stories. I find it very effective. And it's only half a step from doodling. You just draw. If I'm on Morph, I start to draw him, and something happens subconsciously. It's like, 'Oh I see, he's climbing out of a hole.' When I started drawing I didn't know that. Or he's trying to reach a very high shelf. It's in the line. I draw in biro quite a lot. I use it quite softly. When I was at school, I was highly criticized for using a black Bic biro. But I use it like a pencil, starting with a lovely soft line, then getting darker. So drawing for me is the way back into stories. When you sit down you don't have a story. Another thing I might do is write a list of situations. Like ice skating. Is there a story in ice skating? Then you start drawing him ice skating and maybe something suggests itself through the drawing.

I've not had a long-term creative block, but here's an interesting thing. I've talked about Morph. I'm working on stories most days in some form or other, but I've also thought to myself, as I'm approaching what's considered retirement age, that I should do some short films again. But I haven't got an idea for a short film in my head at the moment. Isn't that interesting? You would have thought that over these years I would have had a few stashed, waiting to come out. But I don't. So when I finally get around to this project, I will definitely have to go back to drawing in a sketch book, with pencil and biro, and start from scratch. I've started once or twice. So I might get there.

How do you stay fresh in your work?

I think it's a difficult question because it's maybe hard to spot when you're not fresh, in truth. I don't find that much of a problem. Every story that I approach, whether it be a minute long for Morph, or whether it be 85 minutes long for a movie, it's always such a challenge. I think that's the truth. Maybe that's why you don't feel stale. It always seems like a challenge, and a puzzle, a wild beast to be hunted down. So I always find that exciting.

So staleness I don't know, but creative blockage, yes, that certainly happens. You think you've got 90% of the thing, but for the life of you, you cannot think how to finish it.

Conventionally, the middle is the most difficult part of a story. I find that the set-up for the story is usually the thing that makes you want to tell that story in the first place. So you've got that. And with the sort of films we make, which are entertainment, it's a fair bet that you're going to head towards a happy ending. So what the end needs to be is quite clear. But then the middle is difficult, because sometimes it feels like you're wandering in a featureless plain without any direction, momentum or shape. Having said that the ending is easier, that hasn't been the case in recent experience. Let's say we know that, broadly, the ending involves the heroes getting together and defeating the bad guy, and ending up much happier than they were at the start. The broad strokes are clear, but the detail of that has, over the past decades, proved to be a lot of work.

What is your relationship with satisfaction in your work?

That's an interesting question. If there's a Morph story that is a minute long, and you get that to just turn sweetly, and you get the ending right, that's very satisfying.

When I see work that somebody else has done for our company, and I haven't had any part in that at all, then that is also an extremely satisfying feeling. That's interesting, isn't it? That's not personal gratification, it's something else. But it's a lovely feeling. And when I see somebody trying something new, that may be new to the whole company, and carrying it out with flair, then that's wonderful.

Frankly, any good piece of work should give satisfaction. We're doing a film now which is stop motion film. I'm not very involved at all, but I've given notes for the story. Otherwise I just stand back and watch. And I can see now that this is going to be so beautiful. And I'll be very proud of it. Being proud of what the company does is a thing that gives me great satisfaction.

But then on the purely personal note, the last film I made on my own was *The Pirates!* That was almost 10 years ago. There are some fantastic moments in that. Making a feature film is like climbing the Himalayas several times; it's an enormous challenge. It goes on and on, and there so many people involved, so many tiny decisions are involved. But when it's finished and it comes together, and you see it with an audience, that is incredibly satisfying.

If it then doesn't do very well at the box office, then that's really annoying. It's deeply frustrating, because you know that creatively you've achieved something special, but for a million mysterious reasons, that success isn't reflected in 'The Numbers'. And I say that not because of the money. Box office success is a weird, extremely unhealthy convention of our business. It's ludicrous. But still, if you succeed in those terms, it makes the next project easier to fund. It makes life easier. If it doesn't meet my expectations, then I try not to blame myself.

What is the relationship between your work and its audience?

We're lucky because we reach a mass audience, and therefore you get a lot of visible, audible, legible reactions. Generalizing wildly, we have a very loving kind of audience. They get what we do. Most of what we do is good-hearted. The end result is meant to be that you feel better at the end than you did at the start, and you've been delighted along the way. That's what we try to do. We do it well, so therefore people are delighted, and so you hear from people the whole time who express that enthusiasm. Of course I like that very much.

A funny little point about our work is that it tends to chime very well with autistic people; kids especially, but I think adults too. I quite often hear from the parents of autistic children who talk about the special pleasure they get from Morph or Shaun the Sheep. I also hear it from quite a lot of autistic people who are animators. It works rather well for them. And I've seen some very good stuff made by kids whose communication skills are otherwise quite limited. They've made some really good short animation. And of course now in the days of social media it's much easier to hear about these things than it used to be.

So generally speaking, we have a very warm relationship with our audience. And again, I think myself very lucky for that. As we speak, the recycling people are going by, and I don't suppose people very often tell them what a great job they're doing. If you do a job because you want to do it, and it's a pleasure and it's quite well paid, and people say, "Well done, thank you," then you are very lucky.

What is the relationship between yourself and your audience?

If it plays out anywhere it plays out on Twitter, I suppose. That's where one communicates to and fro a bit. I don't, I suppose, have a particularly close relationship with the audience. Warm yes, but not intimate. On Twitter, there's half a dozen people who are in the business, young animators, with whom I keep up a conversation. And maybe this is me, but I tend to be a little bit distant. I don't feel intimacy, but I do feel a great warmth.

What have you learned from your audience?

We don't make films for an audience, and maybe that's what the audience has told us. With *Wallace and Gromit*, Nick Park's great creation, he only ever did it for himself. We've found that it communicates incredibly well across cultural, national, gender and race barriers. It communicates everywhere. We don't ever sit down cynically and say, "Which audience should we go for this time?" We do it for ourselves. I certainly do. When I think of a Morph story, do I think about a six-year-old watching it? No, I don't at all. But at my age I might edit something out which would just be bewildering to a child. But otherwise we don't self-edit. We just think about what's funny, what's accessible. And maybe that's what the audience has taught us, by seeing how receptive they are.

When we made *Chicken Run*, which was 20 years ago, a painful part of the process with the America studio was doing test screenings before it was finished. So we took *Chicken Run* to some weird part of California, some strange shopping mall, to show them about three-quarters of the film. And so it was a very nervous time. And Nick and I were standing outside this place, talking with the execs, and then these people started to come wandering over, and everything about them was shocking to me, because they were so American. They wore whatever was the appropriate fashion of the day, which probably hadn't quite reached England yet. And they were talking in that different way that Americans talk, with their very loud voices and the things they articulate. Some of them had on sports shirts from teams I'd never heard of. And I just thought, 'Bloody hell, what on earth are these people meant to make of a story about a bunch of chickens in Yorkshire? Where's the connection?' But in fact it got a really good reaction.

So that was a learning. Just do what you want to do, with confidence, commitment, passion and honesty. And it will be good. And they will like it. Maybe not as many as you hope, but they will like it. It's always a sad thing with releasing a film, when they tell us not to bother with the Midwest. And so with a film like *The Pirates!*, they wouldn't even try to release it there. It might be a pretty token effort. But I always think they really would like it if they saw it. There are things I do understand about the US market. They can be a bit insular when it comes to accents. Someone told me that when they hear English regional accents, they think they're watching a foreign movie. But at Aardman we absolutely persist in making films with English regional accents. So we don't go chasing the audience.

What has been the greatest challenge in your creative career?

With regard to the fire we had, where we lost much of our archive, I think I must be a very level-headed sort of person. Because when we won the first Oscar, I don't remember going crazy. And when the fire happened at the time, I wasn't particularly upset either. The news was given to me at work by the guy who was in charge of the archive. He was mortified. I was sad, but I wasn't horrified or stunned or anything like that. And the main reason was that I didn't really know what we'd lost. It was only once or twice in later years that I thought much more strongly, 'Oh gosh, that's a real loss.'

I remember noticing it when we had an exhibition in Paris, a big retrospective of our career. It was fantastic, by the way. I remember stepping into the first room and seeing all the stuff laid out there. There were old photographs, some sets and models, even an Oscar statuette, and some films were playing on monitors. I was really stunned. For the first time, I felt that I had some objectivity about what we'd achieved. To stand back and look, almost as an outsider, rather than being in the middle of it, was a great thing.

But for that exhibition, there were some things that should have been there that weren't, due to the fire. And that would be the pie machine from *Chicken Run*, and the airplane the chickens fly away in. Both of those beautiful objects were lost. They were glorious things. And we lost a lot of stuff on paper too, of course, such as storyboards, early designs and stuff like that.

The company is called Aardman because one of the first things we did was a very badly-drawn superhero called Aardman. And of him, as archive material, almost nothing remains. The little that we'd retained was burnt in that fire. So in retrospect that's sad. But at the time I wasn't dismayed. Maybe it's because we're always moving forward, and looking forward to our next production. That's the important thing. In those days we had no notion of retrospectives and archives and stuff like that.

There's a detailed list of things that you put in the store in big cardboard boxes. One of them was listed as 'Awards: various'. It was a box full of strange lumps of brass and crystal and stuff – prizes from film and animation festivals all across the world. *The Wrong Trousers* in particular had won so many prizes. And they got put in a box, and put into storage and then—in due course—vaporized.

Ultimately I think that the biggest achievement is actually the studio as a dynamic, living community of artists, filmmakers and other creative people. And then the historic factor is important too. By the simple expedient of staying alive and keeping going, those things are continually shared down the years. People are now watching *Morph* with their grandkids, and they themselves watched it when they were children. That's marvelous. And that warmth from an audience is palpable. It's interesting to think about those things, but I rarely do so. Because most of our experience with the audience has a screen in the way. Our stuff is shown on the screens and then the reaction comes back on the screen. The premiere of *The Pirates!* was wonderful because it was a group cultural event, a human event. And that's what the exhibitions have been.

What has been the high point of your career?

I might say the time when we won an Oscar—our first one—for *Creature Comforts*. That was a pretty astonishing thing to happen. Of course it was simply fantastic. We were a small group of people. Three of us were in California for the ceremony. And we came back to Bristol with the Oscar, but I don't remember what happened, which is interesting. Maybe we just went to the pub. It was a defining moment, but it doesn't feel like it.

With *The Pirates!* there was again a shared experience. When you're finished you do the test screenings, then you show it to the people who made it. Which is sometimes a little bit quiet, because the audience is watching their own work, either happily or unhappily, thinking, 'I remember that moment.' They may be anticipating that thing they did, or that thing they made that only appeared on the screen for two seconds. But for *Pirates!* we had a riotous screening for the people that made it, and for friends and families, and some press, in London. That was memorable. It felt like a pure, feel-good moment. But honestly the career has been so blessed. I'm sure I could mention a dozen other great moments I'm sure. To pick one is really difficult.

What is the most important thing your creative practice has taught you?

I'm thinking all sorts of complicated things, but maybe the simplest thing is: collaboration. Because when you think about it, it started out with two of us working together. Though actually the parts of the job we did were quite separate from each other. Our small early success was already based on collaboration.

And then decades later, like on *The Pirates!*, you find you're supported by 250 people, all working together to carry out your vision. And of those 250, in almost every case, they could all do their job better than I possibly could. That's a wonderful feeling. You feel that you have harnessed all this energy and passion. Somehow, by some great alchemy, you've taken all this prodigious talent and focused it on one thing. And you learn that it's better to work with people who are better than you.

When we started, I think for my time I was a very good animator. Because in a way that's what the whole business has been based on. Good stories and good animation. And that stuff we did with Morph, I think for its time was really good. But now, most of the animators I work with could do it better than I could. Puppet animation is a very interesting art form, because it's physical, you're working with your hands. It's a craft. And it's incredibly expressive. And it's also a performance. So it's a strange, mysterious hybrid creature between the actor and the sculptor and probably some other things in between. And it's very demanding.

How did it feel to reflect on and discuss creativity today?

Well, it's been very interesting actually, Miguel. Although I don't produce something tangible every day, to wax romantic for a moment, it's like a gardener. I don't produce the seeds, but I plant, water and nurture them. And it's the same with the other people at Aardman, the other super talented directors, designers and artists. To help to maintain that environment every day is a great thing.

I've seen the effect our work has had over the years. And I know that we do it very well. It is an incredibly creative process. And everyone's still striving. We haven't talked about that very much, but for some reason we strive in every part of the creative process. You just keep at it. You can't even define what you're reaching for, but you just keep going until you've got it. And it feels good when you get there. And I think that's what most people at Aardman are doing so much of the time. And that is a crazy environment. It's collaborative. In normal times people are close together, and on different levels, picking things up from each other the whole time. For us, for me, creativity is absolutely a shared or communal experience.

Rama Mani

Dr. Rama Mani is a peacebuilder, poet and performance artist whose life, work and art are devoted to human and global transformation. She received the Peter Becker Peace Prize in 2013 in Germany, the Excellence in Leadership Award of the Global Thinkers Forum in the UK in 2018, and the Visionary Leadership Award of the Visioneers' International Network in Canada in 2020.

Dr. Mani is the Founder of Theatre of Transformation Academy, whose purpose is to champion and support the creative power of humanity to shape our shared future. She is the Convenor of the Enacting Global Transformation Collaborative Initiative at the University of Oxford's Centre for International Studies, which seeks to redefine paradigms of power, and shape creative and humane responses to current global crises. Rama and her husband, Professor Alexander Schieffer, co-founded Home for Humanity, whose mission is to nurture the potential of each individual, home and culture to be a seedbed for societal and planetary transformation, and whose vision is to transform our divided world into a united home for the Earth family.

homeforhumanity.earth

What drew you to your medium?

The beauty is that my medium drew me to it. It caught and submerged and decided what to do with me. I had to give it a name at some point, and so I began to call it 'Theatre of Transformation'. On the face of it you could say that it is theatre, although what I do has nothing to do with the theatre that we know today. Conventionally, theatre has a playwright, a director and a group of actors, who aim to honor the playwright's vision. The actors rehearse under the direction of a director until they feel it is ready to be brought before an audience on stage. My work, which centers around the idea and experience of transformation, is different, in that it is an embodiment of real life people, and the enactment of their story. I convey the transformative testimonies of people I have encountered, collaborated with, understood and empathized with deeply, the essence of which gets encapsulated in an enacted performance. I aim to convey all of the turmoil, challenges and the turning point of their lives, which took them from what they were to what they have become. Each person's story is conveyed to an audience in two to five minutes. The reason I use 'transformation' is that the audience becomes deeply engaged in the life of the persons I embody on stage, and begins to feel they know them, and feel them working within themselves. It has the effect of activating in the audience members what is common to our humanity within ourselves. So what I do has a different structure to classic theatre, but it has a similar cathartic intent and effect, as the origins of theatre did.

I'll explain how all this started. As a young person I loved art, especially the written arts. I loved poetry and storytelling. I was drawn especially to hear the fascinating stories of resilience of the so-called 'have nots' of society who suffered discrimination. And growing up in India, with its caste, social and economic divisions, I was surrounded by such people, who no one cared about or listened to. But I was not at all gifted at the arts that a good Indian girl ought to be perfecting. I was incapable of learning classical dance, or any musical instrument, and singing was a true disaster. And while I loved theatre, I never managed to make it through any audition. The only plays I was a part of did not have auditions. I think I won one female acting prize, but that's because I was the only female actor in that play. So I kind of gave up on the arts, and convinced myself I was not creative.

But that changed when I was 33. I was living and working on peace building on the African continent, and would go on peace missions to different war-torn countries and areas. And during a mission in Somaliland in 2000, I had a huge epiphany about the power of the arts to prevent conflict and rebuild peace. But believing myself to have no artistic talent, it took me a long time to figure out how to 'act' on it! So my starting point was simply to go and talk to artists on my travels to war-torn countries. I did not speak with famous artists, but with those who seemed to be speaking for the spirit of their community. Their only desire was to contribute to healing the past and recreating the future through their art.

In our home, we have a gallery of Transformation Art, featuring works from artists in countries such as Rwanda, Cambodia, South Africa and Nepal. We have a painting by Wari Zárate Gutiérrez, a Quechua artist from Peru, who was deeply troubled by the Abu Ghraib torture revelations. This made him realize that dehumanization happens everywhere around the world, and that metamorphosis is possible everywhere. Another piece is done by a young Rwandan artist Jean Bosco Bakunzi, who narrowly survived the genocide at age 12 with his siblings, and used art as a way to feed his siblings and heal himself and his society. I talked to artists of every medium imaginable to try and understand the various ways in which art can prevent conflict and sow peace.

That's the background. But it was only in 2013, just seven years ago, that things clicked. I was on a peace mission to Palestine, having won a small peace prize. It is a society that I said I would never visit until there was peace and freedom there. But luckily I have a friend, Zahira Kamal, who is an extraordinary peace activist. She said, "I'm getting on in years, and you need to come and experience my country and speak about it." The stories that I heard on that mission were so powerful. From Palestine, I went straight to the University of Oxford, where I co-host an annual gathering of women scholars. When they asked me to share a report of my peace mission, without thinking of it, I started reciting in the first person the testimonies I had written verbatim of what people had told me, as their stories were still reverberating in me. Everyone was captivated.

The visionary founder of Social Artistry, Jean Houston, actually triggered my emergence as a performance artist. She had already presaged that "something big [was] waiting to come through" me. Just a month after the Oxford meeting, in January 2014, on the fringes of a conference of the Rising Women Rising World movement we had co-founded with peace activist Scilla Elworthy, Jean convened her city's leading cultural creatives and artists, and summarily ordered me to give my first art recital. It was an electrifying evening for all present, and I was astonished at my own performance. Theatre of Transformation took form from that moment on.

I had met many people in situations of crisis and conflict, of genocide, who had deeply touched me. In most cases they were people who did not get stuck in their crisis. Something within them enabled them to transcend their circumstances, and transform themselves toward their deeper purpose. And this self-transformation inevitably led to a transformative impact on their societies. So within the first year of performing, I gravitated towards the testimonies of such people, those who became the lights in their societies, because they became a light to themselves. And that's what the Theatre of Transformation became: enacting that trajectory from breakdown to breakthrough. The stories were unique to each individual, different across cultures and contexts, yet possible for us all.

Because I am so passionate about humanity and all of its cultural diversity, I always give the audience a tour of the world in each performance. I typically perform seven or eight testimonies of people I've encountered or worked with across Latin America, Asia, Africa and Europe. And these are people of all ages and backgrounds.

The next phase began with the realization that I was not satisfied with just performing, hearing the applause, then having a drink with the other performers and going home, as professional actors or musicians normally do. I was interested in awakening something in the audience, being a co-creator with them, and seeing them participate in their own transformation. The enactment, the theatre, is the prelude for the transformative process that continues with the audience. I learned from their reaction that it was a profound experience for them. They felt that if I am not a professionally-trained actress, but can still embody all these people, that means that these people live inside me – which means that they live inside us too. So if I, as an Argentine man who doesn't speak English, wept when I heard the story of a Palestinian man, or Nepali woman, that means that that man or woman is also inside me. And it awakens memories of people in my life who have touched me in similar ways. They came to the realization: 'I am the other, and the other is me'. So there was a profound process of transformation taking place as they experienced my performance, which then deepened in the interaction that followed.

Do you feel a connection with the history of your medium?

I especially feel a connection to Greek theatre, which was very aware of its cathartic role in society. Everybody participated in it. They were out there weeping and laughing and experiencing the gamut of emotions. They had these huge amphitheaters, which were extraordinarily well built. And this wasn't just for the elite, in the way it is today in the best theatres in London and New York – this was for everybody. It was a recognition that everybody needed to go through this dramatic, emotional process, to live through and make sense of what's happening in their lives, and in the body politic. I'm sure there was much less need for therapists, because they had such good theatre.

I've recently been recovering from an illness, and I felt a calling to take some time out and convalesce. And immediately I thought about the sanctuary of Asclepius, the Greek god of healing. It is in a place called Epidavros, two hours from Athens. Amidst the pine groves, there is one of the best-preserved theatres in Greece, alongside an athletics stadium, healing baths, and places for every kind of musical and artistic activity. So although you came to this great sanctuary to heal a serious illness, for several days you would simply practice the arts and sports, and watch theatre, and let all of this work through you and open up your senses, until you felt you were really ready to receive your remedy. You would then spend the night in the Thymele, the underground chamber, where you would dream of Aclepius, the god of healing, or of one of his daughters, whose names include Panacea and Hygieia. Their names have been since enshrined in modern medicine. In your dreams they would tell you the cure you needed for your ailment. The medical priests of the temple would translate the message of your dreams and give you the appropriate treatment. It was so powerful for me to learn that exposure to and involvement in the arts was a vital prerequisite of the healing process for the Greeks. I feel a particularly strong connection to this, because that was when the power of storytelling and theatre to create a healthy and participatory society was fully understood. Of course there are some modern aspects of theatre that I feel a connection to, but it is that ancient mode that speaks to me most.

Does your medium offer something unique?

Theatre in and of itself is wonderful, and offers many unique things: one being that it is a forum that allows for a symbiosis of so many mediums of art: enactment of course, but also music, visual art, photography and so on. But speaking specifically about Theatre of Transformation, as it has grown within and through me in recent years, it is really saying to every single human being that what makes us all human is this unique valve of creativity within us. It was dormant in me, having been convinced that I was not creative, but once it was opened, there was no stopping it, and I became myself. But saying 'became myself' is interesting, because in a performance I am not Rama, I am all these characters, these real-life people. This process makes you realize how our humanity is so intrinsically linked to our capacity to create, through whatever expression.

Secondly, and most importantly, is that it makes us realize that at the end of the day, we have to be the screenwriters, the directors, the actors and the stage managers of our own lives. We need to step onto the stage of our own lives. And if we find that the reality—because there's a whole transformative process that I'll go into later—that we see of our lives does not fulfill us, it does not seem to be our calling, it is up to us to pick up the pen again, to become the scriptwriters of our own lives, and re-author the story that we want. And that's not simply a self-centered thing about 'my' life, because it is the collaborative process of co-creating the reality that we seek in our society. So the third part of it is that it is a profound way of discovering that we can be the creators of the reality that we want in our societies. Because everything happens together; there is no question of solo authors. Until every author decides to take up that responsibility, we cannot co-create.

Why do you have a need to create?

What I have recognized is that, if I look back on these last seven years of creating, I have never had quite the same feeling of fulfillment and bliss, as when the universe, nature, art and humanity, flowed through me each time I composed a performance piece. For the artist, when you are creating, the process is in a way beyond you, yet you feel infinitely grateful that it chooses to flow through you. And it gives you something that's quite unexpected. And it goes beyond you and into the world to have an effect that is greater than yourself.

Why do humans have a need to create?

We have a need to create because how else would we be here? Just look at the creativity of every single thing in nature. The very fact that we are not just consciousness, that we have taken all these diverse forms, is due to the power of creativity. And every single creature and plant is an infinite expression of creativity. We humans, being part of creation, are exactly the same. But the difference is that the creativity is sort of stamped out of us as we grow up, except for that very small handful who don't conform to social pressure and continue to create until the end of their lives. But everyone else has that creativity stamped out, because we are told that art is not something serious, and creativity is not essential to professional adult life. That's the tragedy. My peacebuilding work and research has established that it is our lack of creativity that has hindered our ability to innovate appropriate solutions to conflicts and crises, and prevented us from creating better systems of governance. Creativity is essential for addressing every crisis in society. It can transform crisis, rather than simply managing or suppressing it.

We remove ourselves from the universe, from the process of life, when we cease to be creative and simply repeat whatever we have done before – including our old mistakes.

Finally, we have to restore beauty to our daily lives! In the last century or two we have condemned ourselves to living with such ugliness. If we have 'created' at all in recent times, it is mainly ugliness: our urban sprawl, our toxic industrial waste. We have not realized the toll it takes on our humanity, our feelings, sensitivities, sensibilities and our intelligence, to be surrounded by ugliness. Beauty would be a natural part of our lives if we were living in union with life. To be cut off from creativity is to believe that beauty has no place in our lives, and that it is fine to sit in grey buildings, to travel by grey metros and drive grey cars. And to see and smell smoke all day, which is also grey. That is no way to live.

What sacrifices have you made to pursue your creative path?

The interesting sacrifice I have made takes me back to my childhood. Somehow I knew that if I wanted to work on peace and justice I would have to engage with the arts. But sadly, I believed even then that if I went into an artistic career, like film, I would not be taken seriously. I believed I had to develop my intellect, and have intellectual and political answers to be taken seriously. And that's why I locked up my creativity. But it's interesting that it came back in my mid-40s. But a big concern was still operative in me, that I was a serious person, sitting on all these boards, being an academic and professional expert, giving sage advice to all these international institutions. How would my peers regard me if I was suddenly prancing around a stage enacting old women, young men, warlords or victims? So what I sacrificed—if it can be considered as such—is my fear of being judged as not serious enough. We don't realize what a cage we create around ourselves with our beliefs and assumptions. Our intellectual and ideological baggage gets blasted out of the window when we experience artistic expression and freedom.

It's ironic, because some of my first performances were at the UN, in the presence of many colleagues with whom I had sat on boards, or whom I had taught. I discovered that those people, whose opinion I feared, were much more impacted by this mode than they would have been by the best speech or lecture I could have given. Some colleagues did perhaps judge me, but I ceased to worry or care about it, as I had found my element and essence, and nothing else really mattered!

How has your work shaped you as a person?

It has reshaped me. The delightful thing is that it has made me realize, through my own experience, that everything we believe about ourselves is an illusion. Being able to laugh at my old belief that I was not creative, allows me to laugh at anyone's belief that they are not creative, or artistic. It has made me realize that nothing is impossible. And each story I enact is a living proof of that. People with no resources, having lost everything they had and everyone they cherished, still managed to achieve the impossible of re-storying their own lives and impacting the people and communities around them.

I'm not sure I've ever realized this before, but life is creativity. It's there all the time. And it's when we allow ourselves to be plugged into it that we can become part of that. Human beings are this strange species where we shut off the taps that allow ourselves to be part of the process of life. But we can rediscover the ability to open those taps.

How do you deal with creative blocks?

Earlier, my creative outlet was writing: I would get creative spurts, then hit a dead end before the last stage. But with Theatre of Transformation, I don't get creative blocks. Maybe this is because I'm not trying so hard, and because intellect doesn't come in as much, and I surrender to the creative force, rather than making it an object of my will. So, though I'm very familiar with creative blocks as a writer, I'm able to recognize with Theatre of Transformation that it's been different and less subject to blockages. Unlike with writing, I hold the theme of my next performance in my mind or spirit and just walk in nature around our countryside home, and inspiration comes, in its own time. I trust whatever comes and act on it.

How do you stay fresh in your work?

Unlike conventional theatre, I've never performed the same act twice. Though there are many stories that I've repeated. There are maybe 150 people whose lives I've incarnated so far, from 30 or so countries.

The theme of my performances is different each time, though always centered around human and global transformation: peace, security, justice, leadership, governance and women's power. Sometimes it's a stage performance, but often it's a keynote or a lecture or seminar that I transform into a performative presentation. I set my imagination free while focusing on the topic as I wander in nature, and see what comes. So always there is something new that happens, and something that surprises me. What keeps me fresh is that lack of repetition. I used to rehearse a bit in the beginning, but now I rarely do. I just plan in advance the décor of my stage according to the testimonies I want to share and the 'cultures' each evokes, and the flow of the performance. Often if you're an actor, you have no control over your stage. A professional does the décor. But here, I've realized the joy I get in transforming a grey empty stage into a transformative space hosting multiple cultures – and infinite possibilities. I hate repetition. This is why I could never be a traditional actor. I love creating these magical worlds, and I have to encapsulate them. I have to take people to, for example, Peru, Nigeria, Palestine and Rwanda. I may have to render the essence of 10 countries on this little stage. Usually, I arrive at a performance with just a basket of fabrics and clothes from different parts of the world. By recreating the world on stage it enables the audience to travel with me to all these continents and countries. In a few minutes I create a space of surprise, beauty and mystery. Even though they may be sites of conflict and suffering, they still hold beauty. Sometimes, I embed little secrets on the stage that give a deeper meaning or carry a symbolic intention. It is just a privilege and a joy to recreate our rich, diverse world with a few inexpensive pieces of cloth, so that the tapestry of our humanity can be shared through a few stories.

So the work stays fresh because it's always changing. Therefore I never get bored of myself. In addition, I've been fortunate to perform alongside humanist artists and transformative musicians who aren't driven by profit, but share my desire to serve humanity and foster transformation through art. These include people like musician Paul Grant or visual artist William Kelly. This rich process of artistic and spiritual collaboration makes each performance unique.

In a scripted play you can't innovate or improvise at the last moment, but I remain constantly open to inspiration: even when I get onstage a new idea may suddenly drop in, and I am always willing to change what I had planned, and allow that to unfold instead. So this further adds to the unique nature of each performance.

What is your relationship with satisfaction in your work?

There are three levels. The first is my deep feeling of gratitude, for this unexpected gift of creativity. This is something I would never have imagined myself to be capable of. I get so much joy out of doing something I never expected to, which somehow happens effortlessly through me and has such positive impacts.

There's a second level of satisfaction, which is in seeing the effect it has on diverse audiences, from international leaders to grassroots activists. It never fails to amaze me how such diverse audiences can all be so deeply impacted. Men are usually schooled to hide their emotions, but they often come forward to express how much they were moved or transformed. I remember once, early on, an African chief came up to me after a performance at a major UN awards ceremony. He playfully hit me with his ceremonial stick and said, "You're a very bad person. African chiefs are not supposed to cry!" I was very touched by that.

But my greatest satisfaction comes from the hope and courage my dear collaborators get from seeing me retelling their stories. They may be in Palestine, Syria or the slums of Mumbai, and be in despair or feeling abandoned by the world, but they watch my YouTube videos and see me enacting their stories for a global audience, and know that their stories are inspiring people far away.

For all these reasons, I would love to see Theatre of Transformation spread further. It would give me immense satisfaction if this humanizing impact, that is so vitally needed in today's world of alienation and 'othering', could be spread much further. I would love to perform in places where it is most needed, and for people most in need of transformation. And I would especially love to bring such people to our 'Home for Humanity' which is a simple but immensely transformative space for such processes. And I'd also love to coach and certify many people to develop their own theatres of transformation with their own repertoires of testimonies from their own lives, to perform far and wide to multiply this impact and create societies of inclusion, empathy and creativity.

What is the relationship between your work and its audience?

In the Western world, art has largely become a spectator sport. You go to a concert or museum, both of which are expensive, and you hear the music up there on the stage, or look at something on the wall up there, while you are down here. It is an objective Kantian and Hegelian observation of beauty; it is not experiential, or engaged, so it cannot be emancipatory. For me the question is: how do we release the transformative potential of art? How can it become participatory and co-creative? For me the stage is not separate from the audience. My purpose is not to be applauded for a performance and then leave the audience to deal with whatever it has stirred up in them. Rather, my responsibility as an artist in Theatre of Transformation is to put in the right ingredients that create a transformative space, a place of possibility that transforms the audience into active participants. What I perform on the stage is the prelude to warm up the audience to become co-creators in a collective work of transformation. The interactive workshops that usually follow my performances culminate with the audience-turned-participants performing their own testimonies. So there is no space between my work and the audience, the audience members revisit and re-story their own lives and enact it – they become the main show! They realize that they don't need me; they have the power to witness reality, awaken possibilities, envision change and enact transformation in their own life. That's the whole four-step transformative process of Theatre of Transformation.

What is the relationship between yourself and your audience?

It's completely one of complicity and co-creation. My relationship with every single member of my audience is this: I am here for you, I am engaging in a relationship of profound love and care for you. I profoundly care about what this is going to activate in you, where this is going to take you. And I will be there with you, to help you reach that place of transformation within yourself that you long for. That is why I always aim to hold that space of interaction with the audience after the performance, and wherever possible to offer a more in-depth workshop the following day to support the unfolding of that transformative process. I am not interested in the usual intellectual

Q&A where people retreat into their minds and ask clever questions. As an academic I am used to that and know it is not fertile for transformation. Rather I try to hold a space where the audience can stay in that awakened energy of humanity, of spirit, of creativity, where transformation becomes possible.

What has your audience taught you?

They've taught me how easy it is to reclaim our humanity. How simple, how universal. How in the end it takes so little to reopen us to who we are and what we can be. The human skin is so thin and yet it becomes so thick, so callous. Yet with the right approach, it is easy to trigger a natural surge of humanity, of love and care and concern for the other. I see the depth of care, concern and love my audiences around the world have felt for every one of the characters that I portray. I see their willingness to open their whole hearts to humanity. And I find this incredibly edifying, instructive and hopeful.

What has been the greatest challenge in your career?

I think the biggest challenge is that I didn't grow up with the arts. I didn't learn it formally. It fell into me. So I just didn't know how to operate in the world of artists. I didn't know the business of finding a manager and getting bookings.

It would have been nice to have the two avenues. I created opportunities through the channels I had outside the orthodox channels of the art world, and brought art into the space of peacebuilding, governance and academia. So if a university or international conference invited me to give a keynote speech, I would instead offer them a performance or performative keynote. I gave a commencement speech at a prestigious university as a performance. It was great to see the impact of bringing Theatre of Transformation and its impact into such spaces where art is absent.

But it would have been great if in parallel I had also known how to get into the artistic circuit to perform more frequently in theatres and concert halls, even though what I perform is so different to normal theatre. Interestingly, all the professional actors and theatre directors I've interacted with, have said thank God I didn't have formal training as an actor, or I would never have been able to do what I do. I would have lost that magic, because I would have been so busy analyzing the right theatrical technique instead of letting it happen intuitively. And that freedom is such a gift.

What has been the high point of your career?

There have been many, so I'll just give a couple of examples that come to mind. For the last few years I've been invited to offer an annual performance, followed by an interactive seminar, on Transformative Leadership to the senior leaders of the UN system. And that's meaningful to me because my professional career began with the Commission on Global Governance, helping prepare their seminal report to reform the United Nations at its 50th anniversary in 1995, after the end of the cold War. I offer these performances to UN leaders with one of my favorite musicians, Paul Grant. He is an American who was a rock star in the 60s until he heard Ravi Shankar in California. That took him to India to master Hindustani, Sufi, Afghan and Iranian music. He plays instruments he has made himself, or helped recover from war-torn countries. We compose beautiful performances with his wide repertoire of instruments and musical styles with which he is able to create the sounds of Africa, Asia and the Middle East to accompany my stories. After our performance, we sit in a circle with these 40 or so UN leaders and I ask each of them to express what they experienced. We then go into a deeper seminar on transformative leadership, which is one of my fields of expertise. The impact is palpable. They each share how they feel reconnected to their deeper purpose, and feel re-humanized and re-energized to overcome bureaucratic and political obstacles to fulfill their mission, inspired by these stories of people who achieve so much with so little, having lost all they had.

Part of Theatre of Transformation Academy's purpose is offer peace missions, either funded through my own savings or with the modest honoraria I receive, where I give performances and interactive workshops in Theatre of Transformation to grassroots peacebuilders in societies in conflict and crisis. One that comes to mind was in Soweto in South Africa, where I gave a workshop. It was in a barren, corrugated iron shed which was very uninspiring, so I sent everyone away to do an exercise, while I transformed the place with my baskets of cloth. On returning they were astonished to see what had been created. That workshop was magical. It enabled these black underprivileged youth, who had seen so much violence and deprivation, to tap into and express extraordinary things through their limitless imagination.

In the slums of Mumbai, just a few kilometers from where I grew up, I've partnered since 2015 with a grassroots organization called CORO and the Women's Federation of the slums of Mumbai. I've enacted so many of their stories of how they went from being hapless victims of daily domestic violence to becoming grassroots women's leaders changing legislation and winning court cases! The most moving experience I had with them was when, after just a two-day intensive workshop of Theatre of Transformation, sixteen of these slum women leaders, aged 24 to 65, performed their own testimonies at Mumbai's leading university to an international audience, and moved everyone to tears.

What I love is this: being able to transform both influential leaders who have lost touch with reality, with ordinary people, and to champion these so-called 'ordinary people' who do such extraordinary things in the face of the daily crises that afflict them. So the highpoint of my career is in creating what I call 'circles of solidarity' between the so-called powerful who hold political or economic might, and those with profound inner power though they may lack political and economic means.

What is the most important thing your creative practice has taught you?

We are meant to be creative if we are to be in alignment with life. And every one of us has it in us to be creative. And having discovered that for myself at a later point in my life, I feel it is something I want to give to others, to help them simply access that. I want to be the catalyst, and open that door so that they can become more fully themselves. And that is essential if we are going to create the future we want. We can't do it if we remain stuck in what we are right now.

How did it feel to reflect on creativity today?

With you it was wonderful Miguel. It was very joyful, and regenerative. It was a beautiful gift to spend an hour collecting the treasures of my creative process and journey. It has also reignited in me the passion for why I do what I do. For this I am deeply grateful to you!

Miguel Mendonça

Miguel Mendonça is a native of Olhão in Portugal. He graduated in design at the University of Algarve, in Faro. His artistic career has always been associated with comics. He was part of a small comic group in Olhão when he was younger, and he participated in several local and national contests between 2001 and 2008. In 2013 Miguel entered the American comic book market through the publisher Zenescope, where he designed several titles from the *Grimm Fairy Tales* universe: *Unleashed*, *Warlord of Oz* and *The Little Mermaid* series.

At the end of 2015 he began collaborating with DC Comics and since then he has been developing work on series including *Wonder Woman*, *Teen Titans*, *Green Lantern*, *Trinity*, *JLA*, *Nightwing*, *Detective Comics* and *Aquaman*.

miguelmendoncacomics.blogspot.com

Instagram: miguelmendoncaart

What drew you to your medium?

Drawing is in my blood. I've been drawing since I could hold a pencil. My family says I would draw my toys, and anything I could pick up. That was just something that came naturally. For me that's a little bit of what talent is. It's a natural connection with something. It's easy for me to draw, like it is easy for a painter to paint, for example. And the more you do it, the better you get, so you develop the skills to add to the natural talent.

I had no idea that it was a possibility that I could draw comics for a living. In Portugal at that time there were no examples. Even today there are only five or six people that do what I do. If someone then had told me I would be drawing Batman for a living I would say they were crazy. It's like saying I could win an Oscar without being an actor. So I didn't even think about it. But drawing was always a part of my life. My teachers would tell me I had a bright future in drawing, but I didn't like to hear that because no one could tell me how I would achieve it. So I started thinking about design, like logos, branding and websites. I lived near a university in Faro in the south of Portugal, and I did a degree in design. In the first years of that course it had some art disciplines, like drawing with different materials and observational drawing. After two years it became less about drawing and more about working with software. But this was a path that I could take, and make a living. And I started liking it. So I worked as a designer and editorial illustrator.

In doing this work, I discovered that I liked it, but my real passion was something else. And that part of me was always present. When I was waiting for the computer to load, I would be drawing all the time. I got all my work done, and met all my deadlines, but I was still drawing at every opportunity. And eventually I began to listen to this little voice in my head that started as a whisper. And the more I listened to it, the louder it got. It said, "What if?" And I wondered if drawing comics was really something that I could do. So I fed it by taking more of an interest in comics by other authors, going to festivals, drawing more in my free time and building up my portfolio. When you do this, the voice is no longer a whisper – you hear it clearly. Eventually it becomes you. It's your own voice. And there is no turning back from there. It changes everything. When you get to that point, you make a decision: I will do this. At that point everything becomes clear. You do everything you have to do, in order to achieve what you want. Before it was like I was seeing my objectives through a blurred lens. But now I focused that lens on one thing: drawing comics. From that point on, nothing else mattered. So any obstacle that came up was not a problem, it didn't get in the way. The focus meant taking it seriously, building my portfolio, and thinking about how to get a job doing it.

In 2011, when I was around 27, I had spent about a year collecting emails and other connections on the internet for publishers who were taking portfolios. I sent them off, and the result was: nothing. So what do you do at this point? The work isn't good enough, so you just start over, and do it better. A year later, I sent the new work, and I got a few job offers. Most were backend deals where you do the work, and you only get paid if the work sells. But I was not interested in this because I needed to make a living. I had to do it full-time. So in 2013 I accepted a deal with a small American publisher called Zenescope. They would do more mature versions of known stories like *Grimm's Fairy Tales* or *The Wizard of Oz*. So the author would send me the script, and I would send sketched layouts of the pages, then do the final work. Other artists would do the coloring and lettering, then they would send me the book and they would publish it. That was very important as I was now working in the industry and learning the process. I did 10 pages first, then had to do a whole book, with 40 pages. It was really difficult to get in the rhythm of doing that volume of work, and aiming for the deadline.

Two years later I got an offer from DC Comics, which was one of my main objectives. The bigger companies are not open for submissions these days. They used to be, but now with the internet they would be overflowing with submissions. The way to get in is through comic book conventions, getting to know the editors personally, through word-of-mouth, or through them seeing your work on the internet. If it becomes popular and gets a lot of views it can get their attention.

We do not have big conventions in Portugal where you can meet the editors. So one of the things I did, while working for Zenescope, was to travel to Leeds in England, where a Marvel talent scout was reviewing portfolios at the Thought Bubble Comic Art Festival. I had sent my portfolio and it was accepted, so I went in person to meet with him and some other publishers. I went alone and was trying to find my hotel, at night. I wasn't sure how to get there, so I was told to take a bus. Then the driver stopped, and said, "It's here, but be careful because this is a dangerous place." So I got off the bus with that going round my head. And then it started raining, and I was standing alone in the dark and the rain with no idea where to go. At the time I had no smartphone to get me there. But then that little voice said, "Just keep going forward. Don't look back." So I followed that voice, and soon I found the hotel. So that was another magical little moment.

At the convention, meeting the Marvel scout C.B. Cebulski, it was a great time. He liked what he saw of my work. It was already published by Zenescope, which was a bonus. He said, "This is great. What Marvel characters do you like the most, so I can tell my editor?" And I went completely blank. I'd been reading those comics most of my life, and drawing them for years. But I could not remember a single character when he asked me. It was like, what is happening? He said, "That's okay, don't worry." And I said, "No, but I draw them all the time!" So I didn't get the job, and I don't know if that had something to do with it. Of course it was frustrating, because he liked my work.

So I continued drawing for Zenescope, and through that I had a chance to work with a writer called Meredith Finch. I was doing a series with her, and at the time she was already writing *Wonder Woman* for DC Comics, with her superstar artist husband David Finch. And one day they needed a fill-in artist and she contacted me directly. I did not see the message on Twitter but fortunately she did not give up, and the next day she asked me on Facebook, and of course I screamed around the house and scared everyone here. It was a big moment: DC Comics wants me to do a book! And *Wonder Woman* is not a little character. That was two years after I started drawing for Zenescope.

Do you feel a connection with the history of your medium?

Yes, of course. I think all of us feel that we are standing on the shoulders of giants. Everything I do is influenced by every other great artist that did what I'm doing right now. If it wasn't for that history of great artists it would be impossible to do what I do. And it's very visible in the kind of work I do, in my style. If you study a bit of the history of the medium you can see how artists influence each other. And all the styles are combined. I draw what I like to see. It's like an amalgam. There are many artists that have influenced me at different times of my life, from European, American and Japanese comic books. They are very different schools, and each has their strong points. American comic books are very rich in their character work, like the superhero. And that is very important in terms of the personality of the character as you draw them. That's just one aspect. In Japanese work there is an intensity in both action scenes and slower scenes, which creates a real impact in the storytelling. In the European style, the ambience of the setting is very creative.

When you are drawing a character like Batman or Superman—probably the two most recognizable comic book characters in the world—if you start thinking about this too much, the pressure can become a problem. My first character was Wonder Woman, who has nearly 80 years of great stories and artists. This can be a turning point for most artists, because some don't know how to deal with this pressure. I know some artists who have done one big book then disappeared. They don't do it anymore. And I wonder if the pressure of the history of the character is the reason. You can start thinking that maybe your work is not good enough, and you are now competing with the best artists in the world. And that's really bad for your confidence. And an artist without confidence has a problem. I just had to figure it out myself. Each individual has their own way to deal with it. For me it was really useful doing two years of work with a smaller company. It was just the same thing: it was me, the pencil and the paper. I'm just telling the story, working with the same writer I worked with before. So I held onto those thoughts. I just had to think of it like another piece of work.

Does your medium offer something unique?

First and foremost, comic books are about telling a story in a visually creative way. And it's easy to do, compared to some other mediums. Because it's just me, a pencil and paper. You cannot do a movie like that. It's really direct. You imagine a world, and show what you are imagining. To me those are the strong points. It's easy in a sense, but easy when you have some luck and a lot of hard work.

Why do you have a need to create?

That's a hard thing to explain. We are born with it. My mother is a painter, as a hobby. She has always had an artistic vision in everything she does. My brother is a musician. So I was born into a creative family, and have breathed art all my life. It just comes from within. And I think it's hereditary.

Why do humans have a need to create?

This is an interesting question, but I don't have a definite answer. I don't like the idea of absolute truth. But I love traveling through those questions. Maybe art and creativity is just something built into us as humans. Once we have enough food and warmth, the brain has more space to think about other things, and it has something to do with that energy. And maybe thinking imaginatively is part of that.

Another thing could be that we are all connected as a human consciousness, and we catch a little glimpse of that in our dreams. So we see the worlds that other humans have lived in, in terms of different times and places.

But I don't like to say it's this or that for sure. I like the 'what if?' questions. If something makes sense to you at a particular time, it's your truth in that situation, and it's useful to you in your life.

What sacrifices have you made to pursue your creative path?

It's all about balance, which is kind of the meaning of life. I was talking with a friend of mine about alchemy – turning objects into other objects. But you need equal parts in order to make that transformation. Life is like this. If you want to put time and energy into something, you have to take that from somewhere else. I feel that happens every day. If I want to achieve an objective, I have to sacrifice something else. The trick is to be balanced in this. Achieving a goal has a price, and you may regret it. With a big ambition, you may have to sacrifice something big to get there. The first thing you notice is the time. And there are many things that come with that.

If you want to get somewhere, you have to pull up the anchor. The anchor can be a good thing. It can make you stable and secure, and if you want that, it's perfect. But if you want to go to some beach in another part of the world, you have to pull up the anchor and go for it. There's no way around this.

I probably work more than 12 hours a day. I try to slow down a little at weekends, but sometimes it's not possible. One of my goals is to get much faster at what I do, and that comes with experience. Balancing the deadlines and family life is one of the struggles.

How has your work shaped you as a person?

My work is part of me. It's not two different things. I do what I love. It has always been part of me. But it's still work. There is a phrase that says, "Do what you love and you'll never work a day in your life." I don't agree with that at all. I prefer that line from Jerry Seinfeld, "Choose the torture that you like best." I see what he means. It's work, and if I want to be at my best, and compete with the best in the world, I won't feel good if I'm not doing all I can to do my best work.

How do you deal with creative blocks?

I'm not allowed to have creative blocks! It doesn't work like that. If I'm doing art for me, sure. If I'm doing comic book work for someone else, on a deadline, I cannot have a block. The block means I have to use the eraser more because it's not flowing, but I have to do the work anyway. For a professional it will not work to get blocks.

How do you stay fresh in your work?

By drinking creativity from other people. Talking to other artists at conventions is a great way to keep fresh. That connectivity really gives me this feeling of my creativity level going up again.

What is your relationship with satisfaction in your work?

There are ups and downs, but it feels good when you are happy with what you do, and you get great feedback from your editors, and the writer. Sometimes they will say that the work is better than they had imagined when they wrote it.

What is the relationship between your work and its audience?

It's great to hear from readers who tell you that your book has helped them in some way. It's good to read positive reviews and comments. But it can be a double-edged sword. You can also get bad reviews and comments. Some people will say they hate your work. It hasn't happened much to me, but not everyone will like what you do. And you have to learn to deal with this kind of feedback.

What is the relationship between yourself and your audience?

The audience has an emotional connection to the work I have done, so something is passed from me to them. And the other way around. When they give feedback to me there is this conversation of feelings going from one to the other.

People will sometimes contact me directly to request commissions. And of course you get this at conventions. People have seen my work and they will ask for a little sketch. Not in 2020 of course, in this strange year. But I have had people who have followed my work since my start at Zenescope, and they will give me book editions that I did back then without even knowing me. That's a surreal feeling. It's always surprising when that happens.

What has your audience taught you?

I don't identify with the difference between artist and audience, because I am the audience too. I'm part of them. I've grown up reading comic books. So it's still difficult to make that differentiation between me and them. We're just having a conversation. So that's a hard question to answer.

What has been the greatest challenge in your career?

Right now it's about that balance between work and family life. But the first big challenge was in trying to get into comics. Though it didn't feel like a struggle. The struggle was before making the decision, the things that I had to do to get to that point. Many people don't know what they want to do when they're young. That's very common. Even for me, the path would seem obvious, because I always loved drawing, and comic books. But I didn't know it was even possible. So I had to do those other things to get to the point where I knew for sure that this was the way I wanted to go.

What has been the high point of your career?

The high points are where I fulfill objectives along the way. Like I want to work for this or that big publisher, or that I want to draw a certain character. When that happens I always give a big scream, and now everyone in the house knows that means I achieved another big objective. Like getting the email from Meredith Finch asking me to work for DC. Or getting a script for *Wonder Woman* and in the middle was a Superman page. And I screamed, "*Superman!*" And getting to do a Batman series was the same. These are all things I dreamt of, and when it happens it is wonderful and surreal at the same time.

What is the most important thing your creative practice has taught you?

One of the most important things is to keep yourself motivated, every single day. And that's not easy to do. But you have to find a way in yourself to do that, that suits your mental mechanism. I stay motivated by talking to other artists, going to conventions, reading books, and creating objectives I want to achieve. For everyone it can be different.

It's easy to add objectives to the list, but it's also easy to be without objectives. I see that in people who do one book and then lose their motivation. For me I haven't achieved everything I want to achieve yet. But in any profession you can see this. A football player can win a cup or a league title and lose his or her motivation. Or they can be like Ronaldo or Messi and want more and more and more. But it's all the same: it's all in your head. You do what you have to do to keep yourself motivated.

How did it feel to reflect on creativity today?

These are things I normally think about. Because this is a very lonely profession, and your mind has time to go all over the place. So I'm always reflecting a lot on these things, and it's good to have a conversation with another person about them.

Maggie Murphy

Maggie Murphy is a television development executive with 30 years of experience. In that time she has been involved in the development of some of the biggest shows globally, including *X-Files*, *The Simpsons*, *Buffy the Vampire Slayer*, *Veronica Mars* and *Malcolm in the Middle*. She has specialized in sales in international markets, and also the digital space, where she develops shows for alternate platforms before bringing them to television. She also consults at Universal Studios with Vin Diesel's company One Race.

She has acted in over 100 theatrical productions in regional theatre and tours throughout the US, as well as dozens of episodes of TV.

Ms. Murphy previously taught in the UCLA Producer's Program for 10 years and now teaches as an Associate Professor at Loyola Marymount University where she is Head of the Producers Program, creating the curriculum for a new producer's track for undergraduate and graduate students in the School of Film and Television.

What drew you to your medium?

It was something I always did. Not TV per se, but writing and telling stories. Probably at three or four I began writing, and putting on plays in my neighborhood with the other kids. And I usually charged five cents. So I was a producer even then!

I was born in Kentucky and that was not exactly the entertainment capital of the world. And we were really poor. So I never knew I could make a living doing this. I just loved doing it. I feel like it chose me, rather than me choosing it. It was just who I was. And then through things that happened in my life, I found myself here. It's been almost magical. Because there was no reason in the world that from where I started, I would end up in LA, working as a big entertainment executive and producer.

In school I did the SAT test just because everyone else did, so I never studied for it. My father and brothers are brilliant, and I'm not a stupid woman. I took the test for fun, and I scored the highest in my school, so I got a college scholarship. So all of a sudden it was like, okay, I guess I'm going to college. At the time I had a boyfriend, and in my town, you were supposed to stay put, get married young and start having kids.

In college I was studying computers and doing plays on the side. And the director of Actors Theater of Louisville saw me. It's a Tony Award-winning theater. They did *Night Mother*, *Crimes of the Heart*, and the American premiere of *Whose Life is it Anyway?* The director had come through and he saw me rehearsing, and asked if I would audition for him. I didn't know what that meant. So he asked me to do a monologue, and I did something from a high school play and they hired me! I was in the American Premiere of *Whose Life is it Anyway?* My name wasn't posted, because I wasn't in the union, but it made me aware that I could make a living acting. So, I changed gear and became an actress.

I did very well. But after five years acting I wanted to live in one place. I worked all the time touring and living in many different cities. That was a lot for a woman, because at that time, in every play, there was usually 10 men and two women in every show, so parts were few. I decided to move to LA in the hopes of having a home. I started working part-time in a chiropractor's office and was acting here and there. I was on the soap opera *Days of Our Lives* and did an episode of *Designing Women*, but I wasn't getting any major parts. Then a friend I worked with went into television development. She said she thought I'd enjoy doing that. She got me an interview with the head of Creative Affairs at 20th Century Fox, which was doing comedy and drama. I thought the chances were slim, but he was an ex-actor himself, and he hired me. And that's where I learned development. We did *The*

Simpsons, *X-Files*, *Married With Children*, *In Living Color*, *Buffy* and so on. It was an amazing time to be there.

We then began developing with David Kelly, and he hired me to be his development person. We did *Ally McBeal*, *The Practice*, *Chicago Hope*, *Picket Fences* and *Boston Legal*. I was at the right place at the right time. On *Ally McBeal* I had input on the character, in terms of keeping her human, and like a real woman. Being a woman is a lot harder. I'd always have to say, "This is a little over the top for Ally. If she acts like this as a woman, she would get fired. No one would listen to her as a woman." I contributed those kinds of insights.

My whole career has been like this. Regency Films opened up a television division and one of the patients from the chiropractor's office worked for them. We were friendly, and she followed my work. My thing in life is to be friendly and help people out where I can. I do believe it comes back to you. So they started the TV division, and I like startups. Being at 20th I met great people and enjoyed the work, but the political side of the business is not for me. I like having a lot of creative input. And with Regency we worked on *Malcolm in the Middle*, *Bernie Mac*, *Roswell* and many others. *Wonderfalls* was one of my favorites but the network did not support the show. I had many of my favorites not get picked up or even shot. I wanted to know why, so I decided I wanted to go to the network. I wanted to understand what went on behind the curtain. And one of the patients at the chiropractor's office was the president at UPN (United Paramount Network). She needed a number two, and she hired me. My career has kind of been like that. UPN became the CW and that's where I did *Veronica Mars*. I worked really hard and learned a lot but I wasn't happy. I wanted to produce again. That's when I went into 'international', as around the time after the writer's strike, the market crashed. In fact I recently spent 10 months in England shooting the show *Houdini & Doyle*.

My father was upset when I stopped acting, because he loved seeing me on television. I had a pretty good recurring role on *Chicago Hope*. But I like development better, because I have more control of my life.

Make/Manifest

Development is hard to describe because it's everything. It's like the keeper of the flame. You develop the project from the very kernel of the idea, and then you develop pitches and shows, and then you sell them. And you oversee the pilot script and see if it's good enough. Depending on where they are. When I started it was generally just the pilot, but now you get straight-to-series orders. If they pick it up, you oversee all the hiring, the firing, the set, all of it. You'll be involved in casting. And you're responsible. If your show is over budget they're coming to you, for not taking control of your baby. And then you're also in the rooms fighting for it with the executives. And then when your shows go down, which most of the time they do here—it's a 95% fail rate—then I go to talk to everybody. I always do that, because I don't want anyone else telling them they lost their jobs. I go to the set and tell 120 people or more that the show is shutting down. And I do it in a way that's compassionate.

It might be that I read someone's spec script, and if I like it, I buy it for whichever company I'm working for. Or if it's me by myself I make an arrangement with the writer for the script. And I'll take it around with the writer who is selling it. And I help break stories with them sometimes. The showrunner will do most of that work here. It's different in Europe. I've been teaching in Europe a lot. In Europe and Canada they give the producer the power, instead of the writer. But the writer has the story in their head, and are doing that lifting. I'll do the other lifting, including hiring, taking care of post, the editing, all of that. With *Breaking Bad*, Vince Gilligan writes and has enough control to get across his total vision for the show. And that's what makes it magical. It would be a different show if it was made outside the US. I always say, "You dance with the one that brung ya." If Vince comes to me with an idea like that, it's my job to protect him, and give him his props, and give him what he needs to make that show. You make sure that they listen to notes from networks and studios, but you try to keep the writer golden. I'm the one that fights for them. I don't want them fighting. I want the network to love them. I tell the students this story but they don't believe it. Seth MacFarlane's show *American*

Dad has been canceled twice. And not because the ratings were bad, but because they felt he was difficult to work with. So he needed someone like me, a non-writing producer, an executive producer, to tell him to go away, and I'll fight. Because they're used to that from me, but not from him. So it's like, "Seth, hold my beer."

Part of the creative executive producer role is to sell that show internationally. With *Houdini & Doyle*, I sold it to Canada and England, then came back here and sold it to Fox. We did a treaty co-production between Canada and England, then came back to the US for distribution. We did that from the beginning, because often networks don't support shows if development executives don't feel like it's their baby. So I got them on board from the start. And everybody was giving notes. You can imagine.

There was a lot of moving parts, like England needed each episode to be five minutes longer. They also don't like what's called 'needle drops', where you put songs with lyrics under scenes. That's really big in the US, but many countries feel it's just horrible, that it's screwing up the scene and the dialogue, because you can hear the lyrics underneath. So we had to put the needle drops in for Fox and for Canada, but then we'd have the composer write music in place of the needle drops for other territories. This means that instead of making 10 episodes, you're really making 20, because you have two different cuts. I had needle drops in the budget, but they're expensive. And some of our partners had never heard of them, and asked us to take those out, because they didn't want to pay for them. And I said, "Fox will kill you, and Canada will kill me, if I don't have those songs in here. We have to have them." We had that fight every week. David Shore, who created *House* and *The Good Doctor* was executive producer on it, and he said they should send me to the Middle East to handle the peace talks. You learn to become a real peacemaker.

Do you feel a connection with the history of your medium?

Yes. I feel like I'm part of it. I came into television 30 years ago, and there were only four networks: ABC, CBS, NBC and Fox. Now there are over a hundred, just in this country. When I started there was no such thing as international. We didn't do international shows together. People did their own shows.

It was the heyday in the sense that with only four networks there was so much money coming in from advertisers. Those networks served the entire US audience. The sponsors and advertisers were paying a ton of money to reach that many people. And the higher the ratings, the more you can charge for your ads. People were making money hand over fist. At Christmas the gifts the shows gave out to executives were amazing. Like pinball machines, bikes, leather jackets. But as the market grew, the viewing figures shrank, and so did the ad revenues. And the gifts disappeared. So the big question now is: how do you monetize content, especially when people can just zip through the commercials?

Fox broke in around the time I started. They came in like a lion with *The Simpsons, X-Files, Married With Children, In Living Color.* It was huge. And other people wanted in. Paramount came in with UPN. These are major studios, and they wanted to get in on the money. And then Universal came in with USA. And now AT&T, Amazon and Apple are coming in. You also have Peacock and Disney+. Again, we're watching television history being made. When I started, TV was the bastard child of film. TV was something you did on the side. Like, 'I guess you need money.' But then there were more and more networks.

I then started teaching at UCLA. I just got to a point where I wanted to give back. I taught one class a year, which was still a lot given that I was traveling the world making and selling shows. I worked for a Canadian company Shaftesbury, so I would be gone 10 days a month. When I started with them their TV department was very small and it was all about film. But now it's all about TV.

With Disney+, it should have been huge, given their huge library, but they made some weak decisions. *Mulan* hurt. And the pandemic hurt too. And they have a split in their catalogs with Hulu, which they own most of. And Peacock, which everyone was making fun of, has 15 million subscribers already. I think people didn't really understand their library.

About a year ago, when *Friends* left Netflix, it started this huge bidding war for these old shows. That's what they were really paying money for, to have it for their library. And some of these platforms have to learn the lesson which Netflix did, which was about creating their own original content. Amazon is doing well on that. That's why they make so much new stuff, because they know people want that.

With some shows, even highly successful ones can get canceled. If they make a deal for five seasons, and it's still doing well, the studio is going to gouge the network for more money. Plus all the actors' contracts go up. It's all negotiated. They can get five to seven years in that deal. So they license the show from the studio. They pay two thirds of the money, and they get a third or more from international, and they put up what's left. The network gives one third of the money for each episode. So the studio pays two thirds, but that includes revenue from the international. Sometimes the international covers more than the two thirds, other times not so much.

Now we have second windows and second platforms, but the networks are in essence renting the show for five to seven years. When that lapses, they have to make a new deal. All the deals are different. With new contracts, an episode can cost an extra million dollars each, but if you have a 22-episode season, that's an extra $22m for the show. *Brooklyn Nine-Nine* was on Fox, and had those multiple seasons. So they canceled it at the end of the five-season deal. It was then picked up NBC, and it's now renewed for an eighth season.

I optioned the book *Roswell*, and the international was so big on that show, that from the beginning, we as a production company/studio made $200k per episode. But you don't tell the network that, because then they would cut their license fee. When it came to renewal time we more or less said we'll give it to the network for free, as long as they keep it on the air. And that happens, depending on how they're doing internationally.

Or it might be that the network is doing great, but the international sales aren't. So the studio is not making much money, but the network is. So then that negotiation goes the other way, where the studio says it's done making that show, because it's throwing money away. And in that case the network may up their offer, because they're doing well. This is what I teach. Because you have to know the business in order to be in it. It's important to know who is putting up what money.

I don't know anyone else who has done exactly what I've done, especially from Kentucky. When I was at Fox we used to do readings of scripts, to see if we wanted to pick them up to shoot the pilot, so we would bring actors in. George Clooney knew that, and this was before he'd made it big. He used to hang out with me in my office, because he was also from Kentucky. George and I went to the same school in fact, but we didn't know each other, as he's older than me. There were so few of us in the business from Kentucky.

I started at a studio, then went to a production company that is responsible for making shows. Then I went to Regency, which was a studio and a production company. So we made the show and got the international funding. And then I went to the network. So I saw why they bought what they bought. They call it 'the dark side', going to the network. But some of my favorite shows wouldn't get picked up, or would get canceled, and I wanted to know how and why it happened. If I knew how the decisions were made, it would help me sell better. It wasn't the happiest time of my life, but I learned a lot about how it worked and how to sell better.

I then went back to production, but at that point the writers' strike happened and I was out of a job for the first time in my 17-year career. So I looked at what the next thing would be, because reinventing is important. And I figured it was going to be international sales. The US couldn't keep being an island; they were going to need money. So that's when I started traveling. I was going around the world, to learn about people and culture. Everyone makes different kinds of shows. And I wanted to figure out what makes a successful international show. Then I got a job with a Canadian company who has deals with every country around the world. So I worked on development, and deals selling shows in and out of a lot of countries. With *Houdini & Doyle*, I had already sold it to Canada and England before I came to the US and could give them a more attractive dollar figure per episode on that basis. How can you turn that down? I loved the pitch, and could see it working, and wanted in. The writer was not really big, but to do international you need a gorilla, you need big talent. So I got David Shore to attach. And I got Sony to come on as the studio. I was with Shaftesbury, the production company in Canada. David and I called the head of CBC, and we sold them 13 episodes. David is Canadian, which helped with the treaty co-production. Then we went to England. It was myself, the president of Sony and the three writers, and we sold it there. ITV asked us to write a script. At that point, all we had was the idea. So the guys wrote the script, and ITV loved it. So when I came back to Fox I had the script, and didn't need much more.

I then went into digital and making shows which start on a small platform and then graduate to regular TV. So my career has always been about learning and staying current and adapting to different platforms and markets as they evolve and develop.

Does your medium offer something unique?

Television brings people right into your home. And you can really touch people's hearts. It becomes such a close experience. You can so affect people. I've never done an unrelentingly dark show, though there is a place for that, and I've watched some of those shows. I've always liked levity, and having a positive message. I feel that our job is to inspire, and make people empathize, or see other worlds. It lets you into people. When I was president of Kiefer Sutherland's company for a minute, we'd go out to dinner, and people were always coming up to him. When I did the show *Bernie Mac*, we would be shooting on the streets, and people would be coming up to Bernie like they knew him. It's like they become your friends. But if you're sitting at a table with Angelina Jolie no one's coming up to you; they're intimidated. They're used to see this big persona on a fifty-foot screen. But TV is right there in your living room. And nowadays you can hold it in your hand on your phone or computer. So it's a really personal, intimate medium.

Why do you have a need to create?

Again, I think it's just what I do. I also think that when I first started, it was my escape. I was from a poor neighborhood, and it was a rough, scary place. So you learn to fight. Which has probably helped in my career. I've never backed down from a fight. But TV is an escape from all that. To this day, if I'm watching a film or a show, you can't talk to me. I'm not being rude, but I just don't hear you. I'm not going to be interrupted. I'm in the experience. It's like being on a ride. I want to get into the people and the place. I love it. I love escaping and going to a place I can relate to. I have three older brothers, and I'm lucky I'm alive. That's just boys being boys, fighting all the time. So I can relate to *Malcolm in the Middle*. And that's what makes a big international show. People would never have thought that. Everyone has brothers or has been around boys that are constantly roughhousing. People relate to that. There's an idea that for an international show to succeed it has to have someone British, and someone German and so on. But that's not what makes an international show work. It's about finding universality. And recognizability. *Houdini & Doyle* hit a niche audience that likes scary shows and everyone knows who Harry Houdini and Sir Arthur Conan Doyle are. So it already brings an audience and an interest.

Why do humans have a need to create?

I think it's innate. Growing up in Kentucky this was certainly not fostered in me. It's like, why can someone play the piano? It's just in them.

For me, I'm just trying to make the world a better place. Whether that's entertaining someone by scaring the hell out of them, or making them laugh or cry. And hopefully exploring what makes us all different, and what makes us all one. They say that's part of the Irish, that they have this altruistic tendency, that they want to help others.

What sacrifices have you made to pursue your creative path?

I've sacrificed a lot of my life. I love my family, and when I took vacations in the first 20 years of my career I went home to Kentucky, rather than travel. But my life was my work. I don't have children. And I would have liked that. But it just got too late. I missed time with my family, and my parents – who have now passed. I got home as much as I could, but that was not much. So it's a lot of sacrifice. I have six nieces and nephews, and 20 great nieces and nephews. I love them, but again, I don't get to see them as much as I would like. But I'm trying to slow down now.

How has your work shaped you as a person?

I think I learned a lot of lessons fast. It shaped me in terms of learning to listen and intuit. And also being able to say, "I screwed up. I was wrong." I might push for a cast member, and then they're not right. You learn to listen to other opinions, and you learn that you don't have to be right. That's been a big one for me. And there have been so many lessons like that.

In my role I'm the architect of all these different people, including hires for shows and staff. You're bound to make mistakes. And hopefully you learn from them. I've been in big enough positions and stuck my neck out there. And you have to be ready to learn. When I was at Regency I went to the set of a show called *Ryan Caulfield*. It was my first show with them. And again, we were a studio and a production company. And I wasn't quite grokking it. I'm good on a set, and I'm good with actors, because I was one. But on this set, I got there at call time, and I'm sitting in a nice chair with my name on it. And people were coming up to me asking, "Mag, do you like this costume? Do you like this color?" And was saying, "Sure. I like that a lot." And then it was, "Come and see this set and this wall color." And I was thinking, 'Wow, everyone's so nice.' So F. Gary Gray was directing, who did *Set it Off, Straight out of Compton, Fast & Furious 8* and others. But he'd never directed a TV show before. And then the line producer came up to me and said, "Gary has not got the first shot off. And we're four hours in." And I said, "Well somebody's gotta talk to him." And she said, "Yeah Maggie – you." And then it hit me: 'Oh my god, I'm in charge!' Lucky I didn't fall out of my chair. So then my acting came in handy, because I acted like I was in charge and learned to be.

How do you deal with creative blocks?

They come up all the time. Right now it's pitch season and I work with Universal, and Vin Diesel with One Race Productions. So there's a pitch and it needs a topspin. It's like a B, but it needs something. Like maybe the lead is an alien – something that makes it a little different. Something that gives it that extra oomph. And I haven't come up with it yet. I try not to stress. That's really big. Don't get bogged down in the frustration of trying to get to the idea you need.

I try to have fun. So I take big swings at it. Like, they're a trapeze artist, and come up with stuff and make myself laugh. But you'd be surprised; if you keep at it, you might find that one of those big ideas could actually work. I always tell my students, "If you're struggling, get together with a friend and a bottle of wine, and relax. But don't buy bottle two unless you think you've figured it out." People know that about me. When Bryan Fuller and I came up with *Wonderfalls*, it had taken three months. We had Todd Holland attached to direct, who was the director of *Malcolm in the Middle*. So Bryan and I pushed through and we eventually came up with the idea. And we pitched it to my old boss, who is now president of Fox. And she called me afterwards and asked, "Is this one of those pitches you came up with while you were drinking?" So I said, "Yes." She didn't really like the idea. But in the end it was made and was a hit. It would have been big if they'd supported it. It was on a major list just this year, of the top 25 shows ever. It only received an order for a season, but it aired five times. If you talk to a number of the main people involved in that show, they all say it was their biggest heartbreak. But that's TV. You have to learn rejection, and to say no. Not only saying no, but hearing no. You can put your heart and soul into something, but when it's over you just have to move on and find another baby.

How do you stay fresh in your work?

I stay on top of the industry by watching the latest shows, reading the trades, and talking with my students. For the first 15 minutes of each class we talk about what's happening. My students tell me their favorite shows and I'll watch them. Like *Derry Girls*. It's hilarious. It has great writing. I can't breathe when I watch it. So part of my job is to figure out trends, where things are going next.

What is your relationship with satisfaction in your work?

One of my students said he watched all the episodes of *Houdini & Doyle* in one day. Ten hours. And he said he loved that he could watch it with his wife and daughter, and they all enjoyed it. To me, my job is done. When I was acting, my highest compliment from viewers was, "You're just like my Aunt Bee." So they saw me as a person not an actress. That's what it's about for me – the small things, the human experience that you make people feel.

What is the relationship between your work and its audience?

For me I really want that relationship to be intimate. It's a real love/hate thing, honestly. Because you can think you have a great show, and it gets great reviews, but then it airs and not many people watch it. And it's like damn, what the hell? So then you're pissed. And then you have to figure out what you have to do to get them there.

Even if it's not a big hit, it's meaningful to get feedback from people about how the show touched them, how it changed them for the better, or how they were having a bad day and then watched the show and laughed their ass off. They needed that. That rewards me exponentially. I feel like I've made a difference.

What is the relationship between yourself and your audience?

I love gardening because I get to see it when it's done. If I make a show I get to see it, but it's not the same as being on stage, where the audience is right there. It's immediate, and it's so symbiotic. If the audience is warm and receptive, your performance is just better. You feel their love. If they're cold and standoffish, it's like ploughing a field – it's hard work. So if they're not there, I wonder why. When they are there, it's about the specifics of touching them, and making them laugh, or scaring the hell out of them. Whatever makes them feel.

At the end, I was getting sick of the career of acting. If you're a writer you can write, even if you don't have a job. But if you're an actor and don't have a role it's really hard to act. So for me it became about control. In development I have jobs and do move around, but I can do my job all the time. So that's fulfilling.

What has your audience taught you?

Humility. That's a big one. You've heard that line from Shakespeare, "The play's the thing." That's it. It's not about me, it's about the work. And that is what I've learned. I need to care about my message. Did I make this show the best I can? And then you let the audience fall where they may. But the play is the thing, the work is the thing. And staying true to that is what it taught me. To not be looking for approval. My approval comes from within me. I can look at my work and think I did a good job, even if it got canceled after three seasons. I don't have control over that. I could make myself miserable. And that also comes with age. I don't need external validation anymore.

And when you grow up poor you always worry about making money. So I've worked hard. But I'm good at this point. You have to say, "C'est la vie. I did what I could."

Now I try to impart what I've learned to my students, to make it easier for them than it was for me. It's about courage, confidence and passion. I always tell them to dig into their idea, to their passion. Like they'll pitch an idea to me, and I'll say, "Why are you the one to write that? You could have come to me with a million things. Why did you come to me with this? What is it hitting in you?" And then they really have to dig down to the source of that passion. One kid was pitching a superhero show, and I asked him why. He said, "Because I've always wanted to be a superhero. I don't know what it is. I walked around in a cape for three years." He showed me pictures. You can't make that up. So when you go in to pitch, you have to go in as yourself, be human, and really bare your soul. So he goes into pitch meetings showing slides of him in his cape, telling them he always wanted to be a superhero, ever since he was little. And he has the balls to show those pictures and tell that story. And whoever you're trying to sell it to, you've got their attention. They know you've been thinking about it for a long time. It's important to show your passion, that whether they buy the show or not, you are going to make it.

So I try to give the students all the secrets of how the business works, including pitching. I had one girlfriend break up with me because she was a writer and her show didn't get on the air. She was developing with me. And I said, "I'm flattered that you think I'm the one making that decision, but I'm not." The people making the decision, you don't see. They're all mostly fifty-something white men sitting around a table in New York. They pull me in and I do the best I can to influence them, but they're going to pick what they're going to pick. They listen to me, and I can argue for it, but ultimately, it's not my decision. And I want to share all that with the students.

What has been the greatest challenge in your career?

I got sick, and it was kind of a trifecta of three things in a row. And it was really hard. The last was a broken sternum, and it only hurts when you breathe, right? So I couldn't work, and in this business, being a woman is really hard. Especially if you didn't go to Harvard or Yale, or have family in the business. And when you're weakened, you can't let people know it, or they'll come for you. This is not an easy business. So it was just miserable. But this happened around the time of the 2007 writers' strike, which gave me time to get better. So I was out of work for 10 months. That was challenging.

But then I switched gears and learned about international sales, and that really was the right move. I've been in that area for 10 years now. It was not big when I started but now it's huge.

What has been the high point of your career?

There are many, but one of them was getting *Veronica Mars* on the air, because it was hard to do and I was passionate about that show. And the rape scene was a battle. I fought for it, because I said, "Women need to see this." I was ahead of my time on that one. I fought for months to keep that in. It was not validated so much at the time, but people can look back now and see it was ahead of its time. People said, "Who's going to love her? She's been raped." They actually said that. And I said, "They'll love her *because* she has been raped."

What is the most important thing your creative practice has taught you?

There are so many things. Again I think it's humility. And it's really about having humanity. Most importantly, it's taught me how to listen to people. To really hear what they're saying. If you're going to be good in this business, you have to be a good listener. You have to hear beyond the words. You learn that from listening to pitches, to notes, and listening to what the real problem is on a set. Like, "Why are you so mad? Why did you just lock yourself in the trailer? Don't worry about that crew that's costing $10,000 an hour. Why are you in here?" You have to make them feel better, and help get their ass back out there. And I think that skill benefits your whole life.

And they're actors, so they can smell a skunk. They know if you're authentic, or if you're a phoney. It's the same when you go in to pitch. You're there to sell. And you need to go in there being honest and open. That's what they listen to. This really goes back to my childhood. I was brought up to tell the truth. You might not have any money, and your socks might not match, but you tell the truth. You have your word. So when I say something, it's honest. And people can feel it. When you come in and show those pictures of you in a superhero cape, they can feel that that's really you. And you are brave and honest. It's important that they feel your burn, that you have to make this. You have to tell this story. And you can spend five or six years of your life telling that story because you love it that much.

The end result generally makes it obvious that it was made with love. Though I have had some hellacious casts and crews, and the shows were still successful. But the bigger ones, that's not true. Like in the beginning of *X-Files*, the actors did not get along. In the pilot they were supposed to be attracted to each other, as was customary for shows at that time. But we saw the dailies from the first day of shooting and realized it was not happening. They were combative. So Chris Carter went in and rewrote the hell out of those scenes so that they were adversarial in the show. That relationship was so unique and truly made the show. This was Gillian Anderson's first TV show, and she'd come out of theatre. We cast her four days before shooting. We were down to the wire. She didn't know about hitting marks. Or that if you are drinking something, you have to take a drink on the same word in every take. She was having some trouble with this, and forgetting lines. And David Duchovny is a perfectionist. He is on it. And he's got a co-lead that is forgetting lines and not hitting marks. He was not happy. But when she got her sea legs he saw that she is a really hard worker and they became the best of friends.

How did it feel to reflect on creativity today?

    It actually feels good. It's kind of relaxing. It makes me feel more meditative. I know that sounds funny. But I'm thinking about something besides my students, or my pitches. So I really enjoy it. And I'll probably think more about it. I have been thinking about writing a book. I don't use many textbooks in my classes, because what I'm teaching is not in many books. But there is such breadth to this subject. I would have to write more than one book, to figure out which segments of my life to draw from. I could do a broader, straight-up biography, but it wouldn't be as interesting to me as something I could use to teach.

Charlotte Mary Pack

Charlotte Mary Pack is a British ceramic artist, based in Rye, East Sussex, with a focus on wildlife and an eye for detail. During the summer of 2013 Charlotte gained a first class honors degree in Ceramic Design from Central Saint Martins. Growing up on a farm and traveling widely across Africa were fundamental experiences that instilled in her an affection for the natural environment. The combination of Charlotte's love for both animals and clay, steers her work to explore different ways to draw attention to the global threats to wildlife and the natural world. Towards this end, Charlotte donates 15% of profits to support wildlife conservation efforts around the world.
charlottemarypack.com / Instagram: charlottempack

What drew you to your medium?

I did a bit of ceramics at school, when I was about six or seven, with lessons during and after school. I was always drawn to creative subjects, including textiles. I liked anything that had textures, and that I could create with using my hands. I loved the immediacy of clay, perhaps because I am a little bit impatient at times. And I love the fact that you can create something from nothing. You can create textures quickly and effortlessly. I then took an A Level in ceramics. I felt confident and comfortable with clay. I did a stint of fashion design for a year, but I got put off that quite quickly.

I wasn't environmentally-conscious at the time. But that grew through working with clay, because you are literally working with the earth. And I've been fortunate to grow up on a farm, and have always been around nature and wildlife. It's always been an inspiration. And when I was in second year at university I went to visit some friends in Kenya, and this opened my eyes to the bigger picture. It was mind-blowing to experience that wildness. I felt we had to do everything we could to preserve these spaces that the animals call home. We know that we're encroaching on them, causing habitat loss. We camped in the Maasai Mara, and I didn't get any sleep. I was nearly sick with fear that we would get trampled by hippos or attacked by lions. Living in Britain, you forget that an animal can induce that much fear. When I went back to university, I was working on functional wares in my ceramics studies. We were going to factories and looking at mass-production work, but I didn't have much interest in that. But we then had more free reign in what we worked on, so I started sculpting animals. The timing was good. I felt I wanted to do something to help raise awareness of endangered species, and help protect them. And it happened that I could make a contribution to that through my work with clay. I find it's always a good motivation. I can always find a new animal, or habitat that needs more awareness and support. So I feel lucky that I can do something about it.

Do you feel a connection with the history of your medium?

I get really inspired when I see tribal artifacts at the British Museum, for example. They don't necessarily connect directly to the work I do, but there is a connection to the earth and the environment. They created both functional and decorative pieces from the earth. But that history has largely passed me by. It's something that I may look at later on, but I've hit the ground running with focusing on wildlife and raising awareness about conservation.

Does your medium offer something unique?

I think ceramics is unique in the way that it can be both functional and beautiful. You could build a house with it. It can make bricks and tiles. And ceramics lives within probably every culture, because it's basically earth. So there is a uniqueness there. You can grab it and create something with your hands. And you can recycle it. Maybe glass has similar qualities, in terms of being both functional and beautiful. But with ceramics you can create anything from it.

Why do you have a need to create?

I've just always been creative. In fact I've shied away from academic subjects. I think art was just my calling. I was always going to do something creative. Neither of my parents are artists or creatives. I just followed what I enjoyed, and was fortunate to be able to do that. And I'm always motivated by creating work that helps raise awareness about endangered species. That passion keeps me going.

Why do humans have a need to create?

I think it's been part of our evolution. There is a link between creativity and problem-solving. You can be creative in so many different ways. It doesn't have to be art or craft. I think it's important for everyone to have a skill, whatever that is.

Being creative is also an outlet for feelings and emotions. Not everyone deals with it in that way, but I think it's important that everyone has a healthy outlet.

What sacrifices have you made to pursue your creative path?

Maybe in the future, but not so far. I'm 31 now. I graduated in 2013, and started my ceramic career in 2014. I took a year out traveling before starting my work. I'd been inspired by the trip to Kenya, and wanted to see more of Africa, and wild places. These last few years I've been lucky to have space on the farm that I could use as a studio. I had to work on the farm to earn money to supplement my earnings from my sculpture, but it wasn't the same level of sacrifice as it would have been to take a job with a contract.

I got married a few years ago, and I knew I wanted to get to a certain place with my art before starting a family. I follow other artists on social media, and have noticed that when they start a family they tend to disappear for some time. So I worry that I wouldn't have time for both. I'd want to get to a level where I could take time away to raise children, and still be able to come back successfully. But I have no experience with children, so I have no idea how much time they take up! It looks pretty intense, and a big responsibility. It's hard to imagine having children and still being able to get into the studio any time I get inspired to start making. So I would be sacrificing my studio work if I had a family. But then I have a very supportive family that lives close by. And that has helped me to avoid having to make sacrifices up until now. I do want a family, so that sacrifice will have to be made in future.

How has your work shaped you as a person?

I like that it keeps me in touch with wildlife conservation. I keep up with the latest news on the issues around the world. That has shaped me in a way, because when I create my work that is a part of it.

On the farm I have done my bit towards conservation here. I have created wild flower meadows for pollinators and birds, which have been heavily impacted by insecticide use in agriculture. So I aim to increase the biodiversity here. I have wondered if I would have been so connected to environmental concerns if I wasn't doing the work I am. It feeds into every part of the work. I try to avoid plastic, for example, and I will not run the kiln unless it's full, and it's necessary to do a firing. I do what I can to reduce my carbon footprint.

How do you deal with creative blocks?

I don't feel like I've had one until now. I feel that I'm at a crossroads with my work. It started at the beginning of the year, and obviously lockdown has prolonged the agony somewhat, because I feel that I can't move forward anywhere. I just take myself off, if I need a change of scene. I can just go and work on the farm, or do gardening, or other things that interest me. I try and switch off from it for a bit, then press reset. Because there are times when you can have that moment of doubt, and you wonder if you are doing the right thing, and if people like it. That's why it's so important to exhibit in public, and meet people. I'm working in the studio by myself, so I don't get that feedback from other creatives as much as I would like.

It's also important for me to be excited about what I'm doing. Because otherwise that would reflect in my work. I knew I wanted to start something new, something different, but on the same subject. I'm always playing with scale, color and texture. But I feel like I've exhausted that in some areas because it started really small, then it got bigger. And I brought in the color palette, then added more colors. Then it got more detailed. So it's always on a journey. It's never the same. But I feel like I've got to the end of one part of the journey. And I'm at a crossroads now. So which direction do I go? Lockdown hasn't helped, because motivation is affected when you don't know where the work will go, in terms of exhibitions and audiences. I was supposed to go to an exhibition in France, so that kept me busy through the spring and summer lockdown, but in the end I wasn't able to go there, which was really disappointing. I like to see the reactions of people to the work. Their feedback is invaluable for me. And I haven't had that for over a year, in terms of personally seeing people at gallery exhibitions. That's prolonged that feeling of being at a crossroads. Because people will often suggest new ideas as they explore the work. So I get left with a sense of doubt, even though I want to continue and know that I will. I just want to be excited again.

Hopefully, Ceramic Art London will be on next April, so I have something in the pipeline. That will be perfect for me. I will create new pieces for that, and see how people feel about them. What's great about that show is that I now recognize a lot of people who go every year. And they will see how my work has progressed, and you get a sense of how it lands with them. At the end of the day, I am creating work that I like, but it has to please other people as well. So I'm thinking about the people I'm making it for. I don't like the sales pitch part, but I enjoy seeing people enjoying my work. And hopefully the work will help raise awareness along the way.

How do you stay fresh in your work?

You've got to have the confidence to know you're making the right choice. They say Libras are bad at making decisions, so that's my excuse. When I'm thinking of keeping my work fresh, I play around with color, form and scale. But I now feel that I've almost exhausted that. I think people still like those pieces, but it's more about keeping up my enjoyment in the work. Even though there is the kind of activist aspect of the work, in terms of protecting endangered species, and educating people about that, they are very similar. It's still a pot with an animal on top. I want to do something along the same lines, but it's about where I take that, and how I present it. Experimenting is a great way. But I'm quite an impatient person, so I want it to happen overnight. I have experimented with much larger pieces, but I've put all this time and energy into it, and then it cracks during firing, because I'm inexperienced at working at that scale. So that can be very disheartening. Which is part of it. I have to keep going. But you also have to consider the investment. At that scale, it costs more in materials, equipment, electric bills and time. Things can go really wrong very quickly, but you won't know until you open the kiln. I back myself to be able to do it, but you have to keep practicing and learning.

My work has certainly developed, but I only really see it when I put together old and new work. You can see how the form has improved, or the life in the eyes, or the color choices. Naturally you just get better, and your confidence improves.

There is pressure from the art world itself, but that's good pressure. You're always on a creative journey, but it prompts you to bring something new to the table. It doesn't have to be completely different, but it does need to be a development. There are people who do the same thing every year, but I don't feel I would get picked up and noticed as much if my work was always the same.

There are times when I feel I would like to be represented by a gallery, but then I feel I don't need or want that. And then suddenly I do, and I get disheartened that I haven't been picked up by a gallery. I set the bar high, and there will be disappointments along the way. But that's just life, isn't it? You just have to keep going and not be affected by it. I feel that if I was in a gallery that had a lot of backing behind it, then I could showcase my work further, and more people could see it, which would raise more awareness for wildlife conservation. It can feel like little old me on Instagram isn't enough, and I would like to reach out to everyone. I don't want to be famous or anything like that —that's not me at all—but I would like more people to see my work, and hopefully it would have a positive impact on them. I do worry that some people might think that I'm not sincere about it, that's it just an ego trip. But self-promotion is definitely not my strong point. I'm not a business person. I've been lucky that what I enjoy doing works commercially. If you look at it as a business I think it takes the enjoyment out of it. You can end up being driven by what you think the market wants, rather than what you feel compelled to make.

Some makers say that you shouldn't put prices on your website if you want to be picked up by a gallery or represented, as they don't want to see that you are selling your work privately. I sell my work through the studio, but the customer has to contact me. I prefer it that way, as you have a connection with them. I don't think it would work in a shop format. Usually the people who buy my work have an affinity with the particular animal, and I find that quite interesting. I would miss out on that feedback if it was all done electronically.

What is your relationship with satisfaction in your work?

I get a lot of satisfaction when I finish an animal, because each of them is different. I might start one and think, 'Why did I do this to myself?' I find the more familiar ones easier, and ones with key features, like a monkey. But even things like crocodiles and frogs are very challenging in their shape. Like a frog is way harder than making a very detailed monkey. So getting that right is very satisfying.

And when you open the kiln and the whole piece has worked, that's wonderful. Because you don't know if the color will come out the way you want it to. That gives you the sense that you have enough knowledge of the materials and the techniques. Typically people say that you can expect to have 10% wastage, in terms of pieces that haven't worked, but I hardly have any. That's quite satisfying. I have enough control now that if I know something is going to go wrong I'll start again, rather than bothering to fire it. So any kind of ceramic work that comes out well is satisfying.

When I'm working on an animal I start with images from every possible angle, to get it right. And sometimes I will avoid bias by assigning numbers to a list of endangered animals and use a random number generator to pick the animal for me. How do you choose what to make otherwise? And each animal is important, so I don't want to avoid making something that needs to be protected. But when doing an exhibition I make sure that the more familiar animals are there, because that tends to draw people in. They want to see animals they recognize.

What is the relationship between your work and its audience?

The audience are usually drawn to my work because people are subconsciously attracted to animals. And once they look at the different species we will end up in a conversation about the fact that all of them are endangered. They're usually shocked to hear that. And I tell them that I've barely scratched the surface of the numbers of endangered species. There are estimated to be over 7,000 critically endangered species in the world, and between 200 and 2,000 go extinct every year.

The audience tend to be like-minded people, and enjoy talking about the subject. And many will tell me about their holidays, and animals they have encountered in different places. The work makes them think of those experiences. Everyone tells me I need to go to Costa Rica. Underneath the pot, where the back stamp would be, I always list the name of the animal and its status in the wild. That might lead them to research a bit more about the animal. And it's nice for me to see that happening.

What has your audience taught you?

As I've discussed, I find the feedback from the audience invaluable. Their reaction to my work, and their feelings about it, are so important. Although I make things because I want to, I still want others to like them. We all want that reassurance that we're doing the right thing.

And it's always down to practice, practice, practice. You may be able to make things quickly if you're naturally gifted, but most people are going to get to that level through a lot of practice. And I hope other students and creatives can take something from that. I only graduated seven years ago, so I can show others that it is possible to pursue what you want to do successfully, and that you can get your work to this kind of level if you work hard at it.

Also, people pick up on your passion in the work. This will make them believe in it more. But if you're only doing something because it's trendy, it's not the same. So I feel reassured by the audience that I'm doing the right thing. And you need that when you work alone in your studio.

What has been the greatest challenge in your career?

The 100 Elephants project was definitely my greatest challenge. It was not just the fact that I had to make an elephant every 15 minutes for 24 hours. It was because my work is high detailed, and I had to let that all go. I did practice modeling elephants for a whole week, making each piece in 15 minutes. But it had to look at least a bit like an elephant. And it was important to create an impactful piece that would challenge people's opinions on ivory, and animal products in general. And that number had meaning, in that it represented the number of elephants killed every day for ivory.

There was also the challenge of creating a platform for it, and worrying if anyone was going to watch it because it was all done live. So there were all these technical elements that I was not familiar with at all. But I enjoyed the challenge. I mostly let go of my awkwardness when it comes to self-promotion, because I felt it was important work. I just didn't want people to think it was about me.

What has been the high point of your career?

Exhibiting the 100 Elephants project at Collect in London was certainly a high point. Collect is a really big craft fair, and I created the project for that event. I knew that there would be galleries representing there that may have had collections of ivory, and maybe my work would make them reflect on that. These are the top craft galleries in London, so there were very wealthy people attending. And I like that my installation piece had a bit of weight there. I wanted it to be impactful.

My work is really about celebrating what we have on this planet, and protecting it. I don't like the idea of making elephants or rhinos without horns, which a lot of people suggested. I prefer to celebrate the animal itself, and what we can protect. And it can be that people shy away from images of mutilated animals. It's easier to start a conversation if someone is attracted to the animals, rather than repulsed. I see horrific, upsetting images of that kind online and I have to skip past them. My work is a type of activism, but I don't want to use shock tactics. I'd rather people have positive feelings about the images I create. I find that's a much better way to start a conversation about the issues.

Another high point was being on the cover of *Craft* magazine with the 100 Elephants. I never imagined I would find myself on the cover of *Craft*. It's a magazine I follow, along with *Ceramic Magazine*.

I saw David Attenborough looking at my elephants at the show, but I didn't get to speak to him, which is really sad. It will always be a deep regret, but that's just the way it is. So I'm not sure if that's a high point or a low point!

What is the most important thing your creative practice has taught you?

The most important thing is to do something you're passionate about, but it motivates you in so many more ways. It gives you an extra edge, but it also makes you feel that something is worthwhile. That could mean doing something for a cause, so you're not only doing it for yourself. And it can give you and the audience a sense of the bigger picture. It's a sense of giving back, in your way. It just feels right. A lot of my friends wish they were doing something that they really cared about, something that has a greater meaning in the world. So what my work has taught me is how lucky I am to have found something that I am passionate about in terms of wildlife conservation, but also sculpture. Being able to blend those things together gives me the motivation I need at times to keep going.

Art is a great way to work with this kind of purpose, because it is a language that crosses all borders. People can get the idea without needing any words. If I had done tableware, I'm not sure I would have had the motivation to keep going. The work I have chosen can contribute to something more than just paying the bills.

How did it feel to reflect on creativity today?

It makes me excited to think that I've got all those years ahead. I wonder where I will be in 10 years from now. That's exciting to me, because at no point have I thought that I'll quit. I will always want to be doing this. So in reflecting on the last 10 years of studying and working in ceramics, it makes me look forward to the future.

Lee Pepper

Music is Pepper's life. He has worked in all areas of the music industry for over 30 years. He is a composer, singer, arranger, engineer, director and UK-based music producer. Music has been in his heart and soul since childhood, taking him on a lifelong journey of self-discovery, community and enlightenment. He began as a student of classical piano and violin, then moved onto synths, guitars, rock and rave.

Music has been his rock, his guide, and an endless source of magic and wonder. He has seen decades of artists come and go and feels blessed to be alive in a century that has given us so much color, from classical to punk, rave to opera, and all the richness in-between.

peppermusicproduction.com / Instagram: pepps_pepper

What drew you to your medium?

As a child my mum played the piano. I think it was my granddad's old upright piano under the stairs, and I used to go in there and lay my fingers on the keyboard and wonder how and why it worked. Just the tone of that piano fascinated me, and I remember seeing my mum playing La donna è mobile on it. She had lessons when she was a girl. And it was amazing. I used to run my hands up and down the keyboard. She set me a task starting with my thumb followed by fingers 1, 2, 3, 4, 5, 4, 3, 2, 1. I asked her one day how you get to the sixth note if you only have five fingers. She asked if I wanted to learn, and have lessons, and I said yes. She found a teacher, Mrs. Rogers, and I did lessons from then on.

We had *Abba's Greatest Hits* on a cassette, and I remember running around the table as kids with my sister to that music. Abba was a really early musical experience. My dad had a vinyl collection of really odd things. There was a stack of 7" singles that also fascinated me. The radio was on a lot of the time and I remember hearing a song called *Airport* by The Motors that moved me to tears. My parents were sort of amused by this, but not in a nasty way. I think they were intrigued that a song could have that effect on me. It wasn't sadness, it was like empathy with that chord structure. It just mesmerized me. That was the clincher. It was a conscious thought about choosing music; I just fell in love with it. When my mum offered to arrange piano lessons, I jumped at the chance.

Do you feel a connection with the history of your medium?

Very much. It's a lifelong study. I was classically trained. I took violin lessons at school as well as studying piano. They taught us some history along with music language and theory.

But at the same time, in the 70s, there were all these sci-fi films on TV and I was fascinated then—as I still am today—with the future. Synthesizers where happening at the time, these instruments that could make these weird space noises. I remember watching *Forbidden Planet*, and now know it was the first fully analogue synth soundtrack. Anything with a synth sound grabbed me. The theme to *Doctor Who* was insane. It was like music that came from aliens. I had both a strong connection to the history of music through classical training, and the need to go to the future, and see what's next.

In my work now I like to push the boundaries, to discover an odd chord. I like chord structures that I've not heard, or shouldn't work, and mixing up genres that really shouldn't go together but somehow just work. I like sampling and twisting sounds into noise that never existed before, making things that you can only hear from me. And keeping up with the technology is important to me. In my childhood home, we had a phone on the wall at the end of the hall, that felt like hi tech. I remember watching *Star Trek* and their communicator devices were fantastical. Cut to today and we have the equivalent on our phones. We can make video calls, and make music on them. It's like "beam me up," right there. In fact, what we have now is light years ahead of Captain Kirk's communicator.

It boils down to the dream, the imagination. We have to imagine these things first. It pops up in someone's head that that can happen. For example, we wanted to fly, and we then studied birds and their flight, and discovered the physical properties of flight. To go from that to aircraft required someone to have that dream. That's a big part of my life. If you haven't got a dream, then it's very difficult to think of the bigger picture. It's important to have a dream, to have hope. Like, I wonder what it's like to climb a mountain. Or to conduct an orchestra. Or to make a string that can be plucked to make music. All this stuff is man-made, it's very real, and it all begins in someone's imagination.

Does your medium offer something unique?

It's unseen. People perform it, and mould it into something that's traveling through the air. For me it's the magic of making your eardrums wobble in so many different ways. It can stimulate memory, desire, pain, happiness. It encourages wellbeing. It can destroy you. It can lead you in directions you don't like or don't want to encourage. It can change culture. It's diverse. It's multicultural. It's a language that we all understand. You can be anyone on this planet and understand that a drumbeat is a drumbeat. We all have that pulse that keeps us alive. It's a beat in our chest, and I think we relate to that. There is some kind of symbiosis in the fact that we all generate noise. And there's resonance in us. There's a tiny electrical current within us, and the heart muscles rely on that. Kind of a spark that creates a pulse that keeps you alive. So, we're like these little pulsating machines pumping a rhythm. We're all musical instruments. There's something primal in that. We then create rhythms as a communication tool. The voice is also music. A conversation is a musical journey.

Why do you have a need to create?

I find it incredibly attractive and magical. It was my first love, and I'm still in love with it. If I can't hear or make any music, I feel low. I'm not who I am without it. To be my best self, I need it. It feeds me.

If I was on a desert island, hopefully there would be nature. I would be listening to the sounds of the birds and insects, the river, the thunder in the sky, the roar of the ocean on the rocks. That is all musical to me. Even when driving, there could be a tiny sound, a pebble skipping against the underside of the car, and I'll tune into it immediately. That all goes back to classical learning, and thinking about nature, and what is sound. Your mother knows your voice, and you know hers, from an early age. You rely on those tones. It's about hearing, and that process. So, it's quite deep. When I start to analyze it, it all makes sense.

I like to think about whatever the edge of the universe is, and at this moment, no matter how far away it is, everything is now. And for me, I experience that when I go to see a band. I really like being in the moment, the here and now, and music offers that.

Why do humans have a need to create?

I think it's a lot to do with community. In villages or cities or family units, whatever it is you're going through, from birth to death, you have these fundamental moments where you're doing, learning and growing. In community gatherings you all get together to eat, drink, dance and make music, and that's something you remember throughout your life. It's very tribal. You see it in other lifeforms. The creation of life, and the dance of nature. There's music in that. It goes deeper than just a note or a song.

What sacrifices have you made to pursue your creative path?

I've been quite stubborn in my pursuit of music. I've been offered alternative paths that may have been better for me financially, but I need music more than money. I'm happy if I make enough money to pay the rent and eat. I've had to paint walls and do laboring jobs and other things to make it happen. I worked in a factory so I could buy a car, keyboards, amps, mics and stuff. I needed to go out and create live music. As soon as I got that I quit the job and I was off playing gigs. That eventually led to fantastic experiences traveling around the world as part of my musical work. I'm very grateful for that.

Music has been a great focus for me. If I was a painter, I would want to be painting all the time, and that would be my thing. If I was an engineer, likewise. You could be a fisherman and that's your art. Or you could design cards, or walk dogs, and that's your art.

How has your work shaped you as a person?

The work I do within music and my art shapes me every day. The people I work with, the company I keep, all shape who I am. Every day I practice my art, I live it. Over time you develop an ever-deeper understanding of your art.

How do you deal with creative blocks?

I tend to find I have creative bocks if I'm away from it for a while. And then I worry that maybe I've lost the ability to be very close to it. I crave it, and then I dive into again, and it's a bit washy, and then suddenly it clicks into place and I'm there, and I can see it all. So it's time away from it that blocks me. But when I'm in it I'm not blocked at all.

How do you stay fresh in your work?

That's life choices, and being around people that provide enlightenment. I do live my work, and there's a lot online, and historically there is so much music to listen to.

What is your relationship with satisfaction in your work?

In terms of my work there are three things that are really important to me. The first is very introspective, and relates to the creation of something. A new discovery can be surprising, and give you extreme joy. It could be creating a beat, or finding some words, or a top line melody, or even thinking of a whole band. The birth of an idea is insanely cool. I love that. I can't get enough of it. It drives me, because the joy in that moment is eternal, and really addictive.

The second thing is telling someone about it, and sharing that excitement. And the third thing would be to try to make it happen again. To find a route to making that whole thing continue. Whatever that may be. It could be through finding like-minded people. The career path moves forward, and onwards and around and snowballs all the time. You can work with different people, and people you can relate to. And sometimes you'll find people you don't understand, and cannot relate to, but you can get something out of that. Art is full of mystery. I love the mystery of a band getting on stage and making this noise that probably shouldn't work but does. So I find satisfaction in the spark of an idea, sharing the idea, and seeing what you can do with it.

It's also satisfying to have created something that can remain. It's almost like you want it to be eternal. If you can create something that is around after you, that's satisfying. But trying to get to that point can be quite frustrating.

One of the most satisfying things was having my first track played on the radio. I had heard that, scientifically, anything that goes on the radio travels out into space and it just keeps going. So I thought that if I could get one of my songs on the radio, I'm out there, in space, traveling forever. And I really wanted that to happen, so I made sure I got on the radio. I went into a studio, recorded some music, got one of the tracks on the radio and I thought, 'I've done it, I've flown the Earth. It's out there.' For the want of a nicer way to put it, I could have died happy then.

That's the inward thing. But there's also joy in it, to have a conversation musically with someone. That conversation could stimulate, or confuse, or just help us to learn a bit more about ourselves. I find that fascinating.

What is the relationship between your work and its audience?

The audience can be a consumer audience, and not necessarily for music. It could be for a sound or a visually-exciting project, be it a film or an advert. It could also be about someone wanting to look cool and have something on in the background or they want to drive around in their car with something banging on the system, and you're providing that for them. Or it could be someone who comes to you and says, "I've got something in my head and I don't know how to get to it. Can you help me?" Hopefully I have enough knowledge to know what they need and how I can help them deliver their idea. And you could provide that service and open the door to help them achieve whatever they aspire to. So, there's that side.

I think it's important, when you get to a certain point, to know why you're doing it. Some people do it just to do it. They make art which no one else sees or hears. They have a guitar, and can sit and play and feel ecstatic, and that's enough for them. It can be as simple as a very self-centered relationship with an instrument. And that's it. You don't need to provide anything else. It's hedonistic, but it's also about self-awareness.

I do get those moments where I just play my piano and drift off. I find something I like, and I could record it, or try to remember it, but I don't necessarily need to. I just get off completely on the moment of playing. And that, from an early age, was something that happened, and it was about being in love with the music. The gift of being able to do that is amazing. I'm still humbled by the fact that I can lay my hands on something and create things that bring joy to me, and hopefully to other people.

What is the relationship between yourself and your audience?

I like to please myself. This may be controversial, but they can either like it, or they can fuck off. That's the old punk in me talking. It seems harsh, but I mean it in the softer, artistic sense, that if you don't like what you're hearing, there's no point listening to it. If you hate what I do, do you really need to tell me? Are you just trying to channel your anger in my direction? Your anger and hate is irrelevant to me. I do what I do, and if you like it, great. But if you don't that's not my problem. I'm enjoying it. It's not an ego thing. Half the audience will like it, half won't. I don't take it personally anymore. If you're not hurting anyone, I don't think anyone has a right to try to hurt you with it. The self-defense mechanism is: I don't care what you think. If you're going to destroy what I love, then what's the point of the conversation?

With positive feedback, it's great, but I want to push more. If people like it, I think, 'Well, wait till you hear the next one. It's going to be even better.' I like the encouragement. Not all negative feedback is wrong. That's also part of learning. They might say, "It's great, but it hurt my ears. I couldn't listen to that particular part." So that might be a technical thing. You don't want to offer someone a bunch of razor blades in their drink; you've got to make it comfortable. But then sometimes it is about making people uncomfortable.

What has your audience taught you?

I suppose it's the same kind of thing. Some like the work, some don't. I think it can be down to personality. Even if someone likes my music, it doesn't necessarily mean they're going to like me. Which I've experienced. I've met some amazing musicians and loved their music but have come away a bit disappointed. And they may have been quite rude. I try as much as I can to be pleasant about whatever it is. It's a giving thing. It could be seen as co-dependent, wanting to please all the time. If you're a performer, what are you doing if you're not trying to please? You could go out there with a big sound system, rock it up and want to hurt people's heads. That would please some people, but not others. I think performance is all about pleasing, enlightening, feeling engaged, and the togetherness of it. I like to feel that the audience is with me, and can feel that spark. If I'm feeling that spark, I want to know and feel that they're getting it. If I play a beautiful set of notes and enjoy it, I would want someone else to share that. It's important that it's communicated in the right way. So you wouldn't say, "Here is a beautiful, gentle piece of music, you bunch of shitheads." It would destroy it. So there's a way of addressing it creatively in the flow of what it is, and making it a lovely experience, from music to personality. But then sometimes the juxtaposition can be fun too.

It could be that the music demands you introduce it with a big 'fuck you' to the audience. That may be appropriate. I was in a band at 18 years old where the sheer abuse of the audience was seen as a pleasure. That's kids for you.

I'm lucky enough to work in a beautiful venue in Brighton, where I'm the sound technician, and the technical supervisor for incredible shows. I bring in all my skills for those nights. I put myself into the frame of mind of the audience, asking myself what experience I would like to have. How am I going to help create the magic? To have the relationship with myself as an audience member, and as a performer, I think is really important.

In fact I've done that, where I've been playing while in the middle of audience. I co-produced and wrote tracks on a 3D album called *Holotronica*, with Stuart Warren-Hill. When we toured, during the first few shows we were on the stage behind these massive screens. Then we played at Koko in Camden, and there wasn't enough room on stage, as there were so many other acts doing audio-visual stuff that night. So we decided to do it offstage. At that venue we were in the middle of the audience, seeing it and being part of it at the same time. It was lovely, sharing again. Having someone nudge me when I'm playing, giving me the thumbs up, and I'm like, "You like that? Listen to *this!*"

If I think about what I'd say to encourage my 18-year-old self, it would probably be, "Just keep going, don't be afraid to give it a go." When I started with violin lessons I thought I sounded like a symphony, but it was in reality this scratchy kind of thing, sawing away at the strings. I begged my teacher to let me play it in assembly one morning. I was about eight years old. I went up on stage to show everyone this amazing thing I'd learned, then suddenly realized I had 300 kids looking up at me, laughing. But I did my thing and I thought it was amazing that I could actually stand up there and play. I felt like I had to overcome the fear barrier. The only way to do it was to dive in. I'm still like that now. If I find something a bit scary I remind myself of that first solo performance in assembly. The first time I did the sound mix in front of a crowd of 10,000 people it was scary, but exhilarating. The next day I thought, "Well, that's done now. And it was awesome." Quite often a big crowd is easier than playing for two people. Then again, I've never been shy of that. If I make a fool of myself, I don't really care. I suppose I've seen myself historically as a bit of a clown, a bit of a punk. I got the piss ripped out of me in school for walking around with the violin case, so you develop defenses. That kind of bullying built my resilience.

What has been the greatest challenge in your career?

The greatest challenge is always longevity – keeping it going. If I can make a living from music, and not have to go and work in a bar to subsidize the music, I'm happy. I can't think of anything else I'd want to retrain to do. In this 2020 lockdown I've done a bit of gardening, and I enjoy cooking. It's good to get away from your art to appreciate it. You can get locked into it, and you need to step out of it sometimes.

I've definitely created my own persona over the years, because of it. I've decided that I'm going to be rock 'n roll, I'm going to be punk, I'm going to do live music, I'm going to write music, I'm going to be on films, and I'm going to stick to it. That's the person I wanted to become, and I think I've done it. So chase your dreams.

When I was about 17 I was looking for a producer. It used to be that you had to go into the studio, meet the producer, then they would take your idea and help mould you into this thing you want to be. It's taken a while, but I found the producer eventually, and that was me. The one person who I absolutely know would do it the right way, and who knows me inside out. But I had to learn my trade to do that. I found it in a roundabout way.

A friend reminded me recently of a song I'd written for the band I was in at the time. He asked if I would want to pick that song up again and produce it, now that I know how. So that was quite a moment. I didn't want to call myself a producer until I found something that was working, and was public, and was real. But it still took a few projects being out there to say okay, now I'm a producer. Just as I would not call myself a carpenter after I'd made one chair.

What has been the high point of your career?

Some of the highest points have got me through the lowest moments. My love of music has helped me through things that have been quite horrible.

But on the flip side, there has been so much amazing stuff. I'm now 53, and I've seen music grow and change through the last 40 or 50 years. I was aware of music from a very early age, so I've been lucky enough to see the development of the music industry over a fairly long period. I've lived through some amazing eras in music, which have given me knowledge, and joy. I feel very fortunate to be alive at this moment in time, having the advantage of hindsight, and seeing all that music come through.

One of the personal highlights was getting played on the radio for the first time, which I mentioned. Going through a big rig, and having my music played out very loud, was another high point. That's what catapulted me into doing a lot of live mixing. I love creating something, even if I'm not playing. I love the idea of just pushing it out to people's ears and making it work, whether it's a whole band or a single voice. Having that project across a stadium, and getting it just right, is amazing.

One of the recent high points was recording and mixing an orchestra. Having started as a violin player, I was asked to join the youth orchestra, and I went in with my little fiddle, and sat there with the cello, the other strings and so on. When the whole orchestra played together, that was a spark moment. It was exhilarating. I looked at the conductor, in his suit, and I thought I really wanted to do that, to know how it works. Then fast forward to working with an orchestra at AIR Studios in London. From that little kid scraping the violin, to this glorious moment of working with an orchestra for a soundtrack.

Performing the 3D album in India was another high point. I couldn't take a keyboard as it was too bulky for the long-haul flight, so I used my phone, and an iPad, which had a Korg MS20 synth on it. The iPad overheated and didn't work. It was so hot there. But I had a Moog synth on my phone, so we hooked it up to the computer and I was playing my parts using my phone. Technology-wise that was a massive moment for me.

Another moment was being signed to EMI Paris. I took the hovercraft across the channel, to get down to Paris to sign the deal. I was on the hovercraft, with the tracks on my headphones, and the craft inflated and headed out to sea and it was like, "Here we go." That was a life-changing moment that is with me forever.

And now I'm teaching my kids how to play, write and produce music. I met my wife through music. Everything good in my life has been about music, and has happened because of music.

What is the most important thing your creative practice has taught you?

The most important thing is to have faith in your ability, and hope in what's coming. It can be difficult to keep focus, but my advice is always, "Just keep going." You have to realize that you are already living the dream. And you need to learn how to exist in that state.

How did it feel to reflect on creativity today?

It's great. I like to do it. It's an interesting exercise. Sometimes I like to keep my head down and keep going, and I have to achieve the next thing. It's an urge. Right now I'm thinking that I've got a mix to do, and I've got some ideas I want to get to. And I did some things last night that I want to hear out on the monitors. But it's nice to talk about it all.

It's actually encouraging when you put your CV down, and you look at things that have challenged you historically, and realize that you succeeded. Looking at your achievements encourages you to continue. But it's hard to do early on as you've got nothing to go by, apart from your sense of mission.

Funnily enough though, from a young age I wondered about my future self, what I would be like when I was 50-plus. How would it feel? And now I can tell my younger self, "Life is great, Pepps."

Lady Pink

Lady Pink was born in Ecuador and raised in NYC. In 1979 she started writing graffiti, and painted subway trains until 1985. In 1982 she had a starring role in the motion picture *Wild Style*. That role and her other significant contributions to graffiti have made her a cult figure in the hip-hop subculture.

In high school she began exhibiting paintings in art galleries, and at 21 had her first solo show at the Moore College of Art. As a leading participant in the rise of graffiti-based art, Lady Pink's canvases have entered important art collections such as those of the Whitney Museum, the MET in New York and the Brooklyn Museum. She has established herself in the fine arts world, and her paintings are highly prized by collectors.

Today, Lady Pink continues to create new paintings on canvas that express her unique personal vision. She also shares her 30 years of experience with teens by holding mural workshops and lecturing internationally to college students.

ladypinknyc.com / Instagram: ladypinknyc

What drew you to your medium?

As a teenager it was about finding fun things to do. Having adventures with my friends. When I started, my first boyfriend got arrested for writing graffiti on the streets and was sent down to live with family in Puerto Rico. So he was gone, lost to me. I cried for a month, and started writing his name around the middle school, the way I thought he wrote it. His friends took me under their wing and taught me style. Because letters are very specific. You need a lot of practice to get it right.

And then I started in the High School of Art and Design, which is in the middle of Manhattan. Talented kids from every corner of New York go there. You have to show a portfolio and get accepted. You have everything from colorful kids who are obviously gay to hardcore thugs. That's where I met hundreds of kids that wrote graffiti. And then I met and was down with a group that actually knew how to get into the New York subway tunnels and train yards. The boys told me that I couldn't do that, that it was like a boy's club and that girls were not welcome because they would get everyone arrested, and I would be the weak link. So I had to prove myself, and it took months to convince these teenage boys to take me to the train yards. And the other little feminist girls were looking up to me to succeed. They didn't have the courage to do it but I was the crazy one. Crazy enough to sneak out of my mother's house in the middle of the night, go to the worst neighborhoods where they parked the trains, meet up with a bunch of little teenage boys and sneak like ninjas into the train yards and paint at the risk of our lives. And for what? For glory among ourselves mostly. But fame is infectious, fame is addictive. Once you are well-known and you have fame, it's hard to give that up.

I started painting trains in 1980. Through the early 80s there was an abundance of creative energy happening, above ground and underground. And at that time, when I was 16, I started exhibiting in galleries and selling my work. I didn't have time to finish high school as I was booked with exhibits and traveling, and things going on that they didn't give me too much time for at school. I just took my GED and then was done. Why did I do it? Because it was fun. And then I got fame, and then money. So all of that keeps you in the mix.

Do you feel a connection with the history of your medium?

I wasn't there right at the beginning of graffiti writing. There was a long history before me, more than a decade. There were dozens of women who came before me, since the early 70s. I'm not the first, but they just keep calling me 'the first lady of graffiti'. Some of the early women writers were Barbara 62, Eva 62, Charmine, Stoney, Rocky 184. There were loads. But the shelf life of a graffiti writer is often around two to five years. They hang up their cans and move on and grow up. They get a job, or go to school. That's just the way it rolls. Not many of us stick with it forever. I only painted trains for five years, so from 1980 to 1985 I did illegal work. Anytime after that it's all been legal.

The same thing goes for those girls. They roamed in small packs of four or five, boys and girls together, because New York was very dangerous in the 1970s. They did a lot of tagging. They didn't do massive colorful things like I did. I took it to the next level because I was more artistic. I had the opportunities, I went to the right places with the right people. I got to paint big, and do large, artistic work. Most of the girls did a lot of tagging. They got up a lot, they were very prolific, but were just putting up their names, small-scale. There aren't any existing photos of anything large or colorful they painted. The guys were doing that. They call me the first lady of graffiti because I was around just as it was going above ground. I was in the galleries, books, documentaries and the motion picture, *Wild Style*. Everything that was going on above ground, I was at the right place at the right time. And I was the only female doing it, so whenever anyone asked, they would push me to be the front person. And I was more approachable than my friends. The boys were a little on the scary side, a little thuggish. But I was the smiling, friendly, eloquent girl and they could approach me. And I also knew how to show up on time. That's a really important aspect of success.

In graffiti we teach, master to apprentice. The master could be someone your own age, but they just know more than you do. And I had a lot of different masters that taught me different aspects of graffiti, like lettering, cartooning, how to sneak into a train yard, how to steal spray paint properly. Every little thing has to be taught so you do it correctly. This is just a progression of things. You learn how to tag, then you tag the inside of the trains, and by then you get to know the layout, and how to get in and out of the train yards and tunnels. There are a lot of places to go, and it's all very dangerous, it's all pitch black and you could die in an instant. You could get electrocuted, or get found down there by bigger guys and they beat you up or kill you. There are all kinds of dangers.

After tagging you learn how to do bigger pieces on the outside of trains, if you have the skill, and the nerve to stand around for a few hours doing something bigger and more colorful. Some kids could only do bubble letters, which are easy to learn, and it takes seconds to do. If your objective is only vandalism, then it's just tagging, or bubble letters. Different generations call them different things, but we call them 'throw-ups' or 'fill-ins'. They're quick, and you can move on; you don't have to stand in one spot doing something artistic.

The next level, if you've got the talent, is that you draw up fancy letters. They take a long time and a lot of practice to get correct. Fonts are so specialized and specific. You can tell what country, borough and what era they come from, just by the lettering style. It's the same way we can tell where you're from by the dialect you speak. When I do my tag, it says that I'm from Queens, New York, from the 1980s. All of that is in my signature.

When you can do a nice font, and you've got enough spray paint to have a few colors, then you can graduate to a big piece. All of this takes a bit of skill. But not everyone does it as something artistic. They may do it just for vandalism, just to get up, to have fun with their friends. They're not that ambitious. But I took up with a group that was ambitious. They were the best of the best, the elite. This was TC5, or The Cool 5. So we already had people to look up to, who inspired us. They were kings and heroes, and they were villains. They did giant deeds that you had to keep up with. In 1976, during our bicentennial in the US, two groups pulled out 10 whole cars. That's like every car painted in an entire train. When it went rolling by on an elevated section it was just a huge splash of color. One group did something on the patriotic tip, with American flags and stuff, here in Queens. Another group, led by LEE (George Lee Quiñones) did something else around Christmas that same year. So we had to try to match those giant deeds. There was always different levels that you had to get to. You did tagging, then pieces, then whole cars end-to-end, in collaboration with a couple of friends. It could be cartoon characters, lots of color. It would take 50 cans of spray paint and all night to do. If you have the nerve, the courage, the skills, the supplies, the support and the location, you can take it to that level. All those things have to come together. None of those girls before me had much of that, but I am not the first.

In teaching master to apprentice, you also teach history. Who is who, who is to be respected, this is how it's done, and this is how it's not done – because now that guy's dead. There is lots to teach the young ones, so that when they go into danger they're not going to die. A lot have.

Does your medium offer something unique?

Rebellion. If you need to rebel, this is a way to do it. Other kids, they get piercings and tattoos, or date someone from another race or something. As a teenager you need to rebel against the man, against society. This gives your voice a platform. You can go out in the middle of the night and say whatever the hell you want, even if it's just, 'Look at me, I exist!' Just to mark your territory, just for a little bit of an adrenalin rush. To be rebellious is important. Otherwise we would be speaking in a British clip right now. So our country was founded in rebellion. We had some free thinkers shaking things up.

Art itself needs to be rebelled against. It has become just for the cultured elite. It's become abstract, obscure. And regular folks can't relate to any of that. It's all a commodity. Fine art in the museums and the biggest galleries, people just buy it because it's going to increase in value. It doesn't matter what it looks like, just that the artist's career is going to elevate and in 20 years from now, you want it to be worth 20 times what you paid for it. They don't even hang it in their homes, they put it in storage until they can sell it for a big profit. So street art has become the world's biggest art movement. It is a backlash against art that has become for the 1%, for the cultured few that have the time to frequent museums and galleries. Regular folks don't have that kind of time. They're just trying to make ends meet, and are doing laundry and grocery shopping on the weekends. So street art has come out from indoors. It has come out from the elite, abstract and intellectual way it had gone, and is now available to everyone. It's down your street, it's around your corner. You can do it. With a little paint, a good design, a ladder and permission, you can do it. All you need is a little courage, which I can't teach you.

We now have more countries and more people doing street art. You don't need a degree, you don't need to be sanctioned and bona fide and funded – just do your thing. Art is for everyone. We brought the fun and accessibility back to art. And everyone has taken notice, everyone from the fashion world to music and film; it's all of value.

Why do you have a need to create?

That's just the way artists are born. We have to create, like we have to breathe. It's an urge, and it can come out in any kind of way. It could be making cupcakes. You're always nurturing and creating. It's just a need in us. Even if I'm not painting I feel the need to create something beautiful. It could be a garden with colorful flowers. We are born with this creativity. So I tell young people that it's their duty to use it. They are born with talent in this area, they are not ordinary in that sense. They are special and they must use their talent. Sure, it's not easy being an artist. You don't get a lot of support from the family. They will wish you were a lawyer, a doctor or an accountant. But if you are born with the talent to do visual art, or dance or make music, it means you are special, and it's your duty to use it, and not squander it sweeping floors. Don't mess with that. Always be an artist. Even with an unorthodox beginning like mine, I can set an example, and show that this is what you have to do. Aside from that, it's probably the only thing I'm really good at. And I can earn a lot of money doing what I do.

Lady Pink

Why do humans have a need to create?

The oldest bit of art found so far is a piece of cave art in Indonesia, dated to around 40,000 years old. In Argentina there is the cave of the hands, the Cueva de las Manos. It has dozens of hands which are spray painted by blowing red ochre over a hand stencil. They are dated to around 13,000 years old. In France there is the same thing, and some have missing fingers. Mister Forefinger got up in a lot of spots. The reason for that is that same basic reason that we do graffiti now: to know that we are alive, to leave a mark behind. Mister Forefinger is immortal. Some of us don't feel the need to have children, and leave behind a little copy of ourselves. That's our basic biological need, and for most people that's their immortality. For some of us artists, our immortality exists in our creations. My paintings are sitting in some fine museums, and will be preserved for centuries and for other generations.

Culture is in our DNA. To entertain, to make music, to dance and to paint is part of our nature. But it isn't unique to humans. We have witnessed creativity in animals as well, from birds to apes to all kinds of animals. Without art, what do we have? The Taliban in Afghanistan have banned sports, music and dancing. They behead you if God forbid you strike a tune. That is the most oppressive kind of human existence that you can imagine.

But in America we take it a little too far, and only glorify sports stars and the most inappropriate entertainers, and we raise them to the level of heroes and gods. And in this country we give too much value to sports, and not enough to arts. So when money is tight, they'll eliminate art and music from schools, but they'll keep their sports teams. In Europe, art and culture is much more appreciated, and kids grow up with that since birth. Music, art and beautiful architecture. But here in the US it's all about sports. It's disgusting.

What sacrifices have you made to pursue your creative path?

I don't know if I've had to sacrifice too much. I've sacrificed things like traditions that everybody else follows, because I want to be a kooky artist, and I don't want to do traditional craft.

I'm now living in upstate New York, a couple of hours north of the city. Before we moved, we were raided by the SWAT team. Guys like stormtroopers, with shields and helmets and guns drawn, were coming down my hallway. They arrested my husband on trumped-up graffiti charges, and they took everything: my books, photos, computers, a thousand cans of spray paint. I wasn't under arrest, but I had to sit there with a policewoman and watch the police rob me. They took everything out in bags; it took hours. They just make shit up, and torture and harass you. We had to hire a very expensive lawyer to deal with that situation. You still have to prove yourself innocent even when you are. We had to go to court for a year and a half to get all the charges dropped and everything returned. So we left New York, bought some land upstate and it's just nothing but trees and peace and quiet. But the damage was done. This is what the graffiti police do. They do this to any artist who has the nerve to put out work, organize events, write a book or do anything in the public eye. They have this need to crush us. They'll go fishing and raid your house on a flimsy warrant and search for anything incriminating, like a video or a photo of something illegal. So since we always expected the police in our house, we never kept anything valuable here. We had to get a storage space for that. They raided us twice in 10 years. Despite being professional artists that don't break the law, we still have to see these fucks at our door, because they think we inspire young people to break the law. My work is all about inspiring them to do legal work that benefits themselves and the community, but the police have the idea that any kind of work like this is a problem.

The upside is that we now have this beautiful house in the country, and my husband built me this nice little studio on our land, and everything turned out just fine, despite having to waste so much money on an attorney to defend ourselves from them. She's a brilliant woman who completely took care of it for us, and has been taking care of a few groups of graffiti writers in New York, because the vandal squad does this to them all. They'll make your life hell. As if it isn't hard enough to be an artist already.

How has your work shaped you as a person?

I don't psychoanalyze myself like that, so I don't know. I am what I do. I've been an artist since I was 16. I've been a prima donna since I was young. I get treated pretty well. I've never had a job working for anyone else, ever. I've been selling my work since I was very young. I do pretty well. I have three assistants. My husband has been my executive assistant for the last 26 years. He makes things possible.

How do you deal with creative blocks?

Do I get blocks? Shit yeah. The answer to that is that first you stare at a blank sketch pad, then you bang your head against it for a while, then you cry, and then something will kick in. That's usually my process. Honestly there's no time to be blocked. I have deadlines, and people are waiting for shit. One thing graffiti teaches us is how to hit the ground running, how to create art even when your knees are shaking, your heart is in your throat and you're trembling. You're still going, you're still doing your thing. I have situations where folks are waiting for something at the end of the day and I have absolutely nothing. But you have to find something within yourself, or start looking online at different subjects until something jumps out at you, and something starts to build.

Sometimes an artist's work will come as a full, finished image in our heads. Other times we build it piece by piece as it develops. You might change it many times before you're happy. So it happens in all kinds of ways.

How do you stay fresh in your work?

I don't know if I do. Again, I don't analyze it, I just keep going. That's why I employ young people. I have a couple of assistants, aged 20 and 21, and they help keep me up to date. I've always been immature and childlike. I play video games with my husband all the time, and enjoy things that young people do too, so I try not to get old and stuffy.

I am aware that I am very versatile, and that is one reason for my success. I can meet all kinds of different needs for commissions and assignments. I can do all kinds of styles. In 2015 I got a gig painting a mural at Coney Island Walls, an outdoor museum of street art. So I started researching Coney Island, and made a collage of imagery that is associated with the area. Each situation is different, and I like to be versatile. I don't like to repeat the same things over and over again. I get requests to do that, but I try to resist revisiting things I've done before. I always like to do something new. I don't feel I need to be a one-trick pony. People think that I'm a graffiti writer and that's all I do, but that's not true. I like to show off my illustration skills, my painterly skills, my use of color. And scale does not scare me. So that sets an example for other young women. It shouldn't scare them either. They see me in action working with a team, seeing how I command a bunch of guys and how I speak to them with authority and have them do what I need when I need it. That too is a skill. It's important to teach a bit of leadership, so they are not just a follower.

What is your relationship with satisfaction in your work?

Most of us artists don't like our own work. We're never quite happy. We could tweak it, and make it better. I can be fairly happy with something, but I'm never quite satisfied. You can always see something that you could have changed or improved. But it's too late. You're not going back up that ladder or that lift. The paint's been put away, the car has driven away and there's nothing you can do. Maybe in Photoshop you can fix it. Part of it is challenging yourself to keep improving, to make it better next time.

What is the relationship between your work and its audience?

With my fine art I try to tell a story. I've always got something heavy or deep, or a social or political message in the imagery. It could be depressing or whatever, but I say what I have to say. The only clue I give you is the title of the piece. After that, whether you understand it or not, I don't really care. That's fine art. As long as I say what I have to say and I get it off my chest, my message is up there, and some people will understand it completely.

My work in the street is different. I know that the public comes in all shapes and sizes, all ages. The message is softer, but there is often still a message there. And it is crystal clear. People will not misunderstand it. The symbolism and imagery is simple, you get it at a glance, and I want them to understand it in the street. The time for subtlety and obscurity is fine art. People can stand in the gallery, stare at the piece for a while and figure it out. But in the street, it's almost like a billboard. People drive by it, they walk by it quickly, and they have to get your message in an instant. You say what you have to say clearly. So I want them to understand, and to engage. I want this to be part of the fabric of their lives. I want to give them a little bit of my talent in their everyday lives and lift their spirits, give them a bit of color, and something to smile about as they pass it. I do care if they understand it. If they misunderstand something, I will change it so that everything is cool. I am sensitive to their needs. But with my fine art, no one call tell me boo. If I want to do something horrific, or insulting to somebody, I don't care. The message has been said. But in the street, I do care. I'm sensitive to the community and the neighborhood. Sometimes I donate work that is worth thousands. Usually people are appreciative, but if there is a jerk that comes along and spoils it for me, then I'm just going to do a fucked-up job and leave.

What is the relationship between yourself and your audience?

With visual artists, we don't really engage directly with our audiences. We drop a piece and leave. Unless we're at a gallery opening, and people will talk to me. People might see me painting a wall at a spot, but I'm not really there to engage.

On social media I share my work on Instagram. It's for friends to see, and for me to see their work around the world. I see these girls painting bigger and bigger walls every year. It's a good way to stay in touch, and inspire each other to keep going. But I don't do too much social media. My sister runs a fan page for me on Facebook, but I don't get involved.

What has your audience taught you?

I get a lot of love. I have a lot of kids saying that I inspire them. I've become a role model for young people, which is not something I ever aimed for. But as I'm in that position, I never do anything illegal or get myself arrested, to set an example. There was a time when you needed to pay your dues, and get street credibility that way, but once that's over, there is no reason to endanger yourself or set an example for kids that way. It is a lot easier to just get permission for a spot, and flex your artistic skills. I never teach kids how to do graffiti. I teach them how to paint murals. It's a whole different skill to sneaking out at night. I tell them that if they want to learn graffiti they have to go out and learn that on the street like everybody else. But not in my class. It's about murals, about painting something illustrative. I realized that graffiti starts as fun, but it's also dangerous. And I would not send a kid into danger being a grown-up now. You don't do that.

What has been the greatest challenge in your career?

Perhaps being a petite latin woman, in a white people's world. That is always a drawback. In being small and petite I get underestimated.

Guys will say, "A tiny little thing like you, can you paint that big old wall?" I say, "What? You need a penis to climb a ladder? Does it help you hold on?" I don't put up with nonsense like that. I've encountered a lot of sexism, a lot of hostility. If someone tells me I can't write because I'm a girl, I tell them, "Watch me."

Being a female subcontractor, and going onto a construction site to paint, guys can be weird. As a latin woman, I get offered much less than my husband, who is white with blue eyes. When he asks for thousands of dollars, he gets it. I wouldn't get half of what he gets. But that's construction. I was looking for a guy partner really early on, and then I ended up marrying one. He handles all the accounting, the computer work, and all of that stuff. I just handle the creative part. And they're fine with that. I'll talk colors and design with the client, then leave him to talk figures. We work very well as a team that way. I had to learn to play the game. This is the way white men deal. You get a lot more money being another white man. Usually when I work for women, there are no issues. It's the same when I work with people of color. But sometimes those men on construction sites are difficult to deal with. But I'm happy to say that over the last decade I'm seeing more and more women on construction sites. There are lots of them painting, and doing general work. You even get the little pink porta potty for us ladies. I do major work with architects, interior designers, all kinds of folks like that. And they have no problem hiring me and my team.

What has been the high point of your career?

Some of the high points came early, when we were doing things like motion pictures and documentaries as kids. We didn't know how important some of these things would be. They're cult movies now, and still known 40 years later.

One major highlight came around 1982. We painted live on stage on Broadway, for the Twyla Tharp Dance company at the Winter Garden Theater. We did 10 shows, and there was a bunch of dancers who would come out and dance to the Beach Boys. And there were six of us in the background who were painting live during the songs. So we got to perform live on Broadway, and then at the end we all came out and took a bow in front of this whole theatre full of people cheering. That was the most amazing feeling ever. You're just a teenage vandal, then suddenly you're painting during a live performance on Broadway. So that was a wonderful thing.

We started traveling when we were very young. We were treated like celebrities, signing autographs and being whisked around the world and showered with money. We had our names on the door of every nightclub in New York City, and we could just walk in and they gave you everything for free. We would be at parties with Jean-Michel Basquiat, Keith Haring and Andy Warhol.

At 21 I had a one-woman show at the university in Philly, and all kinds of wonderful exhibits. I've gotten awards over the years and things, so it's hard to say what the best moments have been. But being in the mix with such amazing artists as a teenager was incredible. People like Jenny Holzer, Martin Wong and John Fekner. These were some of the original street artists in different mediums. They didn't know what to call them then. They didn't want to be called graffiti writers, because they weren't.

What is the most important thing your creative practice has taught you?

That inspiration is one of my greatest achievements. I'm just rolling along, working, getting a paycheck, selling my work. People think I'm an inspiration and I take that seriously. I always try to set a good example. So what I do is more than my skill alone, and the work I produce. It changes lives, so I try to help out, educate and mentor young people. I want to hand down my craft to these kids. Some may be on the verge of saying, "Maybe I should give this up and be a doctor." I say, "No, you're an artist through and through. You're a free spirit. There is no medical school for you. You're an artist." I give them that perspective. Knowing a real artist can be life-changing for some kids.

How did it feel to reflect on creativity today?

I do a lot of interviews, so I have to do a lot of this reminiscing, and trying to remember my history. I did one yesterday for the Museum of Fine Arts in Boston. They were asking me a lot of obscure questions like, "Why is color important to you?" And I say, "Uh, I didn't know it was. But I guess it is." A lot of artists don't verbalize this stuff, we just do. I don't ponder why I like color, I just know I want to make something loud and beautiful. Remembering my past work is easier than explaining why I do it.

Stan Prokopenko

Stan Prokopenko has devoted his life to the arts since the age of 13. During high school he undertook an internship at Sony Online Entertainment to animate for the video game *Everquest II*. He wrote an article on animation for *Imagine* magazine at Johns Hopkins University, and created an animated short film titled *A Game of Pool*, which featured on all American Airlines flights in 2004.

In 2003 he began studying at the Watts Atelier of the Arts in California, where he got most of his arts training. His focus then shifted from animation to fine art painting. In 2007 he became a teacher at the Watts Atelier and has taught drawing and painting classes on numerous topics. He has won numerous prestigious awards and exhibited across the country. His *Proko* YouTube channel has over two million subscribers.

stanprokopenko.com / Instagram: prokotv

What drew you to your medium?

I have many mediums. I've always liked to create, and it doesn't really matter what medium I'm using, as long as I'm creating something. I've always been drawing, since I was a little kid. I was creating video games when I was a kid as well. Code is a medium that I enjoy, for example. In high school it was all animation. For four years that was my focus. Building companies is a medium that I really enjoy. For several years in my 20s, my main focus wasn't even art, it was about trying to figure out business.

When I was a kid, my cousin and I would make videos. We would come up with a story and film it on a MiniDV camera. We had no editing software back then, so we would record the good takes onto a VHS tape, and put a movie together that way. Video is still one of my main mediums right now. I make a lot of videos on YouTube as my teaching method.

I wouldn't say that oil painting is my main medium; it's just one of many. I was drawn to oil simply because it's what my teachers used. But I love it.

Do you feel a connection with the history of your medium?

One of the ways I study any medium is by studying masters that came before me. That connects me to the history of it. However with some mediums, like programming, it's more about what's happening now. What's the modern coding language? And what's the future? What should we develop? With oil paint, there's not much more that you can do with the craft of oil painting. It's pretty much been explored completely. So the extent to which I look at the history of a medium really depends on the nature of the medium itself.

Does your medium offer something unique?

All my mediums have something unique to offer, which is why I'm drawn to them. With oil paint, I like the permanence of it. I enjoy the physical aspect of it, but it doesn't move. With animation I can tell a story through motion. It's the same thing with video. I can add audio to it and use it as a teaching tool for my students. I can't do that through oil painting, so I have to combine them.

With coding I can build a website, and create tools for students which connect them all. Mediums are much more powerful when they're all connected; you can use the unique strengths of each one.

Why do you have a need to create?

It's exciting. Having something that came out of nothing is very satisfying. The end result is satisfying, but so is the process. I get lost in it. It's like meditation. It feels good being in it. While you're creating it just feels right. The flow state—if you can get into it—is amazing. If I'm not doing anything, I'll be daydreaming about something else I can do. But when I'm creating, it's like I'm supposed to be doing that. It just feels right.

I could try to go back to my childhood and look for reasons why I became that way, but maybe it's just that some people are wired to create. But I think most people like to create, just in different ways. Some people like to create friendships, and they really work on that. People don't think of that as art, but it is. Anything that you're building is an art. You're being creative about how you can communicate with people, how you can navigate that friendship. Some people are really good at that art form, and some people are not.

Why do humans have a need to create?

We all need to create. We all need to change things around us in order to feel satisfied, like we're making a difference in the world. Maybe we want to make a change in the world in order to feel powerful, like we have a purpose. A sense of purpose is a pretty big one. Creativity in general is what gave us an evolutionary advantage over other animals. And so we've developed to be more and more creative, and now we can't not be—it's how we've evolved.

What sacrifices have you made to pursue your creative path?

Friendship, for one thing. Having a social life. When I was in my late teens and throughout most of my 20s, I sacrificed going out and partying, having fun with friends, watching movies and playing video games, all the stuff that young people do. I just focused on work, on my craft, on building a business, and creating art. The only relationship I focused on was the one with my wife. She was my girlfriend since I was 18, so we've been together almost half my life.

How has your work shaped you as a person?

The art is me. If I didn't do that I would be creating something else. I don't think I could have a day job, even if it was creative. I wouldn't be able to have an office job. The summer I graduated I had an internship at a video game studio, Sony Online Entertainment. They made *Everquest*. I had an internship for about two months, sculpting for the game, and doing some animation. But it showed me that this is not what I want to do. I like animation and 3D modeling, but I don't want to create other people's stuff. It felt like the purpose of it was gone. It was about the technical execution, rather than the creation of something that I have in my head. The whole purpose was gone, and the enjoyment was gone. The deadlines are worse. The whole reason I'm in art is to escape that office job type of thing, and to experience that made it clear. I learned that I did not want to get a job in an animation studio. Instead I was going to focus on fine art, which is more about me, and what I want to create. So I went down that path for a while.

I don't know if my work has shaped me, as much as my personality has shaped my work.

I don't think I've been particularly shaped by the video interviews with artists on my channel. I'm focused on my craft, which at that moment is video creation, so I'm not just there to learn from them. I'm not in student mode. I'm there as a professional, with a job to do. If it's an interview I have to make sure I'm focused on asking good questions, and I'm getting good information out of them, because we are recording and this is going to be seen by millions of people. I have to perform, so I'm focused on that.

I wish I could just hang out with them and absorb. That would be a lot more powerful to me as an artist. And sometimes I am able to. We can go for lunch afterwards and hang out. But it's often so short. There's only a few relationships that I've actually developed. Like with Stephen Bauman. He's an amazing artist. I recorded him giving a demonstration and we've stayed friends. Having those kinds of people around me, I definitely absorb some of their professionalism. And some of their love for the craft. As they say, you become the people you hang around with the most. And so being around those kinds of people definitely helps me become a better creator. In all ways. I find their energy, and their approach to art, very motivating. I often don't realize it, but it is. I see them constantly working, every day, so I feel like I need to as well. Even if I don't think about it consciously, it pushes me, because I know that all these people around me are working really hard. So being around successful artists that take it seriously drives me to do the same.

How do you deal with creative blocks?

I don't think I ever have creative blocks. When I have a block in one medium I go to a different medium. I'm always excited about something that I'm creating. I don't think I've ever had a moment when I'm wondering what to create and have no ideas. I have way too many things on my list that I want to do, and I'm excited about doing all of them. It's the opposite problem – I don't have enough time to do all the things I want to do.

I feel like I'm pretty good at problem-solving. And creativity is problem-solving; that's all it is. You're making connections to figure out the best solution for this thing you want to do. What helps me is going for walks. I walk every day. This helps me think, it helps get my blood flowing, and by the time I get home I'm excited to start working on something. I never get back and think, 'Hmm, what should I do now?'

And I think it helps to have so many mediums. If I had only one medium, I probably would have blocks. And not because there's nothing I want to do with it, but maybe I'm tired of oil painting right now and don't want to pick up a brush. But I don't mind sitting down and planning my next video, or writing a script. Maybe I want to think in words, rather than visually. Or maybe I want to think about how to grow my company from eight employees to 20. And maybe I'm excited about people, and managing people right now. I can switch between so many different things that it's pretty easy for me to find something I'm interested in doing at any given time.

The problem is actually that I may be excited about one thing, but I have to do something else. It's not the fun thing I want to do, but it's the practical thing I have to do, because my business needs it. Or I have to make this video right now, because people have paid for it and I have to deliver. But once I sit down and start working, I still get lost in it, even if initially I wanted to do something else. I focus in, get into the zone, and I'm in it. I don't mind working on any of that stuff.

How do you stay fresh in your work?

I don't think I've stayed fresh in oil painting, or animation, or programming. A lot of the things I do, I'm not a master in them. I'm just good enough. So staying fresh is not really the goal in a lot of the things I do. It's trying to just create the best thing I can, even if it's something that has worked in the past.

But with video I am always trying to figure out something new; how can I improve it, how can I make it a more fun video, or a new format? Adding 3D animation was a big one for me. When I entered the YouTube tutorial space, around 2012, it was all about turning on the camera, doing a real-time demonstration and talking. It was like lecturing in a class. Nobody took it any further than that. Some people did time lapses, which I don't like. It was boring. There was no production quality. I had been teaching for six years already by that point, so I felt that I could combine my artistic ability, my experience with making videos, with animation and with teaching, and try to make the best video possible. So this would not just be a spontaneous commentary, but a fully-planned tutorial. I'm a teacher, so I know how to take complex information and organize it in a way that's easy to understand. Using video you don't have to do it live. You can plan it out, record material and combine it in an interesting way. You can add music and animation to make it more fun. And back then that was fresh; no one was doing that kind of thing in art education. So it took off.

Then I wanted to add a personal touch to it, so I started vlogging. And I was always looking for ways to improve the picture. Getting better equipment helps, but I would learn techniques from other people on YouTube who were more focused on filmmaking, and apply that.

So staying fresh has a lot to do with learning more about what I'm doing. Improving the quality has always made it more fresh to me. To me it's not just about being different, it's about being better. When you have a leap in improvement in something, it's fresh. It's something new, in a really good way. It's not just weird, it's a higher calibre. That's what I strive for.

What is your relationship with satisfaction in your work?

It's pretty good. I'm usually satisfied when I'm done with a piece of work. But while I'm working I'm constantly seeing problems. It's one problem after another and then you slowly shift and change and by the time you're done with it, it's like 'Oh, cool, I like it.' I tend to be pretty happy with the end result. I'm not one of those artists who are never happy with the work they produce.

I feel that a lot of the time, people are not satisfied with their work because their craft is not good enough yet. And the way I approach my work, I'm more of a logical thinker. I'm not like Kim Jung Gi. To him it's very natural. It's about feeling and intuition. For me it's about logic. I learn the rules, then they become intuitive to me, and then I get good at my craft. For example, with drawing and painting, it was about learning the science of light. Why do we see things the way we do? What's the science behind this? And when I understand why it works the way it does, it's a lot easier for me to replicate it. So for me it's about understanding things, logically organizing the information in my head in a way that really makes sense, and then I have those as tools to fix the problems that I encounter.

If I ever am unsatisfied and I don't know how to fix something, it means that I don't know something. So I have to go and learn. And I'm really lucky that I live in the age of YouTube and the internet, and any problem I have I can go and learn about it immediately. Sometimes I can figure out the problem within a few minutes. And other times it's a much bigger problem and I might have to go and study it for months. I'm really lucky that the way I learn is perfect for today's age where we have so much access to information.

To me it always starts with the left brain, with learning the craft, the rules, the science. And then it becomes intuitive, and becomes right brain. I don't think of the rules anymore. I create based on all these rules I just learned. Once it's intuitive it becomes easy and just flows out. But the first part is what takes a long time. You really have to practice, and study, to get to that intuitive point. It takes a lot of discipline. As a kid I did a lot of martial arts, and that got me the discipline to get good at something.

What is the relationship between your work and its audience?

That's more complicated. That's one I'm kind of struggling with. I've always liked to get reinforcement from others. I like it when I show my work and I get positive feedback from other people. It makes me feel good that I made something that somebody else likes. But then at the same time I don't want to care. I want to just do something that I feel like doing. Because I found that when I focus on creating something that someone else will like, I don't enjoy it anymore. When I focus on creating something that I like, and I show it to others and they like it, that's very satisfying to me in both ways. I like the process, and I like the result afterwards.

For example, with painting, for maybe six years I was doing portrait commissions. People would send me a photo of a loved one, or whoever, and I would paint it. Initially it was fun, because it was a new thing, and I felt like I was becoming a professional artist, and people were paying me for it. It was exciting and I got to practice my craft.

But after a few years I started really disliking it. Because it wasn't about what I wanted to create, it was about fulfilling an assignment. It was about their vision. I had to satisfy what they wanted. And I just stopped doing commissions. It had become a day job again. So I no longer create work for other people. I focus on what will satisfy me. And usually it aligns. If it satisfies me, other people like it. In my experience, the product is always better when I'm excited about doing it. Because I have way more energy to fix problems when they're my problems. When it's a commission, and someone else is telling me what to do, I settle. I'm like, 'That's good enough, let's move on.' And the product is never as good as when I want to satisfy myself. And I have pretty high standards for myself.

I no longer make paintings to sell them. I do a painting, then I stack it away in my studio and it lives there. I haven't sold a painting in many years. My work is complete when I finish it. I never feel a painting is incomplete unless it's seen by someone else. You work late into the night and get it complete, and you don't have to have someone look at it right away. I show it to others because I like people, and I like to see their reactions. But I don't need someone else's eyes on it for it to be finished.

What is the relationship between yourself and your audience?

That's an interesting question. I guess it depends on the medium we choose. One of my mediums is my *Proko* podcast. And I'm an instructor. I teach through video. So my face is in the videos. I have a relationship with the audience because I'm speaking directly to my students, and they reply. So sometimes we literally have a relationship like any other human would. It's not through the art, like a painting, where I create it and hang it on the wall, and others observe it and have a relationship with the art. But in my teaching, we go back and forth on questions and answers. And when you have a large audience, when millions of people are following you, it becomes very difficult to cater to every individual. Because you have every single personality type, and you can't satisfy them anymore. So then it goes back to being a relationship with me. What do I want to say? And how do I want to present myself?

If you're recording yourself on video it's a lot more intimate than if you're making a painting. With a painting I don't define myself by my work. I've had successful paintings before, so if a painting I made sucks, that doesn't define me. But if I make a podcast episode and say something really stupid, that's me. I can't get away from it. I can't say that's some artwork – it's me. I said that. It's a lot harder to separate myself from my art in that sense. And so my relationship with my audience becomes much more public, and more real. But I've actually really enjoyed it, as it has helped me grow as a person, a lot. I'm constantly looking in the mirror, in the sense that I record myself, and have to edit this. I have to listen to myself speak, I have to watch my face move, so I'm constantly reevaluating myself, not just my art.

What has your audience taught you?

I'm not sure I can come up with any specific things they've taught me, but they're a very important part of my feedback loop. I put things out there and in order to really get good feedback on this thing that I created, I have to listen to my audience. Because they're my students. If what I just created is confusing, that means I'm not doing a good enough job teaching them. And there is that clash there. Am I creating it for them or for myself? I'm creating it for myself, but the success of this project I just made really depends on its effect on people. Because that is the purpose of the art I'm creating, the teaching that I'm offering. It's to affect someone in a positive way. So when I put something out there I listen. When it doesn't do what I intended it to do, it's feedback for me on how to improve. So they're always teaching me by reacting to what I offer, good or bad.

And I can't get away from that. When I put out a video, the comments start coming in, positive and negative. One thing that taught me is who to listen to. What is good criticism, and what is bad criticism? Who is just having a bad day and needs to make fun of someone on YouTube? And who actually cares about what I'm doing and is giving me constructive feedback? So it's taught me to be able to ignore the ugly feedback, the ones that are created to hurt someone, rather than to help someone. That's a difficult thing to do, because when somebody criticizes you, it's easy to get offended and focus on that, and then it ruins your day. But when you're constantly dealing with that, you learn to figure it out. Not everybody does; some people end up quitting. I feel like it's made me stronger as an artist, because I'm able to filter effectively.

When I see my teaching really land, it's a joy. It's satisfying. It's like a high. There's that adrenaline rush initially. Because when I put something out there that I'm happy with, that I'm proud of, I still want that reassurance from others that this is good. And when I get it, it makes me very happy. It's like okay, I'm not crazy that I'm happy with this – other people like it too. And I put a lot of work into this, and it was worth it. And it gives me energy to keep going on to the next one.

What has been the greatest challenge in your career?

There's so many. One challenge as far as painting goes, was figuring out how to make a living as an artist. And I never really figured that out, other than going sideways, and becoming a teacher, a business person. I don't sell paintings, I sell videos. But my focus for a while was about getting to the place where I could sell my paintings for a lot of money and live comfortably. I started doing that in 2007, just before the global economy crashed. That was the worst time to sell art, as it was the first thing that people stopped buying. And I was 21, just entering the professional art world. I started getting into galleries, but they couldn't sell stuff. But I did okay. I was still living with my parents, and I was making enough money to buy a car, pay for my education, go out with my girlfriend and eat wherever we wanted. But I wasn't supporting myself yet.

I ended up shifting sideways from selling art to selling education, because there was a huge demand for that. I started building that up in 2012. And that's when the market was starting to pick up again. YouTube was growing, and it just took off. So that became a new medium, and focus. And it's been much more lucrative than selling paintings. So I never really figured out how to sell artwork, but through this whole process I realized I don't want to. I don't want to sell my paintings. When I create my paintings, they're for me. Otherwise it loses that enjoyment for me.

But as a teacher, it's really difficult to get away from making your product for someone else, because your student is part of your work. As a teacher you cannot separate your art from your student. You can't be your own student, like you can be your own observer as a painter. As a teacher you can't do that; you have to teach someone. I still enjoy the process of creating something for someone else as a teacher, and because of that, I can make more money.

What has been the high point of your career?

I feel like I'm still going up, so I feel the high point is right now. I'm really excited about what's to come in the next few years. We're building something really awesome with our company.

There have definitely been times in my career that I've reached a new high point very quickly, and it's like a landmark moment. But I've never reached a high point, then fallen down again, and looked back up at that peak. Right now I'm at the highest point I've ever been.

But there have been big leaps upward. Winning the Presidential Scholar Award was one of them, as a high school student. It's like confirmation that you can do this; it's recognition from the president of the United States that you are an artist. It's an annual national award. At my time they recognized around 15 high school students as the best artists of that year, from the whole of the country. It's all changed since then, but then it was called the Arts Awards. Every high school senior could apply in the various categories. I won for filmmaking. I didn't get in for painting. I got 7/10 for painting, but

10/10 for filmmaking. I did an animated film. There were a few hundred winners, and they flew us to Florida. We spent a week together, doing all these activities with famous artists, who mentored us. It's all forms of art, including film, acting, dance, painting and others. It's very inspiring. The whole week is made to make you feel that you can be an artist. Then you go back to your normal life, and it's like, "Shit, I'm back to reality."

But then there's the next level. You can then apply to be a Presidential Scholar. So out of those few hundred people you have to write essays and take a more academic approach to our art. And convince them that we're good artists. And from that, they choose about 15 artists. That group got flown to Washington, DC, and got a tour of the White House. George Bush was the president back then, but he had to leave suddenly, maybe to Afghanistan or something, so his wife Laura Bush presented our awards.

So that was a huge thing. It gave me a lot of confidence. Winning awards was a big thing for a while. As I was approaching galleries, I had won an award from the Oil Painters of America. They have a juried show every year with the best artists that they choose. My painting won the Member's Choice Award. So not the judges, but the artists, chose my painting as the best. That gave me huge confidence. And the next day I started walking around the galleries in Scottsdale and telling them I'd won the award, and that got me into a gallery. So that was a big one.

The third high point was launching my first video on YouTube. By then I had a few followers from my blog, where I was writing tutorials. And some of them happened to be pretty big artists. And when I launched my first video, they were really impressed by it, and they shared it on their Facebook. So within the first day of launching that video I got a few thousand subscribers to my YouTube channel. So those big followers shared my video and drove traffic to my channel. That was reassurance that I could now do video. So those are the big three.

What is the most important thing your creative practice has taught you?

That's a really big question. I have to weigh the importance of all the things that are coming up for me.

I feel like with just the process of working, not even the process of creating art, it's the balance between isolating yourself and working on that thing, and spending time with your family. You can't ignore your family. You have to be there. Learning that has been really important. My son just turned three years old, and it's really important that when he walks into the room, I stop what I'm doing and give him attention. So the most important thing is to know when to not do it. And it's to be okay with that, which is difficult. When you're so into what you're doing, and you have to stop for a little bit and change your focus, it's hard. It can be frustrating, because you have to get your thoughts out. But your three-year-old doesn't know what you're dealing with right now. You can't say, 'Hold on one second, I got something here.'

And also, just coming home on time is important. Having dinner with your family every day at the right time, so that your son doesn't grow up not seeing his dad. I guess that balance is the most important thing.

A big one is your craft. There needs to be a balance between learning your craft and making your art. If you don't learn your craft you're always going to struggle making your art. I've learned that from students, watching people learning how to draw and paint. Some just don't take the learning part of it far enough, and don't take it seriously enough. They say, "I have these visions, but I just can't get them out of my head." That's because you just started. You've only been drawing a year. You're not going to be able to produce the things in your head right now. You have to focus the next 10 years of your life on perfecting your craft. It's like, if you can't speak the English language, you're not going to be able to communicate your thoughts. Painting is just a visual language, it's a form of communication. To say what you want to say, you have to know the language, and be able to put it together in a way that is either clear, or poetic, or however you speak. And you have to have experimented enough to know how you speak. I think people miss the language part of it and they just want to speak.

When you get to that really high level, people can call you an artist. You're doing things no one has done before, or doing them in new ways. But the only way to get there is to learn the basics first. You can't solve new problems, or old ones in new ways, if you've not learned how everybody else has solved them in the past.

You don't need to learn the craft to be creative, but you do have to learn the craft to be able to execute on your creative thoughts. Having really good ideas means nothing if you can't translate them. It just means you can entertain yourself in your own head. Which is fine, but that's where it ends.

How did it feel to reflect on creativity today?

It was fun. It's fun to think about these things deeply, and analyze what I do. I kind of do this on my podcast, but I'm never interviewed on my podcast, so it was a little deeper. Your questions definitely require some thought. I stopped doing interviews for a while because all the questions were the same. I got bored. That's why I asked you to send me the questions. That's my litmus test now. Most of the interviews focus on my story. So I recognized that your questions would require a conversation, and some thought.

Herman Rarebell

Herman Rarebell is a German musician, best known as the drummer for the band Scorpions from 1977 to 1995, during which time he played on eight studio albums. Rarebell also wrote or co-wrote several songs for the group such as 'Falling in Love' and 'Passion Rules the Game'. He wrote the lyrics for some of the band's most well-known songs such as 'Rock You Like a Hurricane', 'Make It Real' and 'Blackout'.

Herman has partnered in a new musical collaboration called The Seeing Tree, with Lee Pepper, Eugenie Arrowsmith and Thomas Perry. Their first single is 'I Can See the Signs'.

hermanrarebell.com / Instagram: hermanrarebell

What drew you to your medium?

I felt the love for the instrument very early on. My mother told me that at the age of five I would play pots and pans. I was born in '49, so by '62 I was about 12 or 13 years old, and we were invited to a wedding. And afterwards the drums were still there and I went behind them and it felt very natural to play with them. And then the Beatles released 'She Loves You', and I wanted to play that kind of music and be like them. Everyone thought I was crazy, but I took it seriously. I pestered my mother to buy me my first drum kit. It was an old Trixon, where the bass drum was oval, not round. There was one rack tom, one cymbal, and the stand. And then over time I got the second tom, the second cymbal and so on.

I then started to listen to more British pop music. I lived in Saarland which is very close to the French border, and the only radio station I could hear was Radio Caroline at night after nine, on medium wave. We were only about 400 miles away from the North Sea. That was the first time I heard The Kinks' 'You Really Got Me', and so on. I admired all those great bands as a kid. When I was about 14 I joined my first amateur band, and we tried to play the top 40 songs.

My grandfather was a police commissar, and was very straight. When I got my first brushes for the drums, he said, "Take the brushes away from him before it gets into his blood." He meant: stop this before the passion takes over. But my mother did not stop me, and the passion for the instrument only grew.

Do you feel a connection with the history of your medium?

When you look especially at the African drummers, for them it was a method of communication, village to village. Ginger Baker told me he went to Africa to learn all those African beats, and you can hear it in his work. So I think in Africa it was a language thing. I feel the same when I play a solo. It's like communication with the people, without any words, or language. You know exactly what I want to say. Or at least you feel it.

Does your medium offer something unique?

Absolutely. It is a true international language. With my old band the Scorpions, we were touring all over the world. We were only the second Western band to play in Russia, in 1988. They didn't speak German, we didn't speak Russian, but they understood everything, and completely flipped out. You could feel the wish for change, to be like others in the west. We played there a year later at the Moscow Peace Festival, for over 100,000 people. There was a line of soldiers in the middle to hold the masses apart, and they were throwing their hats in the air and rocking. When you see this you know music is an international language. It can bring people together.

Why do you have a need to create?

That's a good question. It was there from when I was a young child. When I first heard the Deep Purple song 'Hush' I could immediately copy it, and from that copy I made my own song.

Later on I started writing lyrics. I wrote a lot of the lyrics because at the time I was the only one who spoke English fluently. I had been in England for a long time. In '68 I heard that first riff from 'Whole Lotta Love' by Led Zeppelin and from that moment I knew I wanted to go to the place where they were creating that kind of music. In Germany all we had was schlager, which is worse than country music. It's what they play at the October beer festivals and everyone sings along. And I said to my dad I didn't want to end up like this. My dad said, "If you really don't want to become a policeman, and work all your life for a little pension, go and study music. At least you could end up at a radio orchestra in Saarland. Or you could play in the state orchestra." So I studied drums and piano for a while at the Musikhochschule Saarbrücken.

Then in the spring of '71 my dad drove me and my drums to Ostend in Belgium, and I took the ferry across to England. I had 2,000 Deutsch Marks, which was the equivalent of about £1,000. I hoped to find work with a big band like Uriah Heep. Of course no one was there waiting for me, and after a month my money was gone, so I did a few small jobs. I became a gardener in Hyde Park. I worked in a pub. I was a taxi driver.

In 1976 Michael Schenker and I met again, being the only German musicians in England. He said that his brother was looking for a drummer and that I should go and audition. They were going to play at the Marquee Club. We met at the Speakeasy Club, which is where all the musicians went. At the audition there were about 50 drummers there. As each one played a song with them they said, "Thanks for coming. Don't call us, we'll call you." The typical sort of thing. I played three songs then packed my drums, and thought the audition was another waste of time. But the next morning the phone rang and they wanted to take me to Hannover for a gig. There were problems with the plane ticket, but eventually it got sorted out and I met them in Bremen to play on a TV show called *Beat-Club*. Dolly Parton was playing that day too.

But in May of '77 there was no work, and we were getting supported by the two wives, Gaby Meine and Margaret Schenker. We had a small allowance, and I lived in a dump. In the summer the heat was terrible and there was no air conditioning. And I wondered why I had given up England for this. And then Michael said he was thinking of leaving UFO. He rejoined Scorpions and we did the *Taken by Force* album. It hit the top 10 in Japan and that was for us the big breaking point.

From then on things changed, and I started to write more lyrics for the band. And this is why I can afford a good life now, because of the writing. If I hadn't written anything I would be really screwed now because all the live gigs are canceled. In Germany there will be nothing until at least 2022.

Why do humans have a need to create?

This is simple. The artist has a gift. They get it from higher sources, and are able to transform the thought forms of the planet. In other words, we catch with our vibration what surrounds us. I did a new song with Pepper, Eugenie and Thomas which is all about this. It's called 'I Can See the Signs'. I'm not Nostradamus, but I can see what is coming towards us. I watch news channels from France, Britain, the US, China and Russia. And they all say different things about the same events. They're all painted differently. And if we keep going in the same direction we will end up in a war. In history, countries are often attacked when they are weak. At the moment, the US, UK and Germany are all weak.

But to come back to the question, if you want to let people know what you feel in your heart and soul, you create something. In my case I write some lyrics. In the 80s it was easy to write 'Rock You Like a

Hurricane', because that was our world: sex, drugs and rock 'n roll. Now it's different. Now I look at the world and it's about survival. People are wondering: How do I feed my kids? Can I afford my apartment? Can I afford to keep my car? It comes back to the basics. The new song is about seeing these signs. Each country blames the other. Trump blames the Chinese for the virus because he can't say, "I fucked up, big time." And in a hundred days he wants to be elected again. I played that country so many times and those people are easy to convince – you just have to go on stage and shout, "Are you ready to rock?"

What sacrifices have you made to pursue your creative path?

My first sacrifice was when I was a young man of about 15, still in school. My mother didn't buy my drumkit, but she guaranteed the payment if I failed to keep up the payments. Normally I would have had money for the occasional Coke or ice cream to buy for a girl I liked, but now that money had to go on drum payments. But every day I saw the Beatles on the black and white TV and dreamed of being a rock star.

And I learned that if I had joined an orchestra, my creative life would have been over. You must only play Tchaikovsky, Bach, Beethoven. In fact, in January 2020, the Saarland State Orchestra invited me to play with them. We played a rock version of Beethoven's 9th Symphony, and the audience flipped out. We had a standing ovation of 10 minutes. When I talked with the members of the orchestra, some of them said to me, "Be happy that you did not become a classical musician. We get a pension at 55, but we are like government employees. We get our monthly salary but we have no creativity in our work. They tell us what to play, and if we want to play anything else they tell us for that we would have to play in some other band." I had seen this already when I was around 21.

I always thought John Bonham was the greatest. The song that really fascinated me on the first album was 'Good Times, Bad Times'.

When I heard that incredible foot pedal work I realized how much you have to learn. Now I have that, but it took me nearly a lifetime to get to this point. Because it's not only the set list that has to go into your consciousness, but all the beats, so you don't have to think anymore when you play. This is another thing I learned from Ginger when we played the last show at the Brighton Dome. It was a Drum Legends show. It was Ginger, myself and Peter York from the Spencer Davis Group.

How has your work shaped you as a person?

In my brain I'm still 20. I don't feel like I'm 71. But when you play drums every day, walk every day, you can stay fit for a long time. My grandfather lived to 94, and could do most physical things until he was 93. People in the West eat and drink too much, then sit on the couch and put on weight and get diabetes. Then your system has no power to fight infection. I'm not afraid because I have a good immune system. My joke is always that I survived the 80s. With my band, we must have taken every drug in the world. One day the whole band went for medical checkups. The doctor asked us how much we drink and what we take and we told him. He shook his head and say, "No way. That's medically impossible."

The people around you shape your personality. From the first album in Japan, our lives changed completely. We had been turned down by record companies all over. They said, "America won't be interested in a German heavy metal band. Don't waste your time." But we wanted to conquer the world and play everywhere. I had come from England and felt we were as good as the metal bands there, so why not? And then we played with all those great British and American bands and had the record labels coming to us. Suddenly we had power, and money. And it changes everyone's personality. But you have to try to keep both feet on the ground, all your life, because it's true that everyone you meet on your way up, you meet on the way down.

When I reached my highest point in '96 I felt there was a big change in the rock world. Grunge was happening, with Nirvana and other bands. I had the best 20 years with Scorpions, and I said to myself that this is the best time to leave, when the band was at the highest point. We have a saying in Saarland where I come from, "You have to leave at the nicest moment, so you have the best memories." So that's what I did.

And things changed. You can't drive a Rolls Royce past 5,000 people sleeping on the streets. You have to learn that it's better to drive a smaller car and give the rest of the money away to people who need it. Share it. This is the most important thing now. And if we don't do that, they're going to take it soon anyway. If the pandemic continues, and the government ends the support for workers, then what do they do? They will have to start stealing. There will not be enough police to hold them. Remember my words.

How do you deal with creative blocks?

I have had blocks. I think this is totally normal. When I go on the road I always take note of things that happened, things that interest me. I kept it all in a diary. Then when I get back from the tour I look through them and start thinking and ideas come together and I start writing. I also write on piano. That was my second instrument when I studied music. So I can write the beat and the melody. Then I start singing and finding the right words to fit the track. For a hard rock song I can't write a really romantic song about holding hands in the moonlight. In the 80s it was easy to write the lyrics to 'Rock You Like a Hurricane' because that was the life I was living at that time: waking up the morning after a show with a groupie, not knowing her name. All we did was party. At that time we only played stadiums around the world, and it was the high point of my life.

And this is part of what happens to you. When women are so available because you're a rock star you lose respect for them. And you lose trust in people. You find out that people have been stealing from you. You lend people money, and even to this day, when they see me they walk the other way. If you want to lose a good friend, lend them money.

These are not experiences I had when I was picking up leaves in Hyde Park each day. Or when I worked in a pub, or drove a taxi. But if I had stayed doing that I would have been bitter that I hadn't pursued my dream. Everything is attitude. All the guys I met in bands had the same attitude: There is no Plan B. There is only Plan A.

How do you stay fresh in your work?

Tell me! I don't know. It's a challenge. I can't travel at the moment. And I can't stand to hear the word 'Covid' anymore. Inspiration now means sharing with other people. And share love with other people, because one day you may need that love. Don't underestimate the old people because one day you will be that old person. And people have to stick together. The pandemic has stopped us thinking about wars, but I'm afraid that this will not last.

What is your relationship with satisfaction in your work?

Nowadays I feel very happy and satisfied when I create something. Whether it's a song or a drum solo, it is something new which came from inside me. But I don't sit down to write every day, as I did before. And thematically you have to think deeper than before. Back in the day it was just sex, drugs and rock and roll. But we also had some successful ballads like 'Still Loving You' or 'Wind of Change'. That song helped make a drastic change in the Soviet Union. I could feel it before it happened. We left the Soviet Union on August the 14th, and we drove back to Berlin. And then I went back home. On November 9th I was sitting in Paris on a promotion trip and I saw the wall falling and it felt like I was watching a science fiction movie. And underneath the footage they were playing 'Wind of Change'. And that helped the song become number one in 20 countries.

What is the relationship between your work and its audience?

In the future it may be that the only way I can connect with the audience is remotely, through making videos and putting them on YouTube. This is exactly what I did with Eugenie, Pepper and Thomas, under the name The Seeing Tree. The whole conversation today is summed up in that song.

What is the relationship between yourself and your audience?

Playing in front of huge audiences is amazing. I had goosebumps every night when I walked out in an arena of 20,000 people, and even more goosebumps when I walked out to play a stadium with 100,000 or more, and they're all going completely crazy. It makes you feel incredible. It makes you feel like you can do anything. So it was worth it to hang in there. If you have a dream, don't give up. When you give up you can fall down. It's when you don't get up anymore that you have to worry.

I was touring for many years, and in terms of groupies, they tend to look up to a man that is successful, who has money and fame. But on the other side, you never know if they love you, or they just love the rock star. And you never find out. At our peak we played around 150 gigs a year. In America we toured for six to eight months, and would usually start in the north in the summer, then would go back down again in the winter. Then we do all of Europe, then we go and do all of Asia, then to Russia, and South America. So some years we may have done 250 gigs. And every night was party time.

On the 17th of May 1977, the day of Klaus Meine's wedding, I joined the band. And on the 18th of May 1996, 19 years later, we did a show in Paris and we played 'Still Loving You' with Vanessa Mae playing the solo. And after the show I said to the band, "That's it for me. In my personal experience I don't think we can go any higher. We played all the stadiums in this world, had the best looking women in this world, I made a lot of money, and now it's time for me to progress in a different way."

I was living in Monaco at the time, and went to Prince Albert and suggested we set up Monaco Records, a record company. We did that and became business partners for five years. We produced different bands. And then in 2001 the record companies started going down because of the internet and pirating. Nowadays there are only three majors left: Warner, Universal and Sony. The rest have been absorbed through mergers and acquisitions, or gone out of business.

At that time I met my wife, who is a saxophone player and writer. We got married in 2003 and since then my life has changed, and I'm very happy. My life is peaceful and I can look after myself much better. I don't have to write a new song every day. If it comes, of course I write it. But those songs don't fit in the mass anymore, because my inspiration is completely different to a 25-year-old kid. For them they write about the same problems I wrote about at that age. And millions of other kids have the same problem, the same vibration. But now, half of my original audience is probably dead from bad diet and heart attacks. That's the reality. And even if you do live healthy, the other half will go in the next 10 or 15 years.

But I did notice towards the end of my time with the Scorpions that many fans started to bring their children. So now they are coming with the grandchildren. And if there are ever live shows again, maybe a promoter will suggest doing shows with the original lineup. It could happen. Our manager Doc McGhee wrote me yesterday about doing a documentary on the Moscow Peace Festival, and its legacy. He signed off by saying, "I hope life has treated you as kindly as you have treated life." He was the manager of Bon Jovi and Mötley Crüe at the time, so he organized the festival with the highest political authorities in Moscow. There was also Ozzy Osbourne, Cinderella and a Soviet band called Gorky Park. It meant a lot to those kids in the audience. And hopefully the kids nowadays wake up. Because in America they think Russia is still a communist state as it was during the Cold War. Doc wants to show the mentality of the young people then. Then we could see the world in terms of wanting peace. There is still a lot of conflict today, but I don't want to write a song about it. I don't want to stand there as a teacher, telling people what to do. We are here to learn in life. I believe this is not the first or last time you are here. We've all been here many times.

What has your audience taught you?

My audience was my life. I made music for them, and they feed me, to this day. If they stop listening to my music I have a problem. But the old hits still sell well. My fans always have my love and appreciation. They keep me alive.

What has been the greatest challenge in your career?

To return to a normal life. From the day I left the Scorpions my life changed completely. Suddenly I went from playing stadiums to playing clubs with Peter York in front of 400 people. It was lovely actually. When we played with Ginger Baker at the Brighton Dome it was 1,500 people. It was so different. For the first time in 20 years I could see the people in my audience. A few years ago I toured small clubs all over the world with Michael Schenker under the name The Temple of Rock. We did some great nights in Japan again.

What has been the high point of your career?

In 1984 it was the success of 'Rock You Like a Hurricane'. Not because I wrote the lyrics, but it was a great thing to see a German rock band having such success in America. The song went to number six in the US Billboard chart. And we sold out Madison Square Garden for three nights. Not even Rammstein did three nights.

Commercially, 'Wind of Change' sold more copies, but 'Hurricane' has more radio play. 'Wind of Change' was more important politically, but 'Hurricane' as a simple rock song is still very popular on classic rock stations.

What is the most important thing your creative practice has taught you?

I think in the early years I learned the most, in terms of technique and performance. We had to play Friday, Saturday and Sunday nights at American clubs in Germany. You had to play four-hour shows, doing top 40 songs for the soldiers. You get a really good routine when you play every night, and you learn a wide spectrum of styles. This was the most influential time.

And you learn about conditioning. If I was to go on tour now I would have do at least 10-12 days of fitness training in a studio to get into condition. This is why I still walk every day. I do four or five miles in the morning and I feel good. Once I get back into playing every night it's the same as working out in a fitness studio. Especially the way I play.

How did it feel to reflect on creativity today?

Looking back over my career, I think the more simply and less greedily you live your life, the more happy you become. That I know for sure. And you don't need as much money as you think you do. All those rich people prove that. If I was made president tomorrow, I would make a law that everyone with more than $10 million would have to share the rest with society. If you can't be happy with $10 million, you can't be happy with $100 million. You can make a good living and be quite happy. But it depends on how you live. If you got out at night and buy drinks for everyone you can spend $50,000. But if you go out by yourself you can spend $50. You have to come back to your senses. Be kind to yourself. Do what you feel in your heart. Your conscience tells you right and wrong. Jesus, Buddha, Krishna, all had a message of peace. And this is what my God tells me in my life. Every morning, the first thing I do is thank my creator for my health, and the same at night. Without health, no amount of money has much meaning.

Red Means Recording

Jeremy Leaird-Koch is a classical music dropout who makes electronic music as Jeremy Blake, and videos on YouTube as Red Means Recording about music technology and music creation.
Instagram: jjbbllkk

What drew you to your medium?

I started playing music in elementary school. There were callouts for the school band, and my family had a flute that my aunt had played and so I picked up the flute. I continued playing through middle school and high school. It was the basis for me getting into music. Even though I was really focused on that and was doing lessons and symphony and all that kind of stuff, my real love was for pop, industrial and electronic music. And music videos. I just loved music so much; it was a really big deal to me. The moment that I could, I started playing along with music that I loved on my parents' old upright piano. There was a jazz band in middle school I was part of which introduced me to non-classical playing, and I was able to get better at improvisational stuff. Music was always a gigantic part of my life, and the more I understood it, the more I wanted to participate.

So there's music on one side, and video on the other side. I dove into that as a hobby—as an offshoot of the music—and it turned out to share a lot of the same language with music, in terms of the way that it's recorded and processed, and in terms of being able to tell a story and set a mood. So I started doing both at the same time. When the YouTube thing took off it became a really good synergy, being able to do the two together.

Do you feel a connection with the history of your medium?

Hugely. With music—writing and producing—there is no way that I see, in the way that I approached it, to be able to write and produce music that will speak to people on different levels if you do not understand the history of the medium. So that's everything from how classical composers did what they did, to how Bowie made his voice sound a certain way on a certain record, to how the people producing music in the early electronica, acid house and UK rave scene did their thing. What were their limitations? What were they trying to say? What was making them excited? All of these things are part of this gigantic encyclopedia of musical knowledge that you can use in your productions now. And I absolutely feel a huge connection to the whole history of music as I compose. It's incredibly important to me, and cool, to be able to draw from all of that.

I was also a DJ for a bit in the San Francisco Bay Area gay scene, and there was a lot of looking back towards the free love, 70s, pre-AIDS thing. A lot of people were playing deep disco cuts at parties, and a lot of house music was drawing from that era. It was really fascinating to get that little bit of history and live in it, even though we weren't experiencing it the same way.

Video is a little different. I love cinema. I love being taught something both technically and from a storytelling perspective from the history of cinema, but I'm also really appreciative of how easy and powerful our new tools are. With music I'm interested in trying some of the older techniques, but with cinema I'm mostly about, 'Wow, that looks beautiful, how did they do that? That's a great story. I haven't really seen someone tell a story that way before.'

Does your medium offer something unique?

If you put music and video together, there's a couple of things that you get that you will not get anywhere else. Like I mentioned earlier, music videos have always been one of my favorite forms of media.

When I grew up, MTV was still about playing music videos. I would watch it all the time. This was in the mid-90s to early 2000s, when the music video was having this explosion of technical artistry. There was a lot of really cool stuff going on in that scene in terms of what people were trying out. Some people were going for very abstract stuff, some people were going for storytelling, and then you had the really flashy dance routine stuff. And I loved all of that.

The power of the combination of music and film really stuck with me, particularly the way they influence each other when it comes to nailing the vibe of the scene, or transforming it. We have everything from orchestral scores to really cool abstract scores for horror and sci-fi, where the music is there to ramp up the feeling you're experiencing. And then we have what I would call the 'ironic' use of music. And this is really big lately, where someone takes an older or modern pop song and rearranges it to be like almost a dirge, or something slower or more emotional. And they put it in the scene and it has a prodigious effect on how you're experiencing the visuals.

Music and film are made for each other, and have this incredible copacetic relationship in making us experience powerful things when you put them together in interesting ways.

Why do you have a need to create?

In the past I would have said that there was just a drive to do it, that it was the only thing that really made me feel as if I was doing something important in the world. I've kind of relaxed on that a bit. I'm doing it because I enjoy it.

Through YouTube I have this feedback loop of creation and response, and that's a really good reward. But through the last couple of decades, where I've been not doing YouTube and still creating, it was about this drive to do something that was outside the inevitable grind that we are all forced to go through. By that I mean the idea that life is relatively predetermined for us, based on our social standing, or our abilities, or whether or not we were able to get a certain job. We don't really have a ton of control over that kind of thing. But creation of art, of music, of video, painting, whatever that creation is, that's the one thing we have for ourselves, and no one can co-opt or take that from us. It's a deeply personal experience. I think that a big part of it stemmed from this anxiety of: life is really difficult to deal with, but I can make stuff over here and feel in control of it, and it makes me happy. And that was a big part of the drive when I was really learning.

Why do humans have a need to create?

I think humans like to make sense of the world. We're cursed with knowledge of ourselves. We are self-aware. And a lot of the world does not make any goddamn sense. And this has been the case since we were painting in caves, and creating myths about the stars. We have always had an imagination, and we have never been 100% sure as to why we're here, or what any of this means. You can see that was expressed in some very rudimentary forms when we were making up our creation myths, and making constellations in the sky. Now things have become rather more meta, but I think that the act of creation gives us a way to describe things to other people: an emotion, a complicated set of feelings, or a concept that we don't really have access to in any other way. As long as there are people that see the world, and see things that they think other people don't, and have the ability to create, I think we'll always be doing this. I think this is part of us. This is one of the ways that we describe the world.

What sacrifices have you made to pursue your creative path?

I'm 40 years old, and I've been pursuing creative output as a musician primarily since middle school, and then in high school, and my first year of college. I was doing music performance as a flautist in college, but I dropped out, having become obsessed with electronic music. So you could say that my first sacrifice was a possible career as a flautist. I was obsessed with production, and always wanted to do it, and the flute just wasn't doing it for me anymore.

My mental health would be the number one thing that I sacrificed over the decades, and I'm trying really hard not to do that anymore. Relationships have been strained, jobs have been lost, and a lot of anxiety has been created over the years. I was thinking that if I wasn't creating I wasn't living, and that's not very healthy. I don't think people should obsess over creation, even though we have these incredible myths about the obsessive artist and the sacrifices they made for their art. I've sacrificed a lot of my relationships, and my mental health, for this, and I don't recommend it.

This year I lost my job with a video production company, and I decided to pivot into talking to people about music technology and production. A lot of people have a drive, a passion, and it can become all-consuming if we don't take care to preserve balance – especially if we have so much to learn and we're not there yet. I'm all for dedication and passion, but very few of us are prepared to deal with anxiety. We're not brought up to really understand what it is. I didn't even know what an anxiety condition was until I was 35. That's ridiculous. There's something wrong if that's how things work. So I see it in other people, and in myself, and one of the things I want to get people to understand is that there is a way to create that doesn't involve obsessing, and sacrificing relationships and mental health.

How has your work shaped you as a person?

Through music I've come to understand that it truly is one of the most important mediums for self-expression. It's also one of the most difficult ones to get other people to pay attention to. A painting is a frozen thing. You can look at it for as long as you want, and come back to it, and it doesn't require any more attention in time than you feel like you need to give it. Music is always a linear experience. It takes a period of time to experience someone's song. Especially if you have a bit of ADHD, it's hard to expect anyone to sit and experience your art or expression, because it's going to take up some of their precious time.

Even when I was hustling to create, and really caught up in that, I realized that not many people are going to hear this. I was a very passive sort of person so I didn't really force it on anyone. It was this constant self-reflexive thing where I knew I wanted to make music, and I thought that the final outcome would be that people would listen to it, but I never understood how to get from point A to point B. So I was always questioning myself, and also steeling myself against the fact that, well, this might never go beyond simply being something I enjoy. So a lot of this road has been about accepting that there is an element of this that, if I don't enjoy it myself, then it's not worth doing. That's an interesting loop that you can get in, that might help a lot of musicians. It's important to get that self-confidence that you can do something just for yourself.

The other way that it shaped me, especially through YouTube, is that my confidence level has gone through the roof, compared to what it used to be. I used to not really be happy talking with people. I was just very shy, not outgoing, not one to want to go out when I could stay in. I'm still like that a lot, but I actually really enjoy talking to people now, and I enjoy sharing things about me, because through YouTube I've learned that apparently people think that what I have to say is actually worth something.

So on one hand I've had to learn how to self-contain and isolate the feedback loop of ideas to creation, as something that I should enjoy completely for myself. On the other hand I've also learned that sharing knowledge—and that feedback loop with other people—can in some cases be a very worthwhile experience. I think that those two things have made me a better person in general.

How do you deal with creative blocks?

That's a good question. As I mentioned before, fortunately I have this feedback loop with YouTube, where if I create something I will likely get positive reinforcement for it. In the past when I would have a creative block I would get very anxious, and I would beat my head against the wall because I felt I couldn't do the one thing that I was 'supposed' to be doing.

One of the ways I'd get around that back in the day, if I had the ability to, would be to hook up a keyboard to Ableton, or something I could make sounds with, and I would just play. I grew up with an upright piano in the house, and that was one of the places I went when I wanted to zone out. I still do that sometimes. I just sit and play an instrument. I really like playing long, ambient pads. They calm me down, and it's a really nice way to interact passively with the medium, without having to dedicate yourself to it. So you can feel like you're in the loop even though you're really not putting in too much effort.

The other way is, I try to do small utility tasks, something that I haven't been keeping up on, like file management, backups, collecting old songs that I might be able to master later. Just non-creative things that I can do to feel like I'm still moving forward.

I'm kind of in a rut right now. I have all this gear, but the ideas keep slipping away from me when I think about what I might want to do with it. That just happens sometimes, and I've learned over many years to recognize that that will pass, and something will happen and I'll get back in the swing of things. Sometimes you just have to be still, and accept that it's not the time to do it. If you really need to push through, then you have to drag your ass to whatever it is you're supposed to be working on and just put pen to paper and go. But recognizing the difference between those two states is sometimes difficult.

How do you stay fresh in your work?

This is probably going to be rather specific to me, but one of the number one ways that I get excited about making something new is by doing some sample digging. A lot of my work is sample-based, especially the stuff on the OP-1 synth videos, that people really like. There's usually some sample in there that's kicked off the whole thing. So every once in a while I go digital crate digging and just find a bunch of interesting or random stuff and those usually become the core for some new project. For me that's a really easy way to stay fresh.

I don't believe in buying a new piece of gear to get inspiration. There are some exceptions, especially with Eurorack. A new module can be very inspiring, but it doesn't necessarily solve any problems, or offer a cure for staleness. You still have to do something with it, you still have to put in the work. In the community we have this thing called GAS, or Gear Acquisition Syndrome. People think, 'If only I had this piece of gear my setup would be complete and I could make music.' People will spend a lot of time online complaining about some feature they wish a synth had, instead of really learning the instrument or piece or gear, and using it to its fullest extent.

I'm guilty of getting a lot of gear through here, and some of it will hang around long enough that I realize that I'm not going to use it, and then it just becomes clutter that I need to get rid of. And then I feel guilty if I haven't used something in a while. There is a certain freedom in getting rid of a piece of gear you haven't touched in a while. I don't know why. Maybe because it frees up space for new gear, or it's the fact that I don't have to think about it anymore. Maybe I didn't really like it, or it wasn't a part of my workflow, and those are important things to realize too.

Sometimes I really try to dig into a piece of gear I've had for a while, and find a new way to use it. That goes back to that sitting down and playing thing. If you have a synth that has external controls you can play with it. Or you can pull up a VST (Virtual Studio Technology) software synth that you haven't used in a long time, and try to make a new sound, or reproduce something you've heard on a record that you haven't tried before. There is no reason not to be excited about sharing the tools you're using, and if you're not excited about them you're probably doing it wrong.

And then of course there's the direct external freshness of consuming new media, whether that's an artist, or a film, or anything. A lot of non-music things can inform music, and I think that's really interesting. Staying receptive to new ideas can be a big part of staying fresh.

What is your relationship with satisfaction in your work?

I think one of the best ways to talk about this is the feeling once you've finished a big project. YouTube videos for me are like maybe a 5k run, versus making an album, which is like running a marathon. I do go back and check them out if I've made something interesting in them, and I get a sense of satisfaction if it came together nicely. I've found that really my satisfaction comes from the process that led up to its completion, but when it's out of my hands, I don't have a relationship with it. I'm glad that I made it, and I'll probably go back and listen to it, but it's not for me anymore. It's for other people.

The satisfaction is in all the little things along the way, like getting a mix just right, or nailing a vocal line, or finding a new way to do a sound. And that process makes me happy. The finished product is not just an artifact at that point. It's not a dead thing. It still has life to it, but it's not as alive to me as it was during the process of its creation.

What is the relationship between your work and its audience?

Now it's really great. I'm in a very fortunate position to be in a feedback loop that's very direct with my audience. I've talked to a few musicans who are getting started and are really talented, and they're trying to figure out a way to make their music and themselves known. I think offering up to the world a glimpse into your process, or education around what you do, will go a long way. This is sort of a target, but we may be beyond, to an extent, the age of the masked performer. Like Burial, the dubstep guy. Those things are intriguing, but you can offer people more through sharing the process. By bringing people into the fold they can be part of a community in which we're all teaching each other things.

What is the relationship between yourself and your audience?

I get positive reinforcement, I get new questions, and I get ideas from my audience to try new things for the channel.

There's a conversation about the education aspect, and about the creative aspect of it. I explore how I can teach while relating it to the act of creation in a way that's meaningful. I'm always feeding back from what people comment on the videos. I don't get comments on my music, because there's no way to comment on Spotify. I try to keep it as much of a two-way street as possible. I'm not interested in shoving things out into the world that are meant to just be consumed. I want to have a conversation about everything I put out on YouTube.

I'm now on the other side of the camera, though I started out with just text on the screen. I really like what Knobs—one of the other guys doing similar things to me—has been doing. We have a little Twitter DM (direct message) group, where we talk about what we do, including some of the pitfalls we run into. I think he was slightly apprehensive about having his face on camera, but when he did that first video, I think it was the one about drum machines, it was perfect. He took all the charm and artistry of his text videos, and translated it into this incredibly human thing. It was great.

I did my 'face reveal' video when I reached something like 100,000 subscribers. And I was very tongue-in-cheek in my presentation. It was kind of a shield, to protect me from having to be authentic in front of a camera. But before that I had done a bunch of music videos, which are on my channel. They don't ever really get watched because the algorithm doesn't like them, so people think that 'face reveal' video was the first, and they still write comments like, 'Wow, he has a face?' There was anxiety, and I used irony and sarcasm to mask it for the first couple of months where I was putting myself on camera. I didn't want to make the videos about me, as opposed to the music, or the item in front of me. I don't know what happened then; maybe it was because I started treating my anxiety, or because of the positive feedback, but it became less and less of an issue, and now I know that a human talking to people on a screen is a useful tool in some cases. It definitely can be used to help cement a point, or help people connect with the point you're trying to make.

What has your audience taught you?

That my hands are dry! That's the number one thing. And no amount of moisturizing will ever fix that. The other weird thing that they taught me is that I have a nervous mouth tic thing, which I wasn't aware of. It's not the sort of thing you pick up on as a normal human talking to other humans; we just do these things without realizing it. But once you start putting yourself on camera, whether it's your voice or your face, you become aware of all kinds of interesting things about yourself.

But the big thing that the audience has taught me is that the years of work I have put into this have not been for nothing. Not only is the 'art' that I've been creating something that people are interested in, but also they find the way that I explain it works. If you had told me that five years ago I would have said you were crazy – that'll never happen. So all in all it's been a very positive experience, and now I just moisturize my hands a lot more.

In terms of negative feedback, I don't think I processed it very well. I was working as a video editor in a small company before I was let go during the lockdown. In that context you are getting feedback from clients, through a producer, on the work that you've done. And generally it's not what you want to hear. About 90% of the time the client does not like something. So you're constantly having to undo or redo, or make choices that you as the creator or craftsman would not think is the best course of action. That was really frustrating. Before that I had done music videos for some very talented people, and I was happy with the end product, but the process was like pulling teeth. I got really frustrated. Again, this was all before I started treating my anxiety. So I know that my brain was very prone to spinning off into very negative and obsessive thought patterns, so if I had been in the state that I am now, I probably would have reacted better, and would have had a different experience.

Through the client experience I had working for that firm, I realized that I had YouTube over here, and that work over there, and

I did not want to do that client work any more. I could do my YouTube work exactly how I want, and I saw no reason to force myself to do work that I don't enjoy. That sort of challenge is not something I'm super interested in participating in. I think that through your creative path, when you recognize things that you just do not get along with, that's okay. Find a way to not deal with them. You don't have to be a master of every human interaction that we could put ourselves through.

What has been the greatest challenge in your career?

It was probably about finding the right balance between 'real life' and this thing that for a long time was just a very fancy hobby. Now I can say that it's my professional career, which is wild. Or at least one part of it. That would not have happened without going through extremely challenging bouts of trying to find a balance. We talked about that earlier, about the obsessive need to be creating all the time – the feeling that I haven't done a video in exactly four weeks and I have to get one out or the world will end. That's just not true. Finding a balance was really the biggest challenge in getting from where this started to where I am now, and making sure that the rest of the world is still being attended to.

What has been the high point of your career?

There have been a few things that have happened that have been unique, on the way up. Starting to get attention from some of the companies that make these products, and developing a relationship with them, has been a cool incremental high point.

If I had to pick one thing, it would be the winter NAMM (National Association of Music Merchants) show 2020. It's a huge music technology conference that runs twice a year. I got to meet a ton of people who are part of this world, that I had only really talked to online. People like Mylar Melodies, Andrew Huang and a whole bunch of really cool people. That, in conjunction with just wandering around the NAMM showroom floor, was great. The space is massive; it's four humongous silos of cacophony and various types of music gear. Recognizing people, and having people walk up to me and say, "Hey, I really like what you're doing," was really cool. I was still working for that video company at the time, so having that experience at NAMM was so different to being told that most of what I did was not right or not good enough. It was just the polar opposite of that, and was foundational in boosting my confidence to be able to move forward.

That's where I first encountered the Sequential Pro 3, and the ASM Hydrasynth. That's one of the amazing things about NAMM, or any of those really big shows, like Superbooth in Germany. If you can think of any synth that you've ever wanted to touch, it's going to be there. You can sit down and play it. It's crazy.

In terms of hitting milestones with YouTube subscribers, it's a neat number, and it's wild if you sit and picture that number of people in a room, but you have to understand that, like all social networks, the difference between your follow count and the engagement, in terms of the number of hits on a video, is enormous. For instance, I have 367,000 YouTube subscribers, and I get on average 6-10 thousand views on each video. I don't know why, and I take those subscriber numbers with a grain of salt. If I had a million that would be insane, and I would never have thought I'd get there, but ultimately it doesn't mean a ton. Because you still have to keep making stuff, and you're not going to get that number of views on a regular basis.

What is the most important thing your creative practice has taught you?

I think the biggest takeaway is that intentional creative practice will improve your skills, when you're paying attention, and pushing through a block, or trying to learn a new idea. Practice for the sake of practice doesn't make as much sense, but intention and focus will help. Anyone who is starting or trying to get better will always be better off if they are actively learning, trying new things, and practicing those things with intention. The only reason I am where I am today is because I spent time with intentional practice, and focused on the thing I wanted to get better at.

I also go back to the joy of the act itself, the joy of the process. That is something we can all use in our lives to separate the part of the world we don't have control over, from the part we do. Learning more about how to better express myself through my creativity and my art has helped me find a deeper relationship with my place in the world.

How did it feel to reflect on creativity today?

It's great. I love talking about this stuff. This is really fascinating to me. Humans are inherently self-aware and self-reflexive, so this is all really interesting. The psychology and philosophy of creativity is wild – I love it. Thank you for having me.

Josh Scott

Joshua Scott is the creator and president of JHS Pedals. His YouTube series, *The JHS Show*, has garnered over 30 million views. Josh also teaches the history and stories surrounding guitar technology in collaboration with various museums, Sweetwater, and Skillshare.

Josh was born in 1982, just a few miles from the musically famous Muscle Shoals, Alabama. He completed a year of college before dropping out to pursue a full-time career as a musician. In the years that followed, he worked as both a live and studio guitarist, songwriter, and studio engineer/producer. After accidentally fixing a broken guitar pedal in 2007, he dove deep into electrical engineering and circuit design, and JHS Pedals was born.

Josh has compiled the most comprehensive catalog of interviews and published works related to guitar effects history to date, and he hopes to use these resources to write books on the history of the guitar and the technology of sound. In addition, he hopes to expand his JHS Show into feature-length documentaries on musical technology history.

jhspedals.info / Instagram: jhspedals

What drew you to your medium?

I could go an hour on this question. The show is like a physical manifestation of what I've always been doing in my head, even with JHS pedal products. So if you think back to something like the Colour Box from 2012, I was obsessed with Rupert Neve, and old British studio consoles. And if you look at the Muffuletta, I got real obsessed with all these versions of the Big Muff fuzz pedal. I was fascinated by the history and was just slipping it into the pedals. Which works really well, in hindsight. But then the show comes along and there's a physical manifestation of that interest, and people say, "He just talks about history. He doesn't really talk about JHS pedals." That is how I have really always been, it's just that it's actually seen now.

I've always hated talking about my own pedals, in the sense of, "Hey, come buy this pedal, it's the best." To me, my pedals will sell well because they sound good, they're made well and we're a very friendly, responsible company. If that's not good enough, there's nothing I can really say. That's how I've always felt about it. I understand that that is both right and wrong. I get it. Someone could persuade me that I should talk more about my own pedals. Sure. But in fact JHS pedals is doing as well as we've ever done. It's actually crazy. When Covid hit, we were at 20 employees. We're at 32 now. We've exploded. We made 40,000 pedals last year. We will get close to 90,000 this year. But the channel and the history and all the work I've been doing feeds that. I have been traveling a lot with my sidekick, co-producer and director of the show Nick Loux. I've gone to London the last four years, and I've been to various other countries, interviewing very important creators before they pass away, in the guitar electronics history realm. And the show is being seen a little bit more. And I'm doing a number of other projects in the background. At some point they will magically appear, but I've been working on them for years.

Do you feel a connection with the history of your medium?

At the beginning, a guitar pedal was just something that made my guitar sound different. But when I was around 19 I worked in a small guitar shop in North Alabama, and I got what was technically my first vintage pedal. A guy came in with a 'Small box' Pro Co RAT distortion pedal. He sold it to me for about $15. And I got really hooked. I loved the pedal, but I didn't think it necessarily sounded better than a new pedal. There was just something about how old it was that really fascinated me. And I can't quite pin down why that was fascinating.

When you start playing guitar you soon hear people talking about vintage guitars. That's in the language of the guitar player. But with vintage pedals, I don't know how much of that is in the language of guitar players when they start. I'm sitting in a room now that has about 4,000 pedals, many of them vintage. For me they're just little excuses to tell stories about people and companies, places and things.

JHS is now 14 years old, and in that time I've learned a lot about circuitry, and about pedals. I can sit and design something, I can fix something from off the wall. I can almost tell you what the circuit topology is just from hearing it. There are only so many ways to do things. It's like food. There's a basic way you do a certain dish. So with distortion pedals, there are about five ways to do things there. And the more I learn, the less interested I am in the sounds. Everything to me sounds fine. There are not many bad pedals. In this room, I can only really think of two pedals that technically sound bad to me. But I guarantee that if I was doing session work again, I could pull one of those out and fit it into a mix and make it sound cool. It's about what you do with it. So to me it's the stories, the creators, the crazy series of events where some of these companies have started, and sometimes gone bankrupt, but it has all led to a mass market in pedals. Everything starts in the 60s, and in the 70s we have this massive boom, then in the 90s it's perfected and pedals are like hot wheels, and then we have the boutique era. I see everything through that lens. To me it's a million stories to tell. It really isn't about making new circuits, which is really hard to do. And we do that at JHS. We do a good job at leveraging what we can do uniquely. I get tired of guitar, I'm surrounded by it, but what keeps me going, and I think what got me started, was the fascination with how things came to be, the people that made them, all the little stories, all the little stuff that nobody even knows they want to know. To me there are so many things like that. I'm positive that when I got that first RAT pedal, it really sparked a curiosity. It was more than wondering why it sounded they way it did. I remember finding out that they were made in Michigan. And I wondered where the name RAT came from. I instantly gravitated that way.

So I'm a pedal manufacturer, but I'm also kind of a pedal historian nerd. I think that there are a lot of people who watch my show that didn't even realize that I make pedals. Which is like a dream for me. That's exciting.

Does your medium offer something unique?

I go back to what I said about companies and individuals. If you buy a camera, they're not as interesting. I have a Sony right here, but I don't know who they are, it's not personal. It's ambiguous almost. There's something about how that feels, compared to looking at an EarthQuaker Devices pedal, for example. In 2020 we're all following Instagram, socials, and you probably know they're in Ohio, and you've probably seen pictures of the guys working. There's something much more personal about the narrative of the product of pedals. It's a very personal gateway into other people's lives. Through the show, viewers have learned that I'm just basically a nerd that makes fun of myself. I've always been that way.

BOSS has started to do a better job of showing more of themselves recently. I've been really proud of BOSS. We did the JB-2 collaborative pedal a few years ago. Yoshi and I became friends and he suggested doing a collaborative pedal for their 40th anniversary, and I just wet myself. It was unreal that BOSS would want to do a pedal with me. One of the things he said was, "I love the way your brand looks and feels. It's personal." I wasn't the only one doing that by any means, but I think they began to adopt that approach more. There's just something about the pedal industry, that when you buy a pedal, you're buying into these groups of people that you relate to. When I go buy a camera, I don't really want to relate to Sony. I just don't care.

I know there are people who don't like JHS pedals. As we continue to get bigger, you'll hear people say it. That's business. But there are a lot of people who relate to my stupidity and self-deprecation. And that's JHS. The brand maybe represents someone they'd like hang out with. That's how it is for me. I've been doing a lot of work on DOD, and their history. I look at that company and I relate so much to the narrative of these guys starting in their basement and so on. I want to hang out with those dudes. The company doesn't really exist anymore, but there's that thing there. And with pedals in general it's a personal thing. But with a lot of products they're not personal. You buy a pedal because your hero plays it, or your friends have it. Only rarely do I think that people have a need and go find the pedal that does that exact thing. I think you end up following a company that you would be friends with, and you start investing in a relationship with that company. That's how it feels. I've said on the show—and it's become almost a theme of how I think—"Companies don't make things, people do." And I think that's been really important to this new era of gear. In the 80s it was all about these companies and it was a little bit like facades. But now it's like you can know this company. For example, with EarthQuaker, Keeley, Walrus, Teisco and Fender, I've talked to these people. So I think that's what we offer. The pedal work is a really unique way to see the world, and people and the things they make.

Why do you have a need to create?

My focus these days is not so much about making new pedals, it's more about my other work of research, writing, documentary, and making episodes for the show. And I end up creating pedals from that. It's totally backwards. My research leads me to discover these amazing things that I can create. So I no longer have to try to think up new pedal designs. I have so many ideas. Even my great-great-grandkids would never work through the list of things I want to do. Like right now I have a circuit open on my desk, a DOD pedal. I'm constantly having new ideas slamming me in the face. But I'm not looking for them. I'm just doing my archive of history, interviewing people, talking to people, and I'm getting inspired, getting ideas, finding problems to fix. And if you look at our products, like the Legends of Fuzz series, that came directly from me researching and interviewing fuzz pedal creators. The Bonsai pedal was born out of my study of the history of the Ibanez Tube Screamer series. The Muffuletta was the same story with the Electro-Harmonix Big Muff series. I could go down the list of our products from the last couple of years and probably only 20% of them came from me trying to design a pedal. So the creativity side of stuff is overflowing, but I'm not trying to create pedals. There are so many things happening. It's like I found a secret back door to inspiration, and that's exciting. I don't know how I would ever run out of ideas. The way our workflow is, I constantly stumble into stuff. I feel so confident about endless ideas that it's kind of wild. I should just open an ideas booth at NAMM.

Why do humans have a need to create?

It's a really fascinating question, especially given where I'm at with trying to understand other creators, and learn from them. It's an important question, because I see a lot of people that feel like they don't care to create. Is it everyone, or is there a specific group that are more creative? I don't know.

There's a legendary guy in the industry called Keith Barr. He co-founded MXR in 1972, and founded Alesis in 1984. Alesis produced the ADAT recording format. I've interviewed people on maybe 10 different topics, that are so far apart that they don't seem connected. But all of those people will say, "Keith Barr was the only genius I knew." His name is brought up in the inner circle of the guys who did things below the radar. And they will all say, "Keith taught me that." This guy was crazy. I want to write a book on him, but there's not enough information out there. It would be a one-chapter book. He makes me feel like I'm lazy. The dude was possessed. He invented the first forms of digital for guitar. He leaves MXR through boredom, then starts Alesis, and guys from there went on to start Line 6. While that's going on, Keith invents the FV-1 spin chipset, which is inside 80% of modern boutique pedal brands. It's a little digital chip. One of the only parts ever designed for guitar pedals. The guy produced endless stuff. He was special.

I'm aware that I have a knack for this, and have a good ear, but more than that, I have a good work ethic. I probably work too much. I understand that that's a lot of the success – I just kept working. When people ask me for advice, I just tell them, "Work hard and stick around." But when I compare myself to Keith Barr, I feel like, am I even creative? Because the dude was next level. I kind of get that feeling from lots of people. Some people really pushed boundaries and did some really crazy stuff. Like a lot of Japanese designers are that way.

So that question is tough: why do we go after that? I think it has to be different for everybody, because the more research I've done—and when I'm honest about myself—I think that everybody has a different motivation. I think with Keith Barr, I've done thousands of hours of research on the history of pedals, and he's like the only actual savant I've come across. But most everyone else is like me; they work really hard and they execute some stuff and they're in the right place at the right time. And that's okay to admit. It doesn't make ideas any less creative or any better, but you can tell there's a difference. So your question poses 10 other questions. Everyone is so different.

There are many stories where people just stumble into stuff, and the result is amazing. Like Roger Mayer meeting Jimi Hendrix at the Bag o' Nails club in London in early '67. Mayer showed him the Octavia fuzz pedal, and when Jimi heard it he decided to use it to overdub solos on *Are You Experienced?* Was Roger Mayer's octave fuzz circuit that genius? It's no better than anything that came later, but it's Jimi Hendrix. You get to go to the studio with your little prototype box and the first time the world heard it was on *Are You Experienced?* So some situations are crazy. A lot of that has happened historically.

What sacrifices have you made to pursue your creative path?

Looking back, I would say that time is the most valuable thing, for sure. I'm 38, and still consider myself youngish. I have three kids. I started JHS when my daughter was just born. I spent endless nights working after people went to bed, or before they got up. I've spent lots of money, I've made mistakes and wasted money. I consider pedal design art, and the work of historical research is a service to art. I believe that to make good art, you have to be okay with wasting time. And I think a lot of people have trouble with that. If you're a person that's hung up on time, you can track a record on something like a 40-hour per week schedule, and I've done stuff like that. But to make art, you have to be okay with knowing that in the wasting of time, you will gain something that wasn't possible when you were in a hurry. Painting is like that, and circuit design is just the same. There are times when working fast can produce results, and historically there are hilarious stories of brilliance under pressure. But at this point, I'm now okay with wasting time. It's not easy starting a business. You have a marriage and kids and a life outside, and you're spending all this time and wondering if it's going to work. Those are sacrifices that I think every pedal maker has gone through. The same goes for guitar makers, or any artist. Certainly any small business. But particularly in art, you need to put time into theorizing, and imagining. That feels really hard in our society. I think you've got to be able to do that and commit to it.

How has your work shaped you as a person?

It's astronomical. I think first off, if you'd met me 15 years ago I was so introverted that I could barely have conversations. I'm serious. I never wanted to talk, to converse. I played guitar for a living. But going from that to running a business has been so formative. It's like a grindstone of personality change. I went into business quietly, not being able to communicate well. But you have to deal with everything. You have a product and you have to talk about it. I have employees, and if something isn't working I have to deal with that. And that might involve firing someone. That's hard, but you have to do it. I've learned so many things I would never have learned otherwise. Like talking on camera. If you'd met me in 1999 and told me what I'm now doing on YouTube, with million-view episodes, I'd be sweating profusely at the idea, and clamming up. But it wasn't all done in one day, it was years of getting used to new situations, like going to Chicago Music Exchange to sit down and do a pedal demo and talk about it a little bit. That's how it started: learning slowly. Then Instagram comes about, and you learn to do a video on your phone. And you get a little better at talking. Then a big dealer picks you up, and you go and teach the sales guy how to use your pedals. And then you find yourself explaining things a little better, and even cracking a joke every once in a while. Then 10 years later, YouTube is pretty easy. But 15 years ago it would have been impossible.

So the work has shaped me tremendously. If you're going to survive, you just adapt. I think that's a problem a lot of people have. You have to learn to be personable. The personal element is so important.

How do you deal with creative blocks?

They're pretty rare. I feel like I've always had too many ideas. The problem is sorting out what is the right idea for this time. And I've flopped a few things, where I miscalculated. The right thing at the wrong time. I think everybody has done that.

We joke around here that we almost wish we had creative blocks so we could narrow down some stuff. It sounds pretentious, but it's not like that. We've built a culture in our business where we make note of all ideas, and no idea is bad, even if it feels weird. And we keep those ideas in front of us, and we're responsible for every little idea. And we all know that hey, it's probably not going to happen this year. But I have a list I can look at, and some of that may be up to 10 years old, but there are always ideas. So we can then choose what to execute on. That's how it works a lot of times. But sometimes it's spontaneous, like, "Here's a crazy idea, and let's just drop everything and do it." So we never really look for ideas, we just write them down when they appear. And we've done a good job of archiving those things.

Most people think they're going to remember everything, but it's impossible. I know there is writer's block, but that's a little different. I think if people are creative, if they would just organize their thoughts a little better, they might be shocked to find that there's enough to work on for years.

How do you stay fresh in your work?

I think that comes from the research. It's a natural result of the work I'm doing. Like yesterday, I was working on location at a restaurant with a friend who's a chef, doing an episode on the first time food names became things on pedals. And now today I'm going to go through tube pedals, and do seven phone interviews with creators. And then tomorrow I do two Patreon talks. One on how to collect pedals, and another on identifying the eras, where I break down around 70 years of guitar effects into historical categories. Thursday I film the most legendary phaser pedals ever. I mean, how is that boring? It's all over the place. It's bonkers. It can be tiring, but that's an example of Josh's life for four days. They are all these excuses for narrative.

What is your relationship with satisfaction in your work?

I'm incredibly satisfied to take a narrative of history, that I feel no one has noticed, kind of like the current under the ocean, then write and produce an episode on it, edit it perfectly, display the story in 15 minutes, watch the edit, then say to Nick, "We're done," and I'm already onto the next thing. To me that is very satisfying.

And then obviously when we have a pedal product, it's the same. I've never done this, but I could probably do a parallel chart of the process, from start to finish. Having the idea, then creating a circuit or writing a narrative, I do the same thing. By the time a consumer sees a new JHS pedal, I was probably done six months to a year ago, in terms of my role in production. Sometimes I'll literally have to look at schematics to remind myself what I was doing. Or I'll find my notes. I joke that my head is like a filing cabinet, and it gets so full that I have to throw things out to make room. So I catch up later. But it's the same feeling, of: that's done, it's communicated well, I taught people something, gave people something they didn't have, and that's over, so what am I going to do now?

What is the relationship between your work and its audience?

That's such a bizarre thing. I don't think about this enough. I think about it when I'm creating the pedal or document of history. Obviously I'm creating them for an end consumer. Then I walk away when it's done and I watch people enjoy it. But I wonder how that affects me. I scroll through emails and comments about how cool something was, or whatever, but I really do kind of move on from it. Getting good feedback is an important part of the motivation, because if you don't get good feedback, it makes the next thing a little harder. We all want to be told how much people love what we do.

I think I do it because I love giving things to people, in that sense. I love offering history and lessons and products that weren't there. I get a real satisfaction out of those things being enjoyed by people. It's probably more of a subconscious motivation. I've never thought about it that way. But I think there is a connection there. It's part of the motivation to keep doing it.

What is the relationship between yourself and your audience?

The social media age is interesting, in the sense that we have relationships that don't really exist. So I think that's a danger on a personal level, but it's also why certain things work so well.

Believe it or not, the introvert in me has really thrived and grown by doing public interaction and teaching others in person.

Covid has been difficult, but I do travel to a couple of places to talk or do lectures, and I do Patreon talks. And I've learned that if I go teach something to a group of people in a classroom, I actually figure more out as I'm teaching. And I can't do that on YouTube. When I start talking through a prepared lecture, it will get twice as good by the time I'm done. I'll have more notes. Something about the realtime interaction stimulates my mind. I'm surprised by that because I was always so introverted. But I feel like that learned extroverted thing that I've gotten into, actually helps me create.

In terms of the relationship with the audience, on the one side there's YouTube. I make a video and 100,000 to a million people watch it. I don't know who they are, I'll never talk to them. But then I'll go to a classroom with 50 people and it can be life-altering, in terms of the content. It's great for me to work through that.

With pedals, I mostly see people liking them. And there's some interaction where people will send us ideas for new pedals, or for improving products. And I've had some people tell me they hate me. You get the full spectrum. So for me it's kind of all over the place. I think there are two worlds I live in. One is social media, and it's hard to read. It's a bit like a fake Disney world. Things are not what they seem. But then I really thrive on the live interaction with people, and learning through conversation.

What has your audience taught you?

I think the main thing I've been taught by the audience is that apparently I'm not crazy. It can feel that way a little bit. Like, why do I like this so much? Am I wasting my time? Is it actual waste, or is there something happening here? And I think that's what they teach me: that the people who are interested are as crazy as I am. That's what makes art work. I went to the modern art museum in London, and sat and stared at a square on the wall for 10 minutes. That person wasted a lot of time making this square, and I wasted time looking at it. There's a give and take. It's encouraging to know that the thing you love is also loved by other people.

Josh Scott

What has been the greatest challenge in your career?

I think the greatest challenge was most identifiable early on, in the first few years. It was admitting and working through how bad I am at certain things. You start a business, and start creating stuff. A creative person is generally not going to be a great administrator. It's like watching a squirrel in your yard, rushing around all over the place. That doesn't work very well when you're needing to pay bills, do taxes and order parts. But when you find a big challenge, that is an opportunity to get much better at what you're doing, or find the right person to deal with that part of the business. So for me that challenge was like: here are 10 things, and I really suck at eight of them. Admitting that was hard. And it was not natural to me to say, "But I'm really good at two of these things." My family is not like that. So you have to identify your strengths and weaknesses, and get other people in who can do the things you're not good at. Don't micromanage them, don't be annoying, just let them do what they're good at. That will always be a challenge for me. But letting that happen has allowed those people to do those things in a really effective, creative way.

Nick started out building pedals for me when he was 16, and he's now running the YouTube show. But what if I hadn't given him that opportunity? It's a great show because I let him find what he is good at. He's worked for me for 10 years, and I think he's kind of soaked up how I do things. I've seen him just explode creatively. I have tried to take my hands off the things I'm not good at. You have to be really secure to do that. You have to be okay with people making mistakes. But you have to let people live in their creative space. Businesses don't generally do that, because it's seen as wasteful. But we've done that here, for better or worse, and I love it. It's made an environment at JHS that is really forgiving, safe, exploratory, and it makes people work really hard. They're doing what they love to do. We're all wasting time, but out of that, some really great stuff happens.

The reason I use the term 'wasting time', rather than 'investing time', is that JHS is technically a business. And I say 'wasted' in relation to the values of corporate America – the way our dads did business. That's the best way to say it. The way I run JHS, I think that previous generations would roll over in the graves. I do see that time as an investment, but I imagine that most classic business consultants would look at our operation and cringe. Yet it works. And it's so important in creative industries that we have passion for it, beyond simply completing tasks. Wasting time is the best investment.

What has been the high point of your career?

Getting to do this every day is the high point. I think it's really that simple for me. I'm sitting in a room that is a little museum, a bubble where we work on the show, and the history of the subject, then I walk downstairs and there are 35 employees making these products that we've all dreamed up together. It has its challenges, and it's hard work—and sometimes you want to start the day over and forget it happened—but ultimately, I've had some really bad jobs, and this is not one of them.

And obviously it's a high point when you meet a hero of yours and build gear for them. Discovering new stories is always great. And getting to do it every day is really exciting.

What is the most important thing your creative practice has taught you?

Time and time again, the lesson is to trust my instincts, my gut feeling. It feels like it's rarely if ever wrong. And I would add this. It's like a chicken and egg thing. I feel like I trust my gut, because is it somehow harmoniously in tune with reality beyond my understanding? Or is it that I work really hard, and make things work? It could be one or the other, but probably both. It's committing to that gut instinct. I've learned to sense the pedal market. I've learned a ton about the industry, and I know what not to do. I have a lot of knowledge to draw on, and that all informs my business decisions. Or is it the commitment to an idea that excites me? Of course it works if I put all that extra effort into it. But that's the lesson: to go with my gut.

Nothing just happens. Even going back to Roger Mayer, meeting Hendrix. But Mayer probably worked on that fuzz pedal for a hundred hours. I don't know that story. So his perspiration met Jimi's inspiration. I'm not sure anyone wakes up an overnight success. Maybe on social media it happens, but what good is that in the long term?

How did it feel to reflect on creativity today?

Great. As I said, talking through stuff in a live environment really helps clarify things for me. That's why I do these calls. I say no to tons of stuff, but this is right up my alley, and really fun. And these questions offer another angle for prying at the brain. It's refreshing to talk through stuff. It's conversations like this that keep creative people from getting stuck in a rut. It's encouraging. It's creative to talk like this. It's a little bit of that work you need to put in. Talking to someone like-minded and interested in creativity is always healthy for creative people. There's nothing worse than talking to non-creative people about creativity. Because there are intricacies that don't make any sense. Like the semantic discussion about wasting time versus investing time. So it's very helpful and useful.

Matthew Shewchuk

Matthew Shewchuk has over 10 years of experience in factual and scripted content as both a producer and a director. A multiple nominee for various awards, Matt has been a mainstay director on factual and documentary series such as the hit Discovery Channel shows *Highway Thru Hell* and *Heavy Rescue: 401*. He also won a Canadian Screen Award for Best Direction in a Documentary Series for his work on *Ice Pilots NWT* (History Channel).

Most recently, he is an executive producer on *Rust Valley Restorers* (History Channel/Netflix), *Dog Dudes* (Out TV), and the upcoming *Backroad Truckers* (History Channel).

Bigtimedecent.com / Instagram: bigtimedecent

What drew you to your medium?

They say that if you love what you do, you'll never work a day in your life. And I always loved TV and movies. That was my thing. My wife makes fun of me because I've only read 10 or 20 books in my life. During road trips with my hockey team I would always pick the movies at Blockbuster. I always had that kind of attachment to it.

I played college hockey in the United States. I got my finance degree, then came back to the small town I grew up in, and my girlfriend of the time was acting in Montreal. The industry was smaller then. It's a lot busier now with all the Netflix and Amazon projects happening in Canada. She was taking acting classes, and I sat in on one of them and thought it was really interesting. It was with Jacqueline McClintock out of Montreal, who taught the Meisner technique. I was mesmerized and signed up for the class. And I noticed that I seemed to be the only guy with a job. I worked for Davidoff at the time, who had a distribution center in our small town. My company car was a sports car, a Nissan 350Z. And the other students were mostly waiters and bartenders, or came from money. I met some people I really hit it off with. They said they were doing a short film and asked if I had any interest in helping out. I said sure, without even finding out what the project was. I asked how I could help, and they said that judging by my car, maybe I had a bit of money I could invest. So I put in about five grand, and helped out as Executive Producer, and acted as production assistant, and did lots of jobs. And I worked with a group of people who became really close friends to this day. They've become writers in LA and have written movies and become very successful. I tend to say yes to opportunities because I like having new experiences.

Because I dealt with management stuff, through those guys I got some work as a production manager/unit manager on small TV shows that were being shot in Montreal. But those shows dried out, and at the age of 30 I spent some time painting houses. My parents were saying that I had my degree and had to get a real job. But I said that if I work hard and keep at it I'll find my way one day.

Then one of my friends from the short film ended up going to the American Film Institute in LA, and they were shooting a documentary series on pornography. He had just graduated, and a company from Montreal was shooting a series in LA. The show was called *Webdreams*. So he invited me to come down and work on it, and I had to do release forms for people on set, help the director track story, and drive them around. And I was basically an assistant. But it paid okay, and I basically got to go live my dream. At the very least I could say that I'd done what I set out to do.

The shoot was eight months, and it was amazing. A bunch of my friends from Montreal were working down there, and I started working on documentaries. I wanted to do scripted stuff, but I was just a production manager, and scripted TV is a lot more expensive and the networks want you to have experience, a track record. So unless I did something on my own it would be hard to get that experience. I always wanted to direct, so I was working on set to see if I could find my way in, because I'm very ambitious.

On the documentary shoot I saw how it works. It's a team of four, and you have to deal with people. Maybe because of my hockey background, it's easier for me to network, to be social, to work as a team. I loved the fact that it's very fluid – it forces you to think on your feet. I had a supportive director, who was very good. But he was late all the time and irritated the characters once in a while. And my thing is always getting along with people. I got to see how he and the other directors work. We had other hubs which were filming in Montreal, Toronto and Chicago. And I realized that it's not really that hard. All the director was doing was asking questions, and telling the camera guy where to shoot. But if the camera guy is good, they know how to shoot a scene. So you're there to be supportive to the characters. And my parents taught me to care about people and listen. And if you do that, you find that people will open up and tell you their story. So I thought this should be easy for me. Then one director got sick and I was asked to step in and direct a bit. This gave me a little taste of it. And once I got the taste, I kept pushing the production company for more opportunities like that. I had no experience, but I was a bit cocky.

The same company got another series in Vancouver called *The Beat*. We followed the police walking the beat in the Downtown Eastside, which is a very sad part of the city. It's like Vancouver's dirty little secret, but everyone knows about it. It's 10 square blocks of people who are homeless and addicted to drugs.

Then that company hired me to be an assistant director for another director in Vancouver, so I did that for eight months. I worked for two directors, doing the same production assistant role. And I just absorbed everything, from every role. I listen and watch and remember everything, pretty much. I got to watch one of the best directors work, a guy called Todd Serotiuk. I worked with him quite a bit. He was a showrunner on *Highway Thru Hell* when I worked on that. Seeing him work, it was exactly what I thought a director should be when I learned some lessons on *Webdreams*. He cared, he listened, he was respectful, and he didn't overly push. He pushed when he needed to, but not all the time, like some directors do. It meant he could get what he needed in tough situations, because he was respected. It's not a matter of manipulation, it's a matter of understanding and respecting people.

During that shoot I ended up replacing a director at the end of it, and directing the last few episodes. And it went great. So from that I started getting traction with other companies. They knew I would direct, and I would work in the cold, and in difficult conditions. So I worked on *Licensed to Drill* for Discovery Channel Canada in Northern Canada, in the Arctic. I also worked on *Bomb Hunters*, about guys looking for unexploded ordinance from military training. So I worked all over the country. Basically, anything that was hard and dangerous, I would do. I figured that everyone is doing the easy jobs, and my way to get in is by doing the hard jobs.

On *Licensed to Drill*, one director had to leave for a few days, and there was just myself and a sound guy left in the field, and I volunteered to do some shooting. So I had my sound guy carry the reference monitor, while the two of us were tethered. And I was calling my friends who were DPs (directors of photography), and got them to explain every dial and button on the camera for the next two days, so I could shoot a couple of simple scenes, like welding. So nothing super action-driven. But I shot everything, and the producer liked it. And he asked if I could send them anything else I'd directed. So the production company who did the cop show were very nice and put together some footage and sent it to Discovery. And they approved me, based on that. So they asked me to be a director/shooter, working with just a sound guy. I would just shoot all day. And the editors loved it because I had every possible angle and I never missed anything.

So this always feels like I can have fun and play every day, and make a living from it. It's something I always wanted to be a part of, and figure out how it worked.

Do you feel a connection with the history of your medium?

I started in scripted comedy, but I consider myself a documentary filmmaker. But with an understanding of scripted, in terms of making sure that we get all the best material. Because in a documentary you can miss a bunch of stuff. So I make sure that if they say something important badly, I'll get them to say it again. I don't take liberties, but I make sure that the full story is told. Documentary is supposed to be straight storytelling, and people have been telling stories since the beginning of times, since people could communicate. For me I absolutely feel a connection to that history.

Does your medium offer something unique?

I like to compare it to photography, but it is unique in the sense that there are so many ways to film a scene, or an establishing shot, or a beauty shot. I find it gives us a huge amount of options to tell a story. And then you're into editing, and you have a lot of options for how you polish and conform and color the final locked product. There are so many different options. The stories you can tell, and the way you can tell them visually, the pacing, all of it can be adjusted to go a different way, or have a different feeling.

People often ask me about how to deal with different aspects of the production, and how to make decisions and develop the story, but in the end, you just follow. You default to following. We do the interviews, but 90% of the show is what we call a 'follow doc'. The way you see the guys on *Rust Valley Restorers*, is the way they are. If you met them, they would be no different to the way they are on TV. If they mumble, I'll ask them to give it to us again so it's clear. But other than that we just keep going.

We get some wide shots to make sure we have it, in terms of them walking down in the field and stuff, but really it's a follow doc, pure and simple.

There is an element of luck to it too. I consider myself really lucky with some of the stuff that's happened. Like the scene with Avery and the spider bite, where he comes into the yard with his face all swollen up. And Mike and Doug were working on a motor, against a deadline, and they needed to push to get it done. Avery is a very confident mechanic, and Mike had never done that before, tapping out a broken off bolt, so Avery showed up and he did it. But those guys are so honest with who they are. They're self-deprecating. They're real. They're comfortable in their own skin, which is so magical.

We're following Mike's dream, which is to have his own car restoration shop. That's all we're doing. He was doing a car a year before, but then his other business was doing well, and his son had a lot more experience in restoration. And it was just time for Mike to do his own thing, and have fun with it. He's worked his ass off his whole life as a rock scaler. Even now he just went away for two weeks to do a job up north. And they're working up to 14 hours a day, drilling on a rope. The drill is not light, and he's 63. But he loves it. For him it was a vacation. We do get on each other's nerves. He said he needed a break, and he went up north and was living in a camp where they got three squares a day, and he makes a pile of money doing that. And he had a blast. He didn't have to worry about being on a deadline, or about getting parts delivered and all that. It's the same thing with Avery – it's just the way they are.

Why do you have a need to create?

I like learning about all different types of subjects, and people and worlds. With banking or finance, it's kind of like a box, and in that box there's a bunch of information you can learn and once you learn it, that's pretty much it. But with filmmaking, new things are always happening, especially in new video and audio technology. I worked on the Discovery show *Cold Water Cowboys*, which was another dangerous show. On the first season drones didn't exist, but by season two they did, so we could get aerials of the guys fishing and the ocean. So you're learning something new every day.

I'm now learning about the nuances of business affairs in Canada for financing. And with Netflix I'm learning about SVOD (subscription video-on-demand). There is so much to learn and adapt to, which keeps you on your toes. And I like that. Can I compare it to hockey? You have to keep on your toes there or else you get run over, or a puck in the face, or scored on. And I like the fast-paced nature of it, the fluidity.

It's not easy though. The first year on *Rust Valley* I was there pretty much every day. We had budgeted for five months to shoot originally, with two weeks on, two weeks off. So when we're not there the guys could get caught up without us annoying them. But the first day off, Mike had a bunch of cars being worked on. And he calls me up to ask if we could work on one of them, and I said no, we had to shoot that when we came back in two weeks. And it went on like that for all the cars. So he said, "So you're saying we can't work an anything?" And I said, "Okay, we'll be there tomorrow." So we packed up and went back, me and my business partner Tyson Hepburn, who can also shoot and direct. He's amazing. And just the two of us shot those two weeks, before our camera and sound guys came back. We were supposed to be shooting April to September I think. And we ended up going to Christmas.

I'm not the kind of guy to go bungie jumping or skydiving, but for me this is an adrenalin rush. We did a shoot this weekend that was amazing, and you guys are going to see it in a year when it's edited. All I can say is that it was insane. We had two days to film an event, and all the prep and their arrival.

I started meditating about four months ago, to help me handle multiple things at once. We now have a second show that we do called *Backroad Truckers*, which is coming out right around when *Rust Valley* airs. We're wrapping up the editing for that now. It features a couple of guys from *Rust Valley* – Big Donnie and Dave Schwan. They do backroad deliveries, salvaging and a bit of towing. Off-road recovery work. So meditation really helps keep focus, and sanity, through all this. Mike and Avery asked why I was so calm and I told them I'd been meditating. But I said they can't start doing it or it would ruin the show!

So I do this because I have a restlessness, and I'm kind of an adrenalin junkie. I call it 'wading in the shit'. When shit goes sideways, I'm comfortable in the chaos, figuring it out. I thrive on that. I think I need it. That's why I work well on that kind of TV show.

Why do humans have a need to create?

I think creativity keeps you young. Kids like to draw, play and create, and I think all humans like to be creative in their own way. But as you get older, for a lot of people their creativity gets pulled away from them. Or the drive to create.

What sacrifices have you made to pursue your creative path?

I've certainly made sacrifices. I've been living in BC full-time the last three years, and I have not been able to see my family much. But we've made some adjustments with our living situation and now it's a lot better. I'm near the office more, and still go out three or four days a week, but I'm home for supper now.

Mike and Avery are like family. I would have breakfast, lunch and supper with Mike. I live next to him when I'm out there. My back window looks out over the 'field of dreams'. We're all buddies. I'm consider him almost like a second father, in a way.

How has your work shaped you as a person?

It's forced me to be more organized. I naturally listen to people, but it's helped me to listen to people more. I feel like I can get a good read on a person quite quickly.

And the person I am has shaped my work. My mother is Roman Catholic, so I was an alter boy until I was 18. My mother was very active with charities, and she has her own charity. My sister has mental disability. And that has all helped shape my work. I think that's why I listen, because my mom is a great listener. And a great conversationalist. She is very sympathetic and empathetic. And I think that's rubbed off on me. It helps me listen and talk to people. They afforded me an education where I could go to a private school in Maine, and meet people from different parts of the world. I come from a small town in Quebec, and we still have a place there. But I lived a pretty sheltered life until I went to school in Maine. And I made some great friends, who became producers. They took me to Abu Dhabi with them, and I got to meet heads of state. So I can hang out with a wide variety of people, from ex-cons to heads of state, from hillbillies to celebrities. People are just people to me.

When Covid hit, it turned me into a stressed-out, anxious person, because I was away from the shoot, and we were shut down for a while. But for the most part, my life and work overlap so much that they're one in the same.

How do you deal with creative blocks?

For the most part, we don't have to deal with that. Because everything that happens on set is real. But it's a matter of what order you do things. We have to figure out how things connect, but generally I have an answer for it because I know the work intimately. That's one thing I've developed. When I get into a job I learn it inside out, which helps me solve problems.

Because it's so collaborative and everyone's so good, if there is an issue we work it out really quick. It's usually solved within a few minutes. Worst case, we resort back to following.

How do you stay fresh in your work?

If I feel like it's a bit stagnant, I just leave. I'll leave the shoot. And same thing at the office. So I change my environment, simply. And if I ever get a chance, I take a small vacation. But that's rarely possible.

What is your relationship with satisfaction in your work?

    Satisfaction is when you plan on a result, or where something is going to go, like this weekend, and it takes you to a whole other level. I need satisfaction in my work. I'm severely disappointed when things don't work out. Like maybe a few days of filming doesn't give you the result you hoped for. I take it to heart if I don't hit goals. But when a plan is executed and the outcome meets your expectations, I'm super satisfied. But if it exceeds it, that's when it's magic. Like with Avery and the spider bite. All they were tying to do was drill that out, but it happened that he had been bitten by a spider the night before. He was not in great shape, but he just showed up and got it done. And they are just so comfortable being who they are. Avery's laugh is special. Someone edited together a YouTube video of him just laughing for two minutes. It's pretty funny.

    I'm super critical of everything, even down to the way the short standing interviews are framed. We like to keep them a certain way, because we want to keep the audience and the viewer engrossed with the episode.

    Sam Beck is our creative producer and head of story, and Dan Devita is our lead editor, one of the lead creatives, and they do a fantastic job. So usually for me I'm super happy and it's great to see the ride come to fruition. They're really great at what they do. And they are able to control the pacing, and that's the special talent that they have. And the way they work with music is great. They're masters, they're the best. In BC we got nominated for a Canadian Screen Award for best direction, but we want to be nominated in every category. In BC the show got nominated in five categories: editing, writing, cinematography, directing and best series, and we won all five. That's the most satisfying for me, when the team wins. I've won a Canadian Screen Award for another show, *Ice Pilots NWT*. But to win in your home province, all five, that was awesome. They deserve it. They put so many hours in, and it's not easy work.

What is the relationship between your work and its audience?

I make shows that I would like to watch. I like cars, and have a few. My dad has had cars too. I come from a small, blue-collar town where the guys had muscle cars. My father worked in the elevator trade. So they're my people, my demographic, and I like hanging out with these people. But it's amazing to reach out from here to a global audience. We have five-year-old kids watching the show on rerun. For some reason they're captivated by it. People in their 60s, 70s and 80s watch it, for nostalgic reasons. They see cars they grew up with being brought back to life. I want to give the audience the best possible TV show that we can. And I'm lucky to be doing this. So it's a privilege.

What is the relationship between yourself and your audience?

Again, I am the audience. I like to think that I'm curating exactly what they want to see. There is so much extra footage that we can't fit in, so we have to show the best stuff and give them the best bang for their buck.

What has your audience taught you?

That I was right. That people want to watch good, entertaining storytelling. Well done, well executed storytelling. Even in the era of YouTube and Instagram and all that, if the storytelling is good they will sit down and watch a full hour.

What has been the greatest challenge in your career?

This series. It's a slog. Most shows shoot in probably two to three months, like these car shows in the States. But we give it the respect and the time it deserves. It's a marathon, not a sprint. You need to have patience and resilience. Every day you'll need one or the other or both. There is so much that goes into producing a season of this show. We work long days, and do six days a week of filming. Mike takes Sunday off, but we're in touch with him all the time, and if he's doing something interesting he'll usually let us know. Hockey is all about anticipation, and we have to anticipate what car Mike's going to buy or sell next. And he might get a phone call about a deal and go and do it without letting us know. So you have to be there if you want to capture that.

What has been the high point of your career?

Getting season one done, and getting the show renewed for a second season. That put us on the map. The reception to season one was good. But when season two aired and hit Netflix it was another level. The History Channel commissioned the show, and they sell it to Netflix internationally. This gave us the chance to show the world who Mike and Avery are – two special people in a special part of the world, with this love of cars. We're so thankful for that. Once it hit Netflix their Instagram blew up. They went from a few thousand to now almost 250,000 followers. Avery now has nearly 100,00. He loves it. He's kind of awkward and funny in his posts, but great. And Netflix also got us to some viewers in Canada who didn't have the History Channel.

I'll go back to what I said about the satisfaction when something comes together they way you hoped and planned it. That's really special. It validated what we'd done in season one.

There are so many great people in the show. Like J. F. Lanier, the car builder. He's just another guy like Mike, trying to follow his dream. He's just a different version. He does some amazing stuff. I was there from the start with the Riddler trophy journey, where he built that incredible car for the Detroit Autorama, the world's biggest car show. I went to Detroit and took my dad. They made the final eight, but I think they were robbed. They should have won. Their car was perfect. And J. F. was part of a race team which runs at Area 27 racetrack, which was designed by Jacques Villeneuve.

What is the most important thing your creative practice has taught you?

To be patient and organized. To respect everyone, and treat them the way you'd like to be treated. I struggle with that at times, because there's so much going on, and you can't be perfect, but you have to try your best. I've had some bosses that have been total scumbags, and my goal is to not be like them.

And the meditation and yoga certainly helps with all that. I do 20 minutes in the morning, and nine minutes at three other points in the day, and write a journal. It's changed my life.

How did it feel to reflect on creativity today?

It felt great. I love talking and shooting the shit with people. I talk a lot. I said I had a half hour at the start, but I've pushed a bunch of stuff because I love talking about the show, and about the guys. And it's fun revisiting how it's all come together. I really appreciate it and it's really positive.

Dave Smith

Dave Smith is a pioneer in the field of electronic music. In 1974 he founded Sequential Circuits, and in 1977 he designed the Prophet-5, the world's first fully-programmable polyphonic synth. Sequential released many innovative instruments and drum machines over the next 10 years.

Smith was the key developer of MIDI, for which he won a Technical Grammy in 2013. After Sequential, Dave was President of an R&D division of Yamaha, where he worked on physical modeling synthesis and software synthesizer concepts. He then started the Korg R&D group in California, producing the Wavestation and other technology.

As President at Seer Systems he developed the first soft synth in 1994, followed by the first professional soft synth, Reality, in 1997.

In 2002 Smith started Dave Smith Instruments. The product lineup has grown to include the Prophet X, Prophet Rev2, Prophet-6, OB-6, Pro 3, and Prophet 12 synthesizers, and the Tempest drum machine. In 2018 DSI changed its name to Sequential, bringing Dave's legacy full-circle.

sequential.com / Instagram: sequential_llc

What drew you to your medium?

I graduated in 1971 with a degree in electrical engineering and computer science from the University of California, Berkeley. So I was working with computers and knew electronics, and played guitar in bands a little bit, and I'd played piano on and off. The next year, a friend told me he had seen a synthesizer in a music store nearby, in San

Jose, California. So I went to look at it, and it was a Minimoog. And I saw this thing with a keyboard and a whole bunch of knobs and I didn't know what it did, but I knew I had to have it. So I bought it. And I still have it. It's in my office in San Francisco. Somehow it survived the last 50 years. With a lot of work of course.

Initially I thought it was a cool-looking thing, but I didn't really know what it did. I had no experience with synthesizers before that. I knew what oscillators and filters did from the engineering side, but not in terms of a musical instrument. It wasn't like I played a few notes and the sound grabbed me. I don't know that the people in the store knew how to use it anyhow. Because if you set the Minimoog wrong you won't get any sound out, or you get horrible sounds out. It took me a while to get into it, and learn how and why it worked and what was cool, and I started appreciating the sonic aspects more than the feeling that this is a cool thing and I have to have it. Part of the appeal of the Moog was that it was a perfect combination of my backgrounds in music and technology.

They had an ARP Odyssey sitting next to it, but there was no question visually which one I wanted. I'd heard the Moog name, from the *Switched-on Bach* album by Wendy Carlos. I liked classical music, but that album had a big effect on me. That was probably before the Minimoog came out, but it connected everything. As soon as I got that, the Teac 3340 tape deck came out, which was the first multitrack commercial product where you could record and overdub and do it all in sync. Before that I used to do it on a two-track. You'd have to buy a cheap tape recorder which only had a single head, because then you could overdub because there's no delay between the record and the play heads. I used to record people, and play around with stuff that was music equipment-related. But when I got the 3340 I did some multitrack demos, just experimenting. I recorded a few bands with it, but just for fun. So I was messing around with a whole bunch of things that had to do with music electronics. At one point I was thinking of going to San Francisco State University where they had a program for audio recording and learning to work in a studio. So I had a lot of interest, and knew I didn't want to keep working as an engineer. But I had no idea I'd end up where I did.

I started playing around with the Moog, and building accessories for it, for my own use. Then one thing led to another. At the time I was an engineer in what was just becoming Silicon Valley. And over the next five or six years I had a day job, eventually working with microprocessors on different levels. So I started the first Sequential Circuits company in 1974 when I made an analog sequencer, then a digital sequencer, then a programmer. So between '74 and '77 I had a day job, and it was 1977 that I finally quit to work full-time on designing the Prophet-5 synthesizer.

Do you feel a connection with the history of your medium?

Sure. In no small degree I think I'm part of that history, having done this for 50 years. The Prophet-5 was the first of its kind, and pretty much every polyphonic synth since then has been a relative of it. When I was first playing with electronic music stuff I had no idea I would end up becoming friends with Bob Moog, Alan Pearlman, Don Buchla and Tom Oberheim and all these guys who actually started it all. We would all meet up at trade shows and have dinner and hang out and have fun. I was just a kid and they were probably 20 years older than me. You can't predict stuff like that. I didn't have a plan. It just evolved, day to day. Ikutaro Kakehashi is yet another person who needs to be mentioned. He was also a little older than me. He was doing the Jupiter-4 about the same time I was doing the Prophet-5. Everybody knew everybody eventually.

As soon as we showed the Prophet-5 at NAMM in January 1978 everybody went crazy over it. We couldn't ship enough for a year or two. There was no question that this is what everybody wanted. It was pretty fun. At the time, everybody had monosynths, and they were not programmable, generally. Tom Oberheim did have his four voice and eight voice, but they were huge, hard to use and expensive. But this was the first time a keyboard player, who knew nothing about a synth, could play chords, and go from a brass sound to an organ sound by pushing a button. The first time Rick Wakeman saw it he got me on the phone and said, "This is magic." Those were his exact words. So just the functionality was huge; it was a breakthrough. It was fun to play, it sounded really good and it looked cool. It looked like nothing else. And nothing since has looked like that. So I think it was all of these things, but ultimately it was the sound, and that's why people still use it today. It's a fairly simple sound engine, especially compared to modern products, but it has a great sound.

Does your medium offer something unique?

There are a lot of obvious things. Synthesizers make sounds that other instruments can't. It's actually interesting, because if you look back historically, when the Prophet-5 came out, most of the musicians bought it because it was the best emulative instrument at the time. Because they could play harmonica, then push a button and play a harpsichord, then an organ, then a synth sound. A synth sound is not emulative of a classic musical instrument.

Fast-forwarding to the release of the Korg M1 in 1988, that was kind of the end of synthesis for a long time. Because that's what most musicians always wanted. Now they had real piano sounds, they had velocity-sensitive keys, they had 16 voices, and horns and real strings, and they weren't synthetic. And of course we can't do a real piano sound on a synth, generally speaking. You can create an electric piano, but not a real grand piano sound. It's not going to happen. So what happened was, for about 20 years, every synth was a version of the M1. Everything became sample-based. Touring musicians are still that way. They have their big FANTOM or Triton or whatever, and they have 88 keys and can cover whatever they need to on a sample basis. So that was part of the reason that the whole synth thing died down in the 80s. By the end of the decade, most players weren't interested, and you had all these vintage synths sitting in garages, and you could buy them for nothing. I call that 'the digital dark ages'.

Dave Smith

I started my company, Dave Smith Instruments, in 2002 and started shipping the Evolver monosynth. It had analog filters and so forth. And Bob Moog introduced the Minimoog Voyager the same year. I point to that as roughly the start of the analog synth revival. And as Moog and I came out with more products, so did others, and they overlapped with musicians buying the old synths. At first they were really cheap, so those players could get a vintage synth for not much money. People could find an old ARP or Moog in a closet and buy it for $50 and start making music with it. What's different this time around is that people buy it because they want a synth. If they want a sampler they can buy a sampler. But synths have a sound and a personality that is completely different. That's why I don't think it's going to go away this time. I think the basic subtractive synthesis engine of two oscillators, a low-pass filter and some envelope generators and an amp, has passed the test of time. It's been around for over 50 years. Everybody knows what it sounds like, everybody knows what will happen if you go to any synth and turn the cutoff knob or the resonance knob. And there's just something magic about it.

The other thing that I think is really cool which we've been able to do at Sequential in the last five or six years, is to retrain musicians that it's okay to spend $3,000 on something that only has six voices. And to teach them that every synth has its own personality. We have a Prophet-6 and an OB-6. They both have six voices, and a lot of similar features. There is a lot of common technology in them, but they sound different. If you play both, one will speak to you more than the other. So I remind people that guitar players will have 10 guitars. Why? They all have six strings. What could possibly be different if they all have six strings and three knobs? They might have three Stratocasters. Why? It's because they are all unique. It's all about the look, the feel, the interaction, the tone, the musicality. All of that stuff is really important. And I think that synth players are just beginning to realize that in the last five or 10 years. Features count, but it's the basic personality and sound of the synth. We have all our synths set up in our demo room, so a musician will come in and play the Prophet-6, then the OB-6, and a lot of them will immediately go to one or the other. But a large amount of our customers buy both. They get one first then the other later, because it's a different instrument. Of course you can make sounds that are somewhat similar if you tweak things just right, but generally speaking they're different. So that's been pretty fun. That's the whole magic of synths. We're making unique instruments that have their own feel, their own sound, and people get it and love it, and are making a lot of great music with it.

Why do you have a need to create?

I don't know. I've never really thought about it that way. There was a period between the two Sequential companies where I was doing a little consulting here and there. Then I worked on soft synths for a while. I did have some epiphanies, because I developed the very first professional soft synth in 1995 called Reality. But although it worked, I quickly realized there was no fun factor. I want to be able to turn a knob and it will always do the same thing. And I don't have to upgrade it, or scroll through pages. To me, software isn't a musical instrument. And if you buy it today it won't work in two years because the operating system has changed. And you spend all your time developing the same product over and over to keep it working.

But from a big overview, the one thing I'm probably most proud of in my career is the fact that I've been able to do this twice. I did the first Sequential Circuits and we had a lot of firsts. We were very successful in a rollercoaster sort of way for a few years. And to be able to come back 20 or 30 years later and do it again with the new Sequential, that means a lot to me. You could argue that I did the Prophet-5 at the right time because everything was ripe for someone else to do it first, so maybe I was lucky. But this time around, it's been a matter of crafting musical instruments, learning again, seeing how people use them, seeing what people want, thinking of new things that could be done. And to see that become a lot more successful than the original company has been pretty cool.

But as far as why I like to do it, even now I'm heavily involved in the design of both the hardware and software side. There is something magical about starting with nothing, and ending up with a new musical instrument that didn't exist before. There are not that many people that can do that. If you build a guitar, it can be really nice, and a better instrument than most, but you're still building a guitar. But here, we're making new instruments and there's nothing else like it. I don't think I'll ever stop. I turned 70 this year, and am slowing down to a degree because I've got other stuff to do, but I always want to be involved, because it's somehow ended up being my life. It was unplanned, it's just the way it happened, but I'm still enjoying it.

And the other major part of all this is that I've got a ton of friends who play in bands at all levels, friends who are DJs, and I love it when they play in town and invite us to their show, or come and hang out in the office. And seeing them playing our instruments live or on records, it's pretty hard to describe how cool that is. Because if you develop a musical instrument and nobody plays it, who cares? It doesn't matter how good it is; if no one is recording with it or playing it live, you're kind of missing the point. To me, that's a huge part of the payoff. So the last six months of lockdown has driven me crazy, being unable to go and see live music, or travel, or hang out with my friends. And probably for another nine months or a year it's going to be like this. This is why I've been burying myself in more synth designs.

Why do humans have a need to create?

I think it's just part of us. I can't tell you from a biological, evolutionary standpoint why that is, but clearly people have been making music forever. Whether it's banging on some logs, or plucking a string, or blowing on something that makes a noise. It's interesting that music has always been technology-driven. So at one time someone figured out how to cut holes in a tube and blow in it to make music. And eventually you had the development of simple stringed instruments. One of my favorite examples is the pipe organ, which is an attempt to be the first emulative synth. And that was all done with metal pipes, wood, felt and leather. I have an old pump organ that's 120 years old that I restored a long time ago. And it was fun to work on it and understand how it works. So synthesizers were just an evolutionary point on that curve.

But as far as why humans are creative, it's just something in our DNA. It's what we do. Most people are creative in some way. I wish I was a better musician, but I somehow don't have what it takes to get to that higher level of inventiveness. But on the other hand, I seem to have an ability to develop instruments that are new and interesting and usable. And that is certainly creativity and artistry, if you think about it that way. So I think we all have our skills, and we are all jealous of people who have skills that we wish we had. But I think it's just part of human nature.

What sacrifices have you made to pursue your creative path?

The first time around, when I quit my job to pursue this, I was living off credit cards and never had money to do anything. I was working night and day. But I was also in my 20s and I was doing something I really liked. I would be hard-pressed to call that sacrificing. And even now I sometimes think I don't really want to be running a company, but to be fair to my employees, I don't really run the company. Everyone knows what they have to do, and I give guidance on a technical and product basis, but our company structure is not top-down. I avoid that as it's not something I like to do. We do run into challenges, but we deal with them. I remind people every once in a while that if this was easy, everyone would do it. And you can have things like parts shortages, or parts not working right, or bugs showing up on just a couple of units. There's always some fire to put out. So it's not just being creative and designing instruments – the fun part. There is the reality of producing lots of units and shipping them around the world and keeping them running. It's not trivial.

But I can't say I've ever really sacrificed, compared to 90% of the world, and how people have to live. I'm incredibly lucky to be where I am, and to have had the career I've had. I've been on panels where people talk about luck, and I do think luck is involved, but it's also about working really hard, and being willing to put your ass on the line. At some point you have to decide to go for it, because you believe in it. Which is what I did when I quit my job originally and started working on the Prophet-5. It could have been a spectacular failure. Maybe it would never have worked, or sounded like shit. There are all kinds of possibilities, but you have to put your ass on the line, and go for it, and work really hard. You have to be lucky sometimes, but the fact that I was able to do it a second time means that it wasn't all luck.

How has your work shaped you as a person?

At times I could be termed a workaholic I suppose. Though I try to get out. I've always had a number of hobbies that I do. When I was raising a family, our two kids, all I seemed to do was work and ride my bike. And that's also because I was working at home. So I was always there, and was quite often working. But that doesn't mean we didn't do stuff as a family and go on trips. In fact, once the kids got a little older, our family outings were usually to go to a concert, or a work tour or to different shows. And they would love it because we all generally liked the same music. And they'd get to meet some of the artists, which was a thrill. The music has been a good connection as they were growing up.

Beyond that, it's funny because I don't usually reflect on the fact that I am who I am. People might see me the same way that I used to see Bob Moog. But I don't really think about this stuff outside of interviews. Because I've always been a person who would rather look to what's next. The whole MIDI thing was definitely in that category. It was something I did part-time for a few months, and sure I kind of got the ball rolling on that, and made sure it happened. I got a Grammy for it, and that's pretty cool. But I consider that a minor part of my career. I would rather be known for my instrument designs than for MIDI.

Right now I'm thinking about my new products. Today we've announced the release of the Prophet-5 Rev4. I think of it as my 70th birthday present to the world. That's a lot of fun. And we're already working on the next products after that. And that's what keeps me going.

How do you deal with creative blocks?

I don't get creative blocks. Part of that is because I work with a lot of great people. That was one of the reasons I changed the name from Dave Smith Instruments back to Sequential. Everybody in the company is a synth freak, and they know their stuff, and all come from a different direction. So we have lively arguments when we're designing new products. Andrew McGowan worked at Sequential Circuits back in 1979, then worked for me at Seer Systems, and he was my first employee at DSI. He's the other main synth designer. We'll always be trading ideas. And when we both agree on something, that usually means that this is something that we have to pay attention to. So there's never any shortage of ideas.

And we've been known to change our minds. We have the Prophet-5 Rev4 we are just introducing. And then we had a product we want to do for the second quarter next year, and another for the end of next year. And that was the plan for a long time. And just in the last two weeks we've changed our mind, and we're going to do something different for early next year. In fact we may do two products at the same time. Because something popped up, and as everyone started thinking about it we got excited by the idea. So there's never been a time when we're wondering what we're going to build next. We're always talking about a lot of things. We talked about making effects pedals, because we have a ton of both analog and digital technology, so we could build almost anything. And we've even gone as far as drawing up front panels, but we never do it because we always want to do a musical instrument instead. We're always talking about projects and what's next, so we've never finished a product and wondered what we're going to do now. And we have a lot of time. It's not like we're writing, and have to produce every day.

How do you stay fresh in your work?

As a company we're all trading ideas, so that never gets stale. Speaking for my employees, they all have jobs, and they're not always fun. If you're doing customer support it's not necessarily a fun job to do all the time, but they still have a great time contributing to the designs and working on prototypes, so it's a mix of all that.

We also have a lot of musicians who use our products that we see from time to time, and a smaller group that we work with more regularly. And they'll make suggestions, which sometimes get incorporated. Generally speaking, that's one of our advantages compared to a big company, when we start working on a new product. They will have a marketing and sales department that produce specs that go to the engineering department who figure out how to make it. The marketing and sales guys are talking to hundreds of people in the company. We don't do any of that. We don't need to ask anybody, we just do what we want to do, and for that reason it's quick. From the idea we'll start drawing on a whiteboard and sketch out a rough front panel, then draw up the real front panel, and will argue over what knobs should and should not be there. I've always been a fan of constrained design. I don't feel a need to put every feature on a product, because I feel it unnecessarily complicates it. You could think of that like recording a song. Some people give the song everything it needs with just an acoustic guitar and vocals. Then someone else might want to add drums and bass. And it might end up with strings and horns too. And maybe some synths and low effects and so on. The same parallel exists in designing an instrument. Sometimes you want to overproduce a song, because it works for that particular song. But other times you want it to be real spare and clean. But the temptation, especially these days, is always to add something else. And before you know it the track has gotten out of hand and you've lost the focus of the song. Likewise, you don't have to have every feature on every instrument. We'll argue back and forth about a single switch. We can see that it would be cool, but is it really necessary? There's a craft to that, and I can't define it or spell out rules to it. It's just us using our experience to discuss all the pros and cons, and make a good decision.

What is your relationship with satisfaction in your work?

Going to the trade shows is one of my favorite things to do. You'll see some kids come up and put the headphones on and start to play with one of our synths. They'll push a couple of buttons and then you'll see them smile, and they'll play a bit more and you'll see them start to laugh. And then they play a bit more and start shrieking and they grab their friends and put the headphones on them.

Another thing that happened back in the 90s was that everyone started using soft synths, because they're cheap and everybody's got a computer. So they're easy to work with. And we'd see people, who were only used to soft synths, come up and play one of our synths, and they'd say, "Okay, I get it now." So that's generally what happened. We sell lots of stuff and business has been great for years now.

One of the most magical parts of development is that you design it, you build the metal, we build all the circuit boards, then get the software ready and start testing, and then there is that day when you press a key and sound comes out for the first time. And that's always a great feeling. It's not going to work all the way, and it might be out of tune, but there's sound, and for some reason for me that's a magic moment, where you are going from development to having a working musical instrument.

I always get serial number one of each new instrument. The Pro 3 SE behind me is serial number one, for example. It's never easy getting something into production and we're dealing with that right now on our new Prophet-5. So there is always a feeling of relief when you finally get there. And there is excitement, because we announce the product on the same day that sales open up. So you get to see the reaction from people. That's the ritual: announcing it, seeing the response, me getting the first unit, and us beginning to sell and ship. At the factory we'll see stacks of units and boxes. And then a week later we're in full production and shipping units around the world.

What is the relationship between your work and its audience?

Our work is building musical instruments, and our audience is the musicians who use them. And they range from many of the top professional musicians, down to hobbyists. There are a lot of hobbyists, who build home studios and have a bunch of synths. And there are a lot of collectors out there. A lot of companies have cryptic serial numbers, but we've always kept it simple and just started at one. Some people like getting low serial numbers, and a couple of people like to always get the same serial number on all our products, so we accommodate them.

Doing NAMM is always fun. When we have a new product we try to announce it the first morning of NAMM. We've done that a number of times. So everyone comes rushing to our booth first thing because they want to be the first to see it and post something on social media or a forum. And we see the whole range at our booth. Sometimes it's just kids who don't know much about synths. Sometimes it's the hobbyists who have a bunch of synths at home, but they're not pros. Some are semi-pros who play in bands. Then there are the real pros, and then the top-level pros. Like Stevie Wonder would come by and see whatever we have that's new and he would sit there and play it for a while. Seeing these guys playing our synths can certainly boost your ego.

Below the elite level there are the pros that maybe you would not have heard, but they could be composers, or studio players, session guys or others that make a living playing music, but they are not household names. So we get that whole range at NAMM come and check out the instruments. We do get feedback from them, but mostly it's just hanging out with our friends. A lot of them we only see once or twice a year. Sometimes we don't even talk about the new instrument, we'll just be hanging out, catching up.

What has your audience taught you?

    They keep the music as the primary focus. As I mentioned, in terms of development we just do what we want. The communication with the artists is more about hanging out as friends and going to their shows. It is a reminder that this is all about music. That's really the bottom line.

    I love live music. When I listen to recorded music, I don't listen to a super wide range of styles, but when I see music live I could watch anything. I'll watch a band at a concert and enjoy it, but I wouldn't want to listen to the album at home. Because there is something about live performance. It's inspiring. I love the energy, everything about it. And to go back after and talk to them about the show is fun. Everything about it is awesome.

What has been the greatest challenge in your career?

    There was a period, probably between 1989 and the early 2000s, where I could say I was somewhat directionless. I didn't really have what I would call a career. After Sequential I worked for Yamaha in R&D for a little bit, then I started the Korg R&D group in San Jose, and it's actually still there. Then I was raising a family. In the mid-90s I got back into soft synths for a couple of years. But I wasn't totally inspired to immediately go out and do something. But that was a pretty big spread of about 15 years where apart from the soft synths I didn't really produce anything. We did the Wavestation at Korg and I was involved with that. It was a pretty cool synth. But I wasn't really doing anything on my own until I did the Evolver. I had to relearn a lot of things because I hadn't designed hardware in 20 years. But that's when I finally got my direction again.

And it worked out, because I couldn't design anything on my own for a while as the costs were too high. You needed custom circuits, and everything was going that sampling route, so even if I had come out with something, the timing wouldn't have been right. So it goes both ways. Now, my company has been going for 18 years, which is a lot longer than the first Sequential.

When I made the Evolver, what happened was that Roger Linn had a product he was working on called the AdrenaLinn. It's a guitar processing box. We were always friends and worked on different things together. He was having a bit of trouble finishing it up so I offered to help. It was a hardware project with a microprocessor and a DSP (digital signal processor) chip and I had another epiphany. I realized how much fun it was to develop a product that I could hold in my hands and it always works the same way. There's hardware and software and the UI, and I thought this is actually cool, and nobody was doing this anymore. So I said I'm going to design a new synth. If you look at the Evolver desktop, there are actually some things that are similar to the AdrenaLinn, because that was my starting point in terms of a matrix front panel for controls. But my original idea for that was to use analog electronics, tightly coupled with digital. I had worked with physical modeling in the late 80s and 90s for a while, and I thought it was an interesting principle. So I used some of those basic principles, but tied it in with analog filters, so there are some unique things in there. When it first came out a lot of people didn't know what it was and no one was buying synths, and this was kind of an unusual synth. But some people loved it. It became a starting point, and for the first time in a long time I had made something I could hold, and it made cool sounds and was very easy to use, and it was something new.

What has been the high point of your career?

The Prophet-5, and restarting this company, have probably been the main high points. It's hard to pick a bunch of specific instruments because there have been so many and they're all awesome for what they do. One highlight has been having two companies that have both been successful in the sense that musicians love the products and play them.

When I got my Grammy Award for developing MIDI, there were hints that it was in the works. Everyone makes fun of Grammys until they give you one, and then of course you're very gracious. What was interesting about it is that I live in a small town, and people never really understood what I did. I would start describing it and their eyes would kind of glaze over. But when I got a Grammy it was like, 'Oh, you're doing something real.' But it was awesome going to the ceremony. They give those out the day before with other lifetime achievement awards and so on. So we had a bunch of friends come down and we had a great time. And I now have a Grammy sitting in the office, which is impressive. But, I would much rather have a Grammy for my work as a musical instrument designer. The chances of that are slim because I already have one. But that's the thing I'm more proud of, career-wise. The MIDI thing was an amazing thing to work on, but it's not the core of what I do.

I'm 70 and could be retired, but retirement can be overrated. I would much rather keep my mind active by designing new instruments and working on a lot of new stuff. But I'm no longer a workaholic. I take lots of trips, and take time off. So I'm not nose to the grindstone all the time. I have a good balance. It's kind of like I'm retired when I want to be, and I can work when I want to. But of course for the last six months I've done nothing but work because I can't go anywhere. A year ago at this time we were in Portugal for two weeks. In late May we always go to the Movement Festival in Detroit because we have a lot of DJ friends and that's always a good time. So those are the kinds of things that we miss. In Portugal there was the BPM Festival, kind of a DJ thing going on, so we went down to the beach where it was happening, and a lot of friends of ours were playing. So we got to reconnect with a bunch of them. Almost any time we travel we'll run into friends. Like Ibiza, Berlin and all these places. Hanging out with the DJ gang is always a good time. It's completely different. I'm not going to get into any arguments over the artistry of a DJ versus the artistry of a band because it's apples and oranges. It's just great fun and I really miss that.

What is the most important thing your creative practice has taught you?

To keep it fun. Creativity needs to be fun. If I'm not enjoying the process of developing something, if it becomes work, then it doesn't have the same spark, the same magic. The first time I get a sound out of a new product is wonderful. But then that keeps going. Now I've got it in tune. Now I've got the filter working perfectly. There's always a point in a design where I'm testing a new thing, and I realize I just lost a half hour because I've just been playing with the instrument because it sounds really good and is fun to use. That's always a good sign because it means that the basic instrument concept and design is good. So the most important thing is to keep it fun. If it's not fun you're probably doing the wrong thing, and I don't want to be creative if it's not fun.

How did it feel to reflect on creativity today?

It's hard to make rules about creativity. Like: what's the difference between creativity and artistry? I don't know. I'm not all that interested in philosophy. You could argue, as people have for the last 50 years, that music these days is not as creative or original, that it's all derivative and all sounds the same. That's probably been the case in any decade. And I think it's true today. But there's still innovation, and creativity. Someone comes out with a good song, but it sounds similar to a lot of others. So is that creative? It's a good song, so I guess it's creative, but it's not original. And how important is originality in creativity? Can you be both derivative and creative? There's always creativity, in any category. When you see something that no one else has done before, that's probably a simple way to define creativity.

Kazuaki Tanahashi

Kazuaki Tanahashi is a painter and calligrapher, exhibiting worldwide. As a Buddhist scholar, he has translated the writings of Dogen, a great Zen master of thirteenth-century Japan. As a peace activist, he is the director of A World Without Armies and a Fellow of the World Academy of Art and Science. He was born in Japan in 1933 and has been active in the USA since 1977.

His publications include *Brush Mind, Painting Peace: Art at a Time of Global Crisis, Peace or War, Heart of the Brush: Splendor of East Asian Calligraphy, Treasury of the True Dharma Eye: Zen Master Dogen's Shobo Genzo*, and *The Heart Sutra: A Comprehensive Guide to the Classic of Mahayana Buddhism*.

brushmind.net

What drew you to your medium?

East Asian calligraphy—Chinese, Korean, or Japanese—fascinated me in my youth. There is so much to learn and express. So, I became serious and eventually started exhibiting my artwork.

I also studied oil painting and Western drawing at the same time. I then began combining these disciplines. For example, calligraphers don't go off the edge of the paper, but painters do. So I did calligraphy in an expressive, Western painter's way.

I studied calligraphy in a small town near the city of Nagoya in the central part of Japan. I was tutored in a class at a local community center. I didn't want to study with a famous calligrapher or painter, because I would be his or her student for the rest of my life. So, I chose someone who was not well known.

Do you feel a connection with the history of your medium?

East Asian and Western calligraphers are generally classicists. In these traditions you study classic works, become familiar with them, then deepen your understanding. By faithfully copying, you learn the aesthetics and techniques to develop your skills. I've written a book called *Heart of the Brush: Splendor of East Asian Calligraphy*. It shows how to compare and appreciate different works from ancient times, and then reproduce certain pieces. I call it 'close study'. This is the best way to study calligraphy.

The brush is part of yourself. It allows you to extend your being. Its bristle has a different shape each time you hold it. It has its own temperament, so you need to feel, listen, and be one with the brush.

Eventually, I started making large paintings. There is the biggest commercially-available brush, and there is a larger one commissioned from the brush maker in Nanjing, China, but all are limited in size. So, I started constructing my own brushes. Nowadays I have my studio assistant make a large flat brush, which is one meter or more wide. I pour paint on the canvas and dance with it. Within a minute, you see a large landscape with a lot of movements in it. In such a creation there is joy and excitement, as well as serenity. It is a feeling of being calmly excited.

Does your medium offer something unique?

What is essential in East Asian calligraphy and painting is for the artist to be present. The brush is soft, and it reflects all your pressure, movement and speed. But there is another aspect, which is your own feeling and thinking. And even further, your being. If you are not present, it is apparent in the work. To be fully present each moment, you must be fully alive and focused. To be focused, you need to be relaxed. All these elements come together in one stroke of even one ideograph. Then I asked myself: if one stroke expresses all my being, why not make a painting with just one stoke? Thus, I developed the genre of one-stroke painting. This is typically done on a large canvas, one meter by one meter, or even larger. But it is done fairly fast. I don't make complex shapes but move the brush from one side to the other, or from top to bottom, without going back and making corrections.

This is an extension of my lifetime study of calligraphy. It is about being fully present, and accepting whatever happens. Not trying to be perfect, but to be complete. In order to be complete, to be whole, you include perfection and imperfection. If you say that you don't like one part of the painting, then try to fix it, this may destroy the whole painting. So, to accept the whole is important. Of course, if you don't like it, you can throw it out and try again. You might create paintings that lack presence many times, but in one particular painting it may truly express your presence. In that way, you learn how not to be not present.

I don't have a particular way of preparing for such one-stroke painting, because I think each stroke should express my whole life. When I perform, I'm not always in the best condition. I may be tired or concerned about something else. But to be present at any time, even in the worst situation, comes from practice.

Why do you have a need to create?

Doing artwork is exciting. It is always different. New things happen each time. Each undertaking is discovery. So, it is a lot of joy. I also write, which is creative. But in writing, you have to be perfect. You keep revising. Some kind of painting is more complex. In oil painting you add more layers and keep improving. But what I do is spontaneous and decisive.

Why do humans have a need to create?

Everyone wants to be different. Or to contribute something in singing, dancing or writing poetry. I think we all have a need for expression, in different ways and in different degrees. Some people are outstanding. Others don't try to excel. But everyone needs to express in some way. Even conversation can be a creative act.

What sacrifices have you made to pursue your creative path?

Perhaps being creative is being different from others. So, in a way, I am not as conformed or living in a repetitious way. I have my own routine, but I'm not doing it with other people.

It is not easy to make a living by being creative. In fact, you must be creative in bringing income. I do a number of things to make a living. I sell my painting and calligraphy, I write and publish books, I do exhibitions and performance, and I teach.

How has your work shaped you as a person?

To do calligraphy and painting, you need to go beyond the normal expectations or rules. You need to be wild and free. I had to train myself to be freer, and to be bolder. So, painting teaches me to shape my own character, and my style of writing. In a way, my painting is always guiding me to transform my own personality.

How do you deal with creative blocks?

Creative blocks are in your mind. If you want to be brilliant, have great ideas, and breakthroughs right away, you may run into blocks. But I think breakthroughs can happen any time. They come when you keep working and encounter problems you need to solve. I sometimes get bored doing one thing for a long time, then I do something else. I might write. Or I might do painting instead of calligraphy, or vice versa.

How do you stay fresh in your work?

What helps me keep myself fresh is to find something that seems impossible, then find a way to make it possible. Like when I write a book, sometimes I don't know the subject so well, but by the time I finish the book, I know it well enough to create my own understanding and theories. I might then come up with a unique perspective.

In Japan if you are a calligrapher, you might specialize in phonetic writing, formal script, cursive script, seal carving or something else. You become famous in one small area and keep showing your work. But you don't invade other people's fields. Calligraphers would not paint, speak about politics, or do peace work. People who take a single path are respected. But that's too limiting for me. I would be bored doing just one thing. So eventually I left Japan. The United State is different. You can do anything. I began to do peace work, and talk about demilitarizing nations. People might say, "You are an artist. Why do you have to worry about nuclear weapons?" I think everyone should. I often think about failed democracy, so I have started an organization called Fair Democracy Think Tank. People might say, "You are not a sociologist." But I can talk to sociologists and learn from them. All these divisions are in your mind. To me, artists are not confined to any kind of compartmentalization.

What is your relationship with satisfaction in your work?

As I suggested, if you aim for perfection, you will never be satisfied. I go for completion. Completion includes everything, perfect and imperfect, beautiful and not beautiful. In a way, I am easily satisfied, so I am always happy.

What is the relationship between your work and its audience?

In terms of viewers, buyers and collectors, some people may just like my paintings and contact me. Most of them, however, are those who have read my books, seen my demonstrations, or come to my workshops. So we have some affinity. They want to have something from me or support my life. I am grateful that people are moved to be interested in my work. I would like to be an artist for everyone, not just the rich. I want my artwork to be affordable to students.

What is the relationship between yourself and your audience?

Sometimes people ask me to do things that open up a new way of thinking and creating. Other people may like one of my paintings and ask me to create something similar. But to imitate my own work is impossible, because a lot of it is done spontaneously. I can anticipate and welcome accidents, but no one can micromanage accidents. As I do not succeed in imitating my own work, I try not to get that kind of commission.

What has your audience taught you?

I have found that many people connect with an idea that came out of painting Zen circles. Zen circles are decisively drawn black circles with a brush. Then, I started doing multicolor Zen circles, using different colors. I don't number them, but instead call every piece 'Miracles of Each Moment'. People like it. It can remind us that each moment is full of miracles.

What has been the greatest challenge in your career?

In 1993 I had the idea of making a painting titled 'The Circle of All Nations', for the 50th anniversary of the United Nations. The UN Charter was signed in San Francisco in 1945. I wanted to make a big circle and install it for its official celebration in front of the building where the Charter was signed. I formed a group of collaborators, got permission from the building, the police, the United Nations Association, and so on. The idea was to have people from seven continents paint together. We therefore made a brush to be held by seven painters, which was designed by two architects. We spread five strips of canvas, in total six and a half meters wide and eight meters long, outdoors in the UN Plaza in San Francisco. We had children pour paint of different colors on designated spots, then seven of us brushed it into a circle. Pleasing the public is not a goal of my painting, but this piece had to be liked by people. So, I said that if the painting we create had some problems, we would touch it up. But we did not have to. We had a pencil line, which we followed, and it worked amazingly well. We then hung it on the front side of the building, which was a challenge of its own, due to its size and weight in the midst of a June wind. The whole thing was a logistical nightmare, but it went well.

What has been the high point of your career?

I think the high point of my career is right now. I am 87 years old but still active and productive. I have a humble but workable studio and a large art storage and display room, as well as a trained studio assistant. I paint four, five or six fairly large paintings (81 cm x 91 cm, or 150 cm x 182 cm) in one hour. I do this once or twice a week. Every three months I get through a roll of canvas which is one and a half meters wide, and fifty meters long. New ideas pour out in every session.

What is the most important thing your creative practice has taught you?

To be relaxed, to enjoy, and to be healthy. To de-age.

How did it feel to reflect on creativity today?

Thinking about my own artistic career, I feel fortunate because I could pioneer in different fields. East Asian artists are largely confined to a medium of black ink on paper, but I started using canvas and colors for calligraphy. East Asian paper is thin, so you cannot strike it with a brush too hard, and splashes can be absorbed and turn into blots, so a brush movement loses its power. But canvas is a great medium. When you strike the canvas with the brush, the paint stays there as it is, so it keeps that explosion forever. I sometimes joke that I am not an expressionist, but an explosionist.

The circle has been drawn for centuries in Zen tradition. It is an expression of enlightenment. In the United States, diversity is important, so I started using multiple colors.

I always wanted to do one-stroke painting, but I thought it was like having a party by myself. There is no interaction between the lines. But now I have been doing this for some decades, and it's a wonderful genre. With one brush movement, using a large brush, I can create a big landscape, with a lot of colors, feelings, energy, spirit, and presence on the canvas. It literally shows the miracles of each moment. In every moment there are many things happening, a lot of thoughts and feelings, a lot of understanding. Each moment is so complex, profound and vast.

I am afraid that in contemporary art, a lot of works are just invention. Like someone paints a whole canvas flat yellow, or flat black, and others do a similar thing in different ways. To me an important thing in contemporary art is to be human. To be alive, focused, to be fully in the present moment. To be fully in the present moment means to learn from the past, to work for the future, to be aware of the space around us, and be socially engaged. The world can be our canvas.

Eda Elif Tibet

Dr. Eda Elif Tibet is a visual anthropologist and an award-winning independent documentary filmmaker. She is the founder of KARMAMOTION, a film collective of cultural media and film creators. She has filmed and produced seven award-winning films, which have been shown at film festivals around the world and been broadcast on television. Her films are: *Aït Atta: Nomads of the High Atlas, Awakening: a Fairy Tale, Refugee Here I Am, Ballad for Syria, Hey Goat!, Amchi, and 28 Days on the Moon.* She is a postdoctoral researcher at the Critical Sustainability Unit at the University of Bern and a multi-modal media communications specialist consulting with various environmental foundations around issues of sustainability, local livelihood rights and mobilities.

karmamotion.com / Instagram: freetibetto

What drew you to your medium?

I think a lot of what attracts us has its roots in childhood. I was born in Istanbul in Turkey in 1987 but I was raised in Madrid, Spain and then in Lisbon, Portugal. So my introduction to the social world was a bit of a displaced one. We were living in a beautiful riviera called Parede very close to Cascais, just next to the ocean. We spoke Turkish at home, but I also spoke Spanish, Portuguese and English outside. I went to a Catholic British school, and we learned English there, but I was surrounded by Portuguese children. So I grew up in mostly a Mediterranean culture. It's beautiful, because I have bits of everything, but it's not easy to be accepted by other children when you are different. So the first year of school was a bit painful, as I got a bit of discrimination. I wasn't bullied, but I was not included. So I started making up little games by myself because no one was playing with me. And this was my way of trying to make sense of things. I was paying attention to things, observing, and trying to understand. I was trying to make plans and strategies on how I can be included. I was looking for an access point. Luckily there were other foreign students, so my best friend became a Japanese girl, Ayakko. She introduced me to Japanese cartoons such as *Sailor Moon*, and I loved her very interesting lunch boxes her mother prepared with great care. Ayakko was so kind, and she shared it all with me. Her birthday parties were also very interesting, with all the Japanese food and games. However my favorite snack at school was the Portuguese milk bread filled with chocolate, which I did not spend a day without.

During the week we enjoyed my mom's Turkish cooking (which was the best) and during weekends with family we would go sightseeing, listen to Fado music, and go to the ocean, where I tried to surf, and enjoy the delicacies that I loved. I don't think I would have had exposure to such culinary variety if I'd grown up in Turkey. So at an early age I had experienced the beauties of migration but also the existential crisis of it, the struggle to belong. But I wasn't aware of it at the time. I was just living the consequences.

I used to have this image of an eye that was watching what I was doing the whole day. A bit like Instagram today. I had the feeling that I wanted people to see what I was seeing. So my filmmaking really goes back to that desire to make sense of my reality and conditions, where I was trying to make friends, trying to socialize and to show the world my point of view, which was a bit displaced.

Moving forward to 2007, just prior to graduating with my BA in economics, I went to India to do an AIESEC internship. It was quite popular among business administration and economics students to do that at the time, but normally people would go to the West. Few chose to go to the East. In fact I was among the first to do that from Turkey. I did my internship at what is considered India's Harvard: the Indian School of Business. It was one of the most amazing experiences of my life. It was genuinely life-changing and transformative. I spent time with highly intelligent people, and learnt so much from them. Not just on how to be an entrepreneurial success, but how to manage the inner self before you manage the world. There I discovered my passion to document cultures. My mind was blown by India's colors, richness, diversity, beauty and heritage. It was like a constant feast for the ears, eyes, taste buds, and senses that you did not even know of.

I had always been interested in photography, but then I wanted to do documentary films. My background did not suit a jump into film school, but I found a middle way, which was visual anthropology. I think I became the first Turkish woman to step into that field. Nobody knew about it at the time. The masters programs were quite new.

Visual anthropology as a tradition has been around for 60 or 70 years. But in terms of specific studies, it may have only existed for around 15 years. It was really social anthropology as a discipline. So visual anthropology opened the way to attract a lot more people who did not want to just be academics, or people who wanted to do ethnographic, observation studies through film. At that point I went to the University of Kent, in England. That institution was very concerned with conservation and environment, so it wasn't just traditional anthropology, or visual anthropology. It was much broader. That is how I connected to the Global Environments Network, and the Global Diversity Foundation. They funded our film in Morocco. We did the film 10 years after meeting those people.

To me filmmaking is very relational. Like one film gives birth to the next. And I do films with my friends. They are not necessarily only with visual people. I enjoy a collaborative, co-creative process, which goes beyond strict rules of who does what, and is non-hierarchical. The film we did in Morocco, *Aït Atta: Nomads of the High Atlas*, was made with my friend Inanc Tekguc, with whom I studied at Kent.

Do you feel a connection with the history of your medium?

I am of course influenced by the pioneers. I love, for instance,

Nanook of the North, by Robert J. Flaherty. I just can't get enough of it. Also *Man With a Movie Camera* by Dziga Vertov, Longinotto and Hosseini's *Divorce Iranian Style*, Reggio's *Koyaanisqatsi*, and Herzog's *Where the Green Ants Dream*. Those luminaries and classics are very dear to me. They had a huge influence. Then there is the French filmmaker Jean Rouch, who created cinéma vérité. I particularly love his film *Chronicles of a Summer*, which he made with Edgar Morin. They were influenced by Vertov. And there are lots of other people. I find them inspiring, more than anything. And it was wonderful to learn about the history of documentary film.

I am also part of the decolonization movement. And I have discovered that there are so many people that we just have not heard of, who did not make it into the historical record. So I am researching this area. I recently attended the Royal Anthropological Film Festival in Bristol, which was showing my film *Ballad for Syria*. The film was nominated for the Best Ethnomusicology award by the Royal Anthropological Institute. During that visit I learned about Safi Faye, who was a Senegalese filmmaker. She did a lot more films than Rouch, but nobody really mentions her within curriculums. I'm interested in rediscovering these hidden heroes of the history of filmmaking. There are so many people that we do not know of because they were not in the curriculum. If I were to become a professor one day, I would include the historical context, and have a broader worldview.

Does your medium offer something unique?

To me, filmmaking is like an umbrella. All the arts can be included within it, like music, poetry, theatre and performance. Whatever you look for, you can have it there. But of course the way you participate in it as an audience is by viewing. So on that level, it's a bit passive. Yet it's very active emotionally and intellectually. But the uniqueness really comes from being like a mother, that accepts all the other art forms.

And it offers a great opportunity to reconcile whatever you are not happy about. You can re-enact those moments. A lot of people use it for therapy. They re-enact their traumas, or they want to re-storify the reality. You can remake your life. Film empowers you in that way. If you do a good film, you get into festivals and you get accredited, acclaimed, recognized. That visibility is very good when it's for a good cause. And you can transform your life completely. It's wonderful to tell stories. It's similar to writing a book. It's just different, in the way you view it and respond to it, but it's about your imagination. As a documentary filmmaker, it becomes your imagination as a collective, whoever is involved.

Why do you have a need to create?

Most people have the urge to create, but I think the difference between those who create more and those who create less is fear. I've been good in overcoming my fears. That's been my strength. Be it the fear of failure, or ridicule, or embarrassment, I don't have that. I just go for it. So courage is the first thing. There is an amazing little book about this called *The Courage to Create*, by Rollo May.

And then creativity is a spiritual freedom. The more you create, the freer you become, and vice versa. Creativity is the essence of life. If you just live a mundane life, who will know you existed, other than your inner circle? So I think there is something more spiritual in there.

On another level, a lot of creators want a kind of immortality. They want their names and ideas to survive. I don't attach importance to having my name live on, but of course I'm trying to leave a mark in terms of my thought, and in terms of doing good in the world.

I am also being creative as a way of existing. As someone between the crossroads of Europe and the Middle East, we have all kinds of drama there in the Middle Eastern region. To deal with the drama you really need the space of creativity, and of your own creation. That's how you feel that something is in your control. Because in that region, when a bomb explodes, or when police aggressively implement state violence on peaceful protestors, or when there is a sudden coup d'état and your parliament is being bombed, you go nuts. And this should not be the norm. So my way of overcoming fear and oppression has been my creative path. That's how I could go beyond my country, and have access and exposure to other places. For instance, with the film *Ballad for Syria*, it aimed to transcend borders on many levels. But mostly, the aim was to liberate Maisa Alhafez, by enabling her to access asylum in Europe, without having to go from Turkey to Greece on a little dinghy boat. We wanted her to fly to Europe, and manifest something. Because it's not easy for Syrians to get visas. In fact at that time, nobody was issuing them visas. These were the people who needed to escape violence and persecution the most, and they were not allowed to leave. They were just left to be bombed. It's like a lockdown for a particular group and region, which now the whole world has experienced due to Covid. People have now learned what it means to have borders closed to them, to be banned from moving. They know that they will soon be able to move freely again, but Syrians don't have that feeling, nor do Palestinians or Tibetans. They feel trapped. So I said to Maisa that she must become the co-director of her life, and rewrite it. But not by risking her life in a dinghy, but by fastening her seat belt.

She had this beautiful project called the Istanbul Mosaic Oriental Choir. She assembled a multilingual choir, where Syrians sang together with other nationalities in various languages, including Arabic, Kurdish, Turkish, Armenian, English, Russian and Persian. Any language was welcome, and they sang for peace and reconciliation. It was a hit, and they became famous. Almost any cultural event that had to do with migration, integration, wellbeing, social justice and human rights opened with them giving a performance.

The funny thing is that Maisa and I really look alike. So suddenly the camera became a mirror. Looking at her, I was seeing myself. And looking at me, she was looking at her own life. And what we were trying to do was to go into the anthropology of sameness, and not into differences. Because with the migration field, everyone talks about differences. But actually people are the same everywhere. So for me, filmmaking and creativity is also a way of overcoming the kind of world that you do not accept, or want to be part of. And making the kind of world you want to co-create. So being creative is recreating the world.

If I was Swiss, or raised as a Swiss, probably I would not have the desire to create as much, at this political level. But now that urge is strong, and expresses itself as deep content creation and evocative storytelling.

Why do humans have a need to create?

We come from the earth, from the soil, from the stars. We feel these vibrations of life, and this is our way of being alive. It's more than breathing and eating. Even with food, some people are artists. I'm so impressed with the chefs, but also the indigenous people. Their recipes are wonderful. Everything is about culture, and culture is creative. That's just the way we are. It's in our DNA. It's the way we vibrate things and mirror things. For instance, you smell this beautiful scent and it's like you're hearing a melody. Or you hear something and it feels like you're eating something. So there is this holistic and sensorial thing about being.

And animals are very creative too. I've seen birds that make these beautiful nests, and that's very creative. So it's part of nature.

What sacrifices have you made to pursue your creative path?

Because I think creativity is so liberating, I don't think I have made many sacrifices. When I took the opportunity to do a PhD, and learn by reading, writing and teaching, that separated me from my family for five years. The sacrifice was going beyond the comfort of my own home. I missed my family a lot, although I visited them frequently. I was supposed to visit them recently, but of course it's very difficult to travel at the moment. As soon as I can travel again I will go home to see them.

How has your work shaped you as a person?

I grew up and I thrived with it. So it empowered me. It built my self-esteem. Also it shaped me in my humanity, because of this constant drive to understand other people and help them tell their stories, which are inspiring. So this shaped me into a very friendly person, a lover of people. So I fell in love with my own kind. But also there are disastrous humans out there. It helps me to be more balanced, when I see terrible things in the world. I remind myself that there are such beautiful people out there too. And I find this calming. It gives me a constant feeling of hope.

How do you deal with creative blocks?

Never. I have been lucky. There has never been a time that I felt blocked. Even if I did, I still found a way to be creative, but more in terms of inner work. Outer creativity comes from inside.

I could also consider the question as: how do I deal with my blockages through creativity? I had a lot of blockages. I think we all do. There is no human being who has realized their full potential and is absolutely satisfied. I don't think that's a level that is easy to reach. So I use creativity to deal with any blockages on the psychological, physical or any other level. Whatever inefficiency or deficiency I have, creativity always helps with those issues.

How do you stay fresh in your work?

I follow the discourses, and worldviews. And I feel I see things coming, like I'm always a little ahead of my time.

I was making a film about where I came from, in Cappadocia. That was my first assignment, in studying anthropology. I had to examine my own roots. And it is this beautiful, surreal landscape of cave dwellings, and volcanic ash soil, and incredible architecture, which is a UNESCO World Heritage Site. I felt so lucky to have ancestors who were troglodytes, living in caves. I didn't need to do anything to get this freshness, it was given to me. So I exploited that, in the positive sense. It was wonderful to make a film there. I found very charismatic, humorous people to film, and it was screened on TV and everyone loved it.

And then I felt that I should not only be a Turkish filmmaker, making films about Turkey. And I did not want to only focus on villages. But then I had the chance to make a film with a Tibetan healer. I was sent there by a British anthropologist who was working on Tibetan medicine at Kent University. He knew I had been to India, and to Ladakh, where Tibetan culture is prominent. And he had this urgent issue with the NGO he was working with. They said they needed someone to go there immediately, who could deal with the conditions, the elevation, and ideally someone who is good on economics, and not only anthropology. So he thought I would be ideal. And also, my surname happens to be Tibet. He felt Tibetans would really like that! It was like destiny.

So I was meant to have the Turkish village, Tibetan situation, then this mobile pastoralism, because also it comes from heritage. And then migration, which I had experienced, though not at the level of being a refugee.

I was in a privileged situation in Portugal, where my father held a senior position with Alcatel, the telecommunications company. I was living in good conditions, yet I still felt the displacement, a kind of exclusion from childhood. And my parents had a lot of fights, which made it stressful at home. So all these things that made me, and built my identity, I made films about them. And about my worldview. So the Free Tibet movement has always been close to my heart. And I resonate with every movement that I would consider to be anti-capitalist, anti-imperialist, anti-colonial and anti-patriarchal.

In Ladakh I met Tibetan medics, and made a film about one of the journeys we took with the healer. I also learned a lot about ethnobotany, about medicinal plants. Again, I didn't need to do anything; I was lucky in having the opportunity to make the film

Amchi. And there weren't many films about Tibetan doctors, so that had a freshness about it.

When I went back to Turkey and people saw the film about Tibetan nomads, they said I should look at Turkish nomads too. It happened that another nature conservation foundation funded me to make that film, which I called *Hey Goat!* It's about a family of nomadic pastoralists who herd 500 goats in Southern Turkey. Then we did the film on Aït Atta. It's so relational in that way. One project leads to the next.

At that time I was dealing with both mobility and sedentarism (village life). Being from Istanbul, I also see the migration there, with the Syrians coming in. And African diasporas and so on. So I made the film *Refugee Here I Am* with a reggae musician called Enzo Ikah. Istanbul for me is a musical city, so I was inspired by music and documentary film. In the end it's about your own experiences, which I think helps maintain freshness in your work.

What is your relationship with satisfaction in your work?

The first time I made a film, I didn't know how to edit in a way that made it compelling. I just put it together sequentially. The part where I needed to get the interviews into a conversation among themselves, I didn't know how to do that. So I collaborated with an editor and learned from him quickly. So it was satisfying to learn how to edit in a compelling way.

And then with the second film, *Amchi*, it was very difficult to edit because it was in Tibetan and Ladakhi, the Bhoti language. So I had to wait until all the material was transcribed and translated. It was crazy. I was really going nuts with that. And also there were political issues with the NGO and I did not want to create more conflict, so I had to be very patient.

Then I went to a prominent documentary TV channel in Istanbul to ask if they would like to broadcast the film. They wanted to get everything from me for free, edit it themselves and give me no credit as the filmmaker. But how could they narrate it without the experience? All of that was happening because they found me so young and inexperienced. But when I shot and edited the film myself, and then saw it on TV, that was huge for me. It was an incredible feeling.

Early on I made a lot of mistakes in presenting and marketing the work. But that's how you learn. And you become more confident. I feel that the maturity is coming, but you want to raise the bar each time. So you're never truly satisfied. But I'm not the kind of person who competes with herself, or other people. I feel that every story has its own goal, and reason to be. And I try to stay truthful to the essence of that vision.

For me, filmmaking is a tool to communicate. It's an activist tool. I always have an agenda for each project, so the satisfaction level is deeper. With Enzo, the hidden agenda was to liberate Enzo. And it was the same with Maisa, and the Amchi. So it was always about empowering people by giving them the recognition they deserve. The kind of work I do is to defend human rights defenders. And also support livelihood rights. The first film, with the pastoralists, was the same. Therefore, because I have this political agenda, the form, the technicality and the beauty of the film is always secondary. But with the last film I felt a level of satisfaction being met in every sense: political, intellectual and artistic. But it takes a while to get to that stage. It's not like you do your first film and it gets an Oscar. You dedicate your life to it, and that is more important than satisfaction.

What is the relationship between your work and its audience?

I always had a really good audience. I'm not interested in how many people watch something. It's about the right people watching it. Because when they come to you, even more amazing things happen. For me, the meeting of the film and the audience, and my meeting with the audience, is the afterlife of the film. Without that, we cannot complete our Nirvana. We need to reincarnate, and that's through the audience. And the more people who watch and respond to it, they can transform their lives. Because a lot of people's lives will be touched. The families, the closer circles, and maybe the NGOs.

What is the relationship between yourself and your audience?

It's a very positive one. It feeds me. It inspires me to make a better film each time. And sometimes I had people who want to put you down. The negative comments are very precious, because when you know about those weaknesses, then next time you make sure you don't have them. If people just pat you on the back and tell you the work is perfect, then there is nothing to improve. So I have a very positive relationship with criticism.

There are some creators who are just interested in their own ego. We all have egos, and they are very important. Without ego, we can't create. The 'I' is needed. But we also need to think about we, us, all of us, together. If you have this negative critique, if you feel this person is a separate entity, then you don't deal with it. But if you see them as someone who belongs to that audience, that community, then you embrace this person, and you try to win them over. I see the negativity, but I try not to let it get to me. Of course this takes time. I used to have sleepless nights over getting harsh criticism. And I would drive myself crazy worrying about why I said certain things certain ways. You have to build up the shield, and the power to deal with that. It's only recently happened for me that I no longer take it to heart.

What has your audience taught you?

I learned that those critiques really come from distrust. They are saying, 'I don't trust you. I don't believe in you. There must be something negative about you. You did this, but it's not enough. You're not enough. You're lacking. Why should I listen to you?'

Maybe this person wants to compete with you. You can provoke a competitive feeling in some people. It may be jealousy. Some creators wish they had made that film, for example. It's very human. When I see the human in them, I just smile, and let it go. And that's even more annoying to them, because they want the fight. But with some people you have to fight, because it's too much to bear.

What has been the greatest challenge in your career?

That was my PhD, but a lot of my creativity was inspired by my PhD. That was a very difficult subject, working with unaccompanied asylum-seeking youth. And I found myself doing activism more than anthropology, because these kids had very difficult lives, and I couldn't just be an observer. In addition, I had a difficult time with some in my department. Most were incredibly supportive, but it was very challenging. During those difficult times, making the films really saved me.

I then wrote up my PhD as a book, called *Learning to be Freed*. It's about the stories of these young refugees, searching for freedom. And I worked with the theory of third space, which is attributed to Homi K. Bhabha. It's really about this fusion of being in a different co-creative and transformative space. It's not about where you come from, or which host country you are in, or where you will be resettled as an asylum seeker, but all the other things that you become in this third space, in this immobility. I will hopefully publish it next year. I want to be faithful to the essence and the power of the youth.

Having experienced migration from a very young age, I have some way of relating to what happens as a non-Westerner in a Western country, and everything that goes with that. And it is not always positive. It can include people taking advantage of you. But when you are an asylum seeker it is different. They are at the mercy of so many people who can abuse them, including employers and officials.

What has been the high point of your career?

I think I'm still not there yet. I don't believe in this career thing. I am a very spiritual person, so I look at things more on the soul level. The career idea belongs more to the materialistic world, which of course I can't hide from. And I can't neglect the fact that that's where I live. But I always think of going into the woods. The highest point of my career will be when I say I have done enough, and I will now go into the beauty of nature and stay there.

But at the same time, I don't think it is possible to stop thinking and writing and filming. I don't know how alive that would be. I think it would be very peaceful, but I haven't reached that point yet.

In terms of productivity and creativity, I think it's going well, but I don't know how high it can go. Does it need to? I don't know. I wouldn't be able to tell. I just live. I just be.

What is the most important thing your creative practice has taught you?

The most important thing is to believe in and trust yourself. And to never give up, to continue producing. And to be proactive, and to stay fresh.

But that self-belief and self-trust is most important, because it then allows you to believe in and trust other people. To live without trust in yourself and others will mean you are always in fear of something, and you don't feel like it's worthwhile to discover or experiment, because you feel that it's going to be awful. But if you have that belief and trust in yourself, you can create a better world for everyone. And that's part of the vision. The creative practice teaches you to not give up on creating a better world for all of us. It's a bit like the story of the starfish washing up on the beach. You cannot save them all, but it means everything to the starfish that you can save.

If you talk to our friend, and my spiritual mother Rama Mani, her vision is about enacting global transformation, and that's why I love her. Her belief is deeper and bigger. It's the macro view. But for me it's about the micro changes that make a difference. It starts with your own circle, then you expand it, and it becomes a huge wave. I think that's what happens with books, for instance. We read a book, and for some of us we act based on that. But for others, it doesn't move them in the same way.

Working so closely with the subjects of my films, despite all their hardships, these people keep going. They are so resilient and powerful, and so transparent in their vulnerability. But despite everything, they keep moving forward. That inner power amazes me. Where does it come from? It comes from their creativity, from their urge to create. That's how they fight against hatred, how they survive wars. It's so beautiful to see that. Because when ugliness and darkness comes into your life, you can become ugly and dark too. But the people I make these films with are like these eternal lights. They just don't get dark, they have the inner strength to not fade away.

And I keep finding this in the most unexpected places. In a youth shelter I was told that these young kids will become extremists and terrorists, because they see so much violence in their lives. But not a single being that I met was awful. They were all beautiful, because they are children. They were from Syria, Palestine, Congo, Somalia and Afghanistan, and came all that way without their parents. Some of them were on the road from the age of 10. That's too young to be traveling by yourself with people traffickers and smugglers. Many were escaping wars, dictators, prison and torture. And I was warned that these young boys could be dangerous because of this. But I met them and they were all wonderfully funny people. What is there to be afraid of?

That's another important thing I learned: you can find the most beautiful things in the most unexpected places. So it's all about going against the current, against the stereotypical images. If we go to Afghanistan, I'm sure all of us will fall in love with the land and the people. But not many of us will experience this, because it's too dangerous to travel there. It's the same thing in many countries.

When Enzo went to Turkey, he began turning traditional Turkish songs into reggae versions, and he was singing them in Turkish. It was the first time this had happened in Turkish history, because Enzo came so far. It was the same thing with Maisa. She is the first Syrian person to conduct a choir singing in six languages, including Armenian and Kurdish, in Istanbul. And she is reconciling not only her community of Syrians, but is reconciling us, the Turkish community, and Armenians and Kurds. So I wanted people to know that there is more to see than just categorizing people as foreigner or refugee. These categories are so harmful. They stop us from seeing the real humans behind them. We should be looking into their creativity, their talents, what they have to bring and share with us.

How did it feel to reflect on creativity today?

It felt like I was really on the right track in doing my thing, doing what I am believing in and that I am doing well. That it is great to be a polymath and be interested in a variety of fields and that I am able to combine them. It reminds me that the transformative power of art relies on co-creation and co-directing, as hierarchies should always be blurred and borders be transcended that way. So thank you for making me reflect and realize this once more.

Conclusion

The joy of creativity is its unbounded nature. In its essence, creativity seems to be one with the force of life itself. Formica and I found ourselves in a labyrinthine discussion about the relationship between life and creativity as we finalized her chapter. It may in fact be my greatest takeaway from the project: if life is fundamentally creative, then everything is an expression of that creative force. So, those who feel intimidated by the idea of seeking and expressing their own creativity can be reassured that it is in every heartbeat, every moment, every thought, word and deed.

Which immediately makes me think of the moral dimension of creativity. One can be a creative torturer, for example. Creativity feeds into the machinery of war, poverty, famine and environmental destruction, and the social, ethical and psychological decay that has increasingly defined our age. The effort to design weapons, surveillance systems and policies which make the rich richer and the poor poorer have surely been fed by the same resource that others draw upon to oppose them, in whatever manner they can. Creativity sits at the heart of all human action.

Being the fundamentally emotional beings that we are, art, I would think, has been fueled far more by the passions of love and anger than by passive philosophical interest in objects or events. But the philosophical aspect of art is of great interest to me, in terms of definition and purpose. Defining art seems to be one of those eternal questions. Having no academic background in art history, all I can offer by way of personal experience is that art serves the processing of experience. It has an element of synesthesia, where the experience of one thing is expressed as another. So heartbreak can be represented in a melancholic melody in D minor. Or the essence of a memory can be caught in a few swift stabs of color on canvas. Some attempt photorealism, an absolute facsimile, while others may move through levels of abstraction until there is nothing but the emotion you take from the form and color before you, or the wall of sound, or the movements of the human form. The depth of what those expressions can evoke is astounding, and this has a way of holding us in the moment, quite against the currents of life which seem designed to sweep us ever downriver with only a dim sense of control.

Art reaches into realms which evoke Taoist principles. As *Poem One* of the *Tao Te Ching* says, 'The Tao that can be told is not the eternal Tao. The name that can be named is not the eternal name.' The Tao is something eternally nameless, yet apparent in our experience of it. It is considered by some as the ground of all being, the underlying principle of existence. Similarly, among its many applications, art is a means to express some sense of the conditions of our existence which may otherwise be beyond language. Perhaps some poets can reflect them, but intellectual understanding can be surrendered willingly and without shame in the face of existential mystery. Yet if one listens to Holst, the cosmic awe is right there. The spirit and imagination can let us play among the stars, released from logical and material constraints.

It would be a true pleasure to list 100 songs that have accompanied me in life, and given formless form to feeling and experience. They take me immediately to times, places and relationships across dozens of countries, and almost five decades. Some of them dash through the mind and body like the Tasmanian Devil, whipping up a storm of memory and emotion. Others are like slipping into a warm bath. Scent, for some reason, has that same ability to snap us back to a point in time and space. And sure enough, there are true artists working in the realms of perfume and incense.

And then there is the skill element in art, as David Hurn discussed. Craft raised to a supreme level may be dubbed artistry. For some reason, images of dancing traffic cops come to mind. They inject so much personality and meaning into their work, and the world is a

Conclusion

better place for it. On a YouTube video of a female dancing traffic cop in New York, set to the music of Billie Jean by Michael Jackson, one commenter wrote: 'You see this and say, "The world is a beautiful place," and you smile.'

So what is it that drives the producers of art and craft? In this book we have heard many stories of passion, inspiration and determination. These people have sacrificed time with their children, their partners and their friends. They have in some cases foregone better paying work, or other opportunities in life. And for what? We loop back around to that creative force. Some of us have an irresistible need to make, to manifest, to bring things into the world. Most of the contributors said that they have simply always been this way. They do what they are, they are what they do.

Sometimes we do not know where the inspiration comes from. In my glass work I would sometimes clear my mind and say out loud, "Show me." And before long that open channel would start to flow with imagery, geometry, color and feeling. It seems that things are trying to get into the world through us. And in so doing, others will benefit. My colleague and mentor Herbert Girardet, whom I interviewed in my book *Wisdom: Now and Always*, once said to me, "We can never know the effect our work will have." He was referring to its life beyond us, when it goes into the world and meets people we never will. I think of Corin driving past crowds of tourists outside Westminster Abbey, as they photograph his sculpture. They do not know him personally, but they take something personal from his work. Likewise Maggie will never truly know the effect of her contribution to 30 years of television, seen by hundreds of millions of people around the world. Many of the contributors have interaction with their fans, but the bulk of their influence will always be hidden. And yet it is the most exciting aspect of creativity to me: the unknowable influence. If we do what we do with love, we are assured of changing lives for the better, to whatever degree.

The immediate effect of working on this project is connected with others from this year, 2020. I interviewed 25 people for *Wisdom*, eight others on their peace work, and half a dozen on the theme of home. The interview with Claudia started a shift that was accelerated notably by the discussion with Rama, and with Jan Oberg. Jan is a peace expert who is also a photographer. He is attempting to articulate 'peace photography', as opposed to war photography. For that book I also had discussions with Yongey Mingyur Rinpoche, Evelin Lindner, Richard Falk, David Krieger, John Avery, Sulak Sivaraksa and Elisabet Sahtouris, all of whom opened my heart and mind in profound ways. And during the interview with Muazzam Ali Khan, I had to take my socks off and scrunch the shag pile carpet with my toes to stay grounded. As we discussed connecting with God during Qawwāli performances, my mind filled with such intense light that I could barely stay connected to the earth. Out of all these experiences, one thing came through more strongly than any other: the desire for integration and liberation.

This was articulated as the desire to move from the left-brain analytical approach, and instead find the place where I feel most real, honest and whole. And that is when I see the world through the lens of art, and express myself likewise. I find poetry spilling out of me through the day, in response to every imaginable observation, memory and encounter. That sense of release, of permission to make art, is a gift from all these people. My fondest hope for this book is that you, the reader, will likewise be inspired and supported in letting your creativity loose, and expressing a more fuller sense of self. Because that is what art offers us, in the end. Most of our processing is done subconsciously. It works itself out in dreams, or finds expression in emotions that we do not fully understand. But to make art is to allow that channel to be open in a more conscious way, and the world becomes a brighter, more colorful and honest place because of it.

While on a peace mission in Africa, Rama had the epiphany that creativity and peace were closely intertwined. This led her into internal conflict about releasing her own self-judgment about people losing respect for her if she came out as an artist. And to her surprise, those same people have been impacted the most by her performances.

Conclusion

Formica similarly shared the story of the Damanhur community letting go of judgment in their quest to explore human potential through art. And the work they have produced is spectacular. This echoes the 'playful investigation' of Claudia's work. That term has for me a special attraction. As children we are encouraged to explore our creativity, but increasingly there seems to be an educational focus on the foundations of the global economy: the STEM subjects of science, technology, engineering and mathematics. Though creativity is fundamental to all human endeavor, the arts are lower down the academic pecking order than ever. As Lady Pink commented, there is often a strong preference for supporting sport over the arts, so if schools face budget constraints, they are typically more likely to cut arts than sports. The take-up of arts subjects has been declining in UK schools, with special mentions for performing arts including dance, music and drama. And yet there has been a significant rise in adult crafting and other arts interests. In addition, art therapy has become an increasingly widespread and popular therapeutic approach for supporting those with mental, emotional and physical health issues. The process of creation has a way of unlocking and releasing trauma, and thereby helping us to heal. Rama shared with us the ancient Greek practice of using art as a means to prepare us for healing, and the way they used theatre for shared catharsis. Returning to the question of the primacy of creativity in existence, it should be no surprise that we have a need to channel creativity throughout our lives. If we suppress the very nature of existence itself, that can never be healthy.

Art and creativity offer a huge variety of benefits and meanings. Above all else, I believe its primary function is its role in developing self-knowledge. Not only can it help us to understand and express ourselves in a positive way, it can also let others into aspects of ourselves that may often be beyond words. How many of us have had the experience of seeing the artwork of a loved one and being surprised, even intrigued? We all have hidden depths, and art can expose aspects of them in a way that can foster more intimacy, both within and between us. There will always be a need to better understand ourselves and each other, and so much is submerged where it could or should find a healthy outlet. We are living through a time of excessive and increasing polarization, anger and distrust. One can readily imagine that if all concerned had a daily creative practice, much of this would be opened up, decompressed and understood in a more honest, and perhaps less judgmental way. As part of a more holistically healthy lifestyle, involving connection with nature and loved ones, good diet, personal time and so on, art can bring us to a more centered, calm, open-hearted and open-minded place. This way lies peace and wisdom, which the world is more in need of than ever.

And as Lady Pink said, the basic motivation for the art that has a through line from cave art spray painted with red ochre, to the graffiti sprayed on walls around the world, is to know that we are alive, to leave something behind, to say to the world, "I was here."

www.ingramcontent.com/pod-product-compliance
Lightning Source LLC
Chambersburg PA
CBHW031607210526
45464CB00004B/1467